Feminism and Families

Feminism and Families

Edited and with an Introduction
by Hilde Lindemann Nelson

ROUTLEDGE

New York and London

Published in 1997 by

Routledge
29 West 35th Street
New York, NY 10001

Published in Great Britain in 1997 by

Routledge
11 New Fetter Lane
London EC4P 4EE

Library of Congress Cataloging-in-Publication Data

Feminism and families / edited and with an introduction by Hilde Lindemann Nelson.
    p.   cm.
   Includes bibliographical references and index.
   ISBN 0–415–91253–9 (hc : alk. paper). — ISBN 0–415–91254–7 (pbk. : alk. paper)
   1. Family. 2. Feminism. I. Nelson, Hilde Lindemann.
HQ734.F374 1996
306.85—dc20   96–28729
                                                                      CIP

This book is for Margaret Urban Walker

Contents

III. INTIMATE KNOWINGS

IV. WHO'S IN, WHO'S OUT?

V. FAMILIES AND MEDICINE

VI. IMAGES WE DON'T NEED

Introduction

Hilde Lindemann Nelson

An upsurge of interest in families has appeared recently in the popular highbrow press, much of it neoconservative, but some of it apparently motivated by the Left's growing resistance to libertarian individualism. This renewed interest has been accompanied by a new political and legal focus on families, of which the Family Leave Act, children seeking the court's permission to disown their birthparents, judicial affirmation of the rights of biological parents over children who have been adopted, and the push to rethink no-fault divorce law are only a few instances.

A great deal of the attention has been fueled by the suspicion that families are "breaking down." The Right has been busy reaffirming "family values" and seeing in the divorce rate (now holding steady at just under 50 percent) a threat to the foundation of society. In the psychotherapeutic community, on the other hand, the suspicion has been that the "traditional" family is dysfunctional, a view underscored of late by the controversy surrounding retrieved childhood memories of sexual abuse. The health care system exacts from patients' families increasingly large sacrifices of care and money at the same time as it also is inclined to suspect families of abuse. The U.S. Senate became so concerned over increasing reports of domestic violence that it held hearings on the topic in 1991. A strong subtheme of the history of families—namely, that they are not to be trusted—has once more become a major motif. There seems to be an increasing dissatisfaction with contemporary familial arrangements, a generalized feeling that things ought to change.

The little attention feminist theorists have devoted to families up to now has been well repaid. Barrie Thorne and Marilyn Yalom, eds., *Rethinking the Family: Some Feminist Questions*, first published by Longman's in 1982 and revised in 1992, is a good interdisciplinary anthology that challenges widely entrenched assumptions about families as it raises questions about family gender roles and family boundaries, among other things. Two recent monograph-length feminist analyses of the family—Linda J. Nicholson's *Gender and History: The Limits of Social Theory in the Age of the Family* (1988), which explores the connection between evolving conceptions of the family and modern political theory as a way of understanding dilemmas generated within feminism, and Susan Moller Okin's *Gender, Justice, and the Family* (1989), which shows how and why theories of justice need to be applicable to families if women are to have anything like their fair share of influence on politics and society—are required reading for anyone who is interested in theorizing families. And *Hypatia* devoted its Winter 1996 issue to the topic as well.

By and large, however, feminist philosophers have taken little notice of families—at least professionally. From its inception until 1996 *Hypatia* had published only three essays having to do with families, and *Signs* had published none. The issue of *Ethics* devoted to feminism and political theory (January 1989) does not address the family at all. *Explorations in Feminist Ethics*, ed. Eve Browning Cole and Susan Coultrap-McQuin (1992), is likewise silent on this topic, as is (with the exception of Christina Hoff Sommers's "Filial Morality") *Women and Moral Theory*, ed. Eva Feder Kittay and Diana T. Meyers (1987). *Feminist Ethics*, ed. Claudia Card (1991), contains nothing on the philosophy of the family, nor does *Feminism/Postmodernism*, ed. Linda J. Nicholson (1990). The reader *Living with Contradictions: Controversies in Feminist Social Ethics*, ed. Alison M. Jaggar (1994), contains a short section called "Family Values," but half the excerpts in it have to do with assisted reproduction. Sara Ruddick's *Maternal Thinking* (1989), like *Motherhood: A Feminist Perspective*, ed. Jane P. Knowles and Ellen Cole (1990), and Nancy Chodorow's *Reproduction of Mothering* (1978), focus on only one element of family life.

Feminists have fared no better in their indirect dealings with the subject. They have had a great deal to say about any number of issues that would seem to cry out for at least ancillary treatment of families, yet by and large this treatment has been oddly absent—as if there were white spaces on the page just at the places where careful thinking about families is needed. A case in point is Alison Jaggar's splendid work on patriarchy in *Feminist Politics and Human Nature* (1983)—a work that is most insightful, for example, about the relationship of human birthgiving to the social connections that are central to human nature, but that confines its discussion of families to a rehearsal of the Marxist/feminist critique of them as an instrument of capitalist/patriarchal oppression. But if, as Jaggar argues, a crucial fact about human nature is the enlarged cranium that makes birthgiving arduous and necessitates a prolonged infancy, and if the attendant vulnerability of this state in turn necessitates relationships of intimacy, then by not offering a positive feminist account of how such relationships ought to be configured, Jaggar has left a significant gap in her argument.

A similar white space is visible in the pages of Judith Butler's *Gender Trouble* (1990). Butler argues that gender is performative, a disciplinary production of the fantasy of a binary opposition of masculine and feminine played out on the body through a series of exclusions and denials of other, more fluid possibilities. Gender is imposed by an unwritten law, namely the taboo against incest; because the incest taboo institutes the exogamy that allows a culture to reproduce itself, it presupposes a prohibition against homosexuality, at the same time that it requires one to be either male or female. Gender is thus not only the identification with one sex, but it also entails the direction of sexual desire toward the other sex. As a critique of hegemonic categories of identity this work is brilliant—brilliant too in its destabilization of those categories. Yet nowhere in her account of how children acquire the fantasy of "I" as female or male does Butler offer any analysis at all of the structures of intimacy within which this acquisition takes place. Nowhere, that is, does she acknowledge the significance of the fact that most young children live within families. This inattention to the situatedness of the process of engendering is really rather odd.

A final example. In Joan Tronto's admirably clearheaded *Moral Boundaries* (1993), the task is to accord the work of caring its full moral value. Tronto's strategy for doing that is to break down the moral boundaries that have confined caring to a domestic activity performed by women and redraw them so that the political nature of caring becomes visible. While she is surely right to widen the boundary in this way, it is nevertheless frustrating to come across that familiar white space on the page—the place where theorizing about the family as a context of care ought to take place but does not. The white space is understandable. The point of the book, after all, is to show that the ethic of care is more than kids and car pools and the domestic labor women engage in at home. But the fact remains that most of the unpaid caring labor most of us do is done on behalf of family members. Given Tronto's insistence that "we cannot understand an ethic of care until we place such an ethic in its full moral and political context," the omission of any theorizing at all about the familial context cries out for comment.

Why have families suffered neglect at the hands of feminist philosophers? Well, the topic is an explosive one. Although the patriarchal structures of intimacy that serve as the hegemonic ideal of family are perhaps the structures among all others that have silenced and exploited women, they are also the structures—or something like the structures—of many feminists' families. To critique them may literally hit feminists where they live. Such criticism also hits other women where they live. Feminism alienated many women in the 1960s and '70s by being outspokenly critical of families and so earning the epithet of antifamily, and this may be one reason why many of us now step around the topic. Although we do not, perhaps, take her advice at the level of practice, at the level of conversation many of us seem to be heeding Shulamith Firestone, whose considered opinion about families in a nutshell was: Shun them.

This advice will not do. Most of us were reared in families, and many of us went on as adults to form new families of our own. Some of us have tried to repudiate the institution altogether, but I note with interest that certain African-American feminists—Patricia Collins and bell hooks spring to mind—conceive of families as a rare safe space in a culture that is multiply oppressive. I also note that in most of the works whose lack of attention to families I just lamented, the acknowledgments and dedication pages thank the authors' and editors' family members. We value these people. We nurture our sons and daughters, look after our aging parents, marry, divorce, enter important lesbian and heterosexual relationships that we or others either do or do not think of as familial, wonder as adults about our responsibilities to our siblings. These activities and the institutional background against which they take place stand in sore need of sustained feminist philosophical reflection. Careful and imaginative theoretical work in this area is an essential basis for good public policy as well as for the ethical stance we adopt toward those with whom we live in intimacy. It is also, as I have tried to show, crucial for theorizing about human nature, about gender, about the ethic of care, and about other philosophical issues.

If theory about families is in sore need of forward movement, this collection aims to provide momentum. Its sixteen essays, representing a wide range of theoretical approaches, examine families from a number of diverse cultural, political, and religious perspectives. The contributors range in age from Mary Midgley at seventy-six to Elise Robinson at twenty-four. Some are bioethicists, some are political theorists, one writes on psychoanalytic feminism, another is a sociologist, others are epistemologists, still others do lesbian theory.

Here, then, a brief overview of the collection.

I. Histories

Susan Moller Okin examines the history of feminism in England and the U.S. for its contributions to the policy debates over practices (such as abortion and welfare reform) that have their greatest impact on families. She argues that feminists ought not to overreact to the recent debate about differences among women by losing sight of these important historical contributions. Much feminist concern about insufficient attention to differences among women and families is unfounded, she thinks, as the insights of second-wave feminism in particular—the challenge to the public/private distinction, for example, and the insistence that housework is real work—are often useful in the very settings of difference they had been thought to neglect.

Linda Nicholson looks to the past for another purpose. She surveys the history of families in America and Europe to support her contention that "traditional" families aren't very traditional. She argues that the distinction between "traditional" and "alternative" functions normatively, legitimating certain family types and unfairly stigmatizing others. Because the distinction gets in the way when we try to evaluate family types, she suggests we drop it and consider instead whether a particular type of family provides economic and emotional sustenance to its own—particularly its children. We can then, she argues, begin mobilizing the political power necessary to make our institutions conform more closely to our familial needs.

Naomi Zack undertakes a historical investigation for yet a third purpose. She examines the history of philosophy for its masked normative assumptions about families and how they relate to broader structures of social and political power. As her investigation reveals, philosophers have often written about "the family" as if a specific form of it were natural, universal, and good, and then used those assumptions to argue for a particular form of government that depends on and supports that specific form of the family. In exposing these assumptions to a radical critique, Zack also reconceptualizes "family" in a way that better acknowledges the diversity of both familial structures and family values.

II. The Breakdown of the Family

Mary Midgley and Judith Hughes survey the most common communitarian responses to the perceived "breakdown of the family"—namely, a denunciation of individualism and a demand for a return to "family values" and community spirit—and find them inadequate. They note that although politicians and social reformers expect families to be stable and self-supporting units, these are not the family values that matter most to individuals, who look to their families for loving and supportive relationships. Midgley and Hughes call for ways of making life more tolerable for families that do not fit conservative norms, by offering them the kind of neighborhood and social support that communitarians have largely reserved for "deserving" nuclear families.

Laura M. Purdy has a different approach to the breakdown of the family—she would like to see women deliberately break them down, at least temporarily. She suggests that if, for a while, women refused to bear children, the degree to which society depends on women's unpaid caregiving labor to assure the well-being of future generations would immediately become visible. Arguing that this burden of care is a serious impediment to women as they try to progress toward equality with men, she proposes a babystrike. Downing reproductive tools, she argues, would make it impossible for women to believe that producing babies is "naturally" their lot and solely their own choice, and force society to take more responsibility for the children it wants and needs.

Michele M. Moody-Adams notes that feminism has widely been perceived to be in fundamental opposition to family life (a perception perhaps fuelled by essays urging babystrikes). Moody-Adams observes that antifeminists have exploited the insecurities of many women by persuading them that to call themselves feminist is to reject their "essential" womanhood, along with the familial practices that are attached to it. On the contrary, she argues, feminism can often be indispensable to the stability and well-being of modern family life. She shows how, especially when families threaten to break down under economic pressures, women often cast off their familially assigned gender roles and get the education and jobs that are necessary to keep the family going. A woman's commitment to preserving her family is thus often inseparable from an equally strong commitment to autonomy and equality for women.

Elise L.E. Robinson and James and Hilde Lindemann Nelson, who are all members of one family, criticize how Americans think about and make postdivorce child custody arrangements, arguing that parents and the courts wrongly attempt to reproduce certain features of the reigning ideal of family life. Replacing this "sentimental" ideal with a model of fluidity, they (we) argue, permits postdivorce families to affirm children's sense of their own moral agency and to assure children that the benefits of family life go on even when the family's structure changes. The proposed model also allows children to feel the advantages of living in two worlds and prepares them more adequately for the families they will form when they too become adults.

III. Intimate Knowings

John Hardwig begins his essay with an argument he made more than twenty years ago—that pluralistic communes are better suited than other familial arrangements to promote the kind of dialogue most conducive to self-knowledge. As he (now) goes on to argue, communes and the other, more usual, forms of families are important places where knowledge is situated; or, put another way, situated knowers are not only gendered, raced, and classed, but also familied. He calls for an epistemology of the family, invoking and blurring both the inside/outside and the public/private distinctions to theorize communes as familial arrangements that contain "private publics" where certain kinds of knowledge—among them, self-knowledge—are produced.

Judith Bradford and Crispin Sartwell also see the need for an epistemology of families. They use recent developments in feminist epistemology as a way of understanding twelve-step programs and the popular self-help literature aimed at "healing" the "dysfunctional" family. The goal of such self-help, they suggest, is to return from deviant knowing as it is practiced in "fortress families" to the baseline of healthy knowing as this is supposedly practiced in the hegemonic ideal of family. But because, the authors argue, the ideal of family itself constrains what one can know, other epistemic communities may be needed to produce knowledge adequate to living. They close by offering criteria for evaluating such epistemic communities.

IV. Who's In, Who's Out?

Cheshire Calhoun reviews lesbian-feminist analyses of lesbians' relation to the family, marriage, and mothering, showing how lesbians' *difference* from heterosexual women is often not visible even to lesbian feminists themselves: the analyses mistakenly center on familial harms to heterosexual women, not lesbians. She suggests that lesbians' distinctive (and problematic) relation to the family is better captured by attending to the social construction of gays and lesbians as family outlaws than by attending to the gender structure of families. She argues that in refusing the outlaw construction, lesbians and gay men rightly bid for the same privilege most heterosexuals enjoy—of claiming that, in spite of their deviations from norms governing the family, their families are nevertheless real.

Mary Romero explores the idea that domestic workers are "just like one of the family," arguing that this construction not only papers over the physically hard work of domestic service, its low status, and its low pay, but also masks the impact this work has on the domestic worker's own family. From interviews with seventeen people whose mothers worked as maids in private homes, she shows how domestic workers' children too pay a price when women employers shift their burden of sexism onto women employees already burdened by injustices of class and race.

V. Families and Medicine

Françoise Baylis and Jocelyn Downie explore the quandary faced by Western health care providers who wish to respect cultural diversity but also must determine whether a child is being abused or neglected by family practices sanctioned in a minority culture. What should be the limits of deference to various cultural beliefs or values? The authors develop a feminist approach to the problem of cross-cultural conflict that allows them to navigate between the extremes of cultural relativism and cultural imperialism: they ask a set of questions whose objective is to assess the claim that a familial practice is culturally sanctioned. If it is, they argue, it must be respected, but only if it does not also oppress a subgroup within the culture.

Sidney Callahan believes that although gay men and lesbians stand to benefit particularly from recent advances in reproductive technology, neither they nor heterosexual couples ought to have children by these means. She argues that the well-being of most children most of the time is best served when those who are genetically connected to a child fulfill their responsibility for rearing it. Viewing adoption as a response to an unforeseen crisis, she fears that intentionally separating the strands of parenting through the use of alternate reproductive technologies will have negative social and symbolic consequences.

VI. Images We Don't Need

Sara Ruddick suggested in *Maternal Thinking* that we reject the ideal of a distinctive fatherhood and instead support the concept of male-inclusive motherhood. Here she examines three defining paternal functions—provision, protection, and authority—and explains why they should not be used to support fatherhood as a regulative ideal. She is, however, more hesitant now about erasing the sexual difference between mothers and fathers, as a denial of sexual difference could affirm children's fantasies of their own sex being the only good one, while denying fathers' distinctive experience of their bodies as procreative. And as most of the world distinguishes between mothers and fathers, she calls for an *ethics* of sexual difference—one that acknowledges different parental genders without falling into old habits of domination and oppression.

Bat-Ami Bar On thinks there is another ideal we don't need: that of Zionism. She argues that in Israel, where the patriarchal family has been one of the cornerstones of the Zionist nation-building project, lesbians and gay men are in danger of losing the social acceptance they have begun to enjoy, unless the Zionist project changes. She uses the film *Machboim* to show that to participate in the Zionist project, a man must be toughly masculine and strictly heterosexual, while a woman's duty is to rear children and to mother soldiers for the state. As Jewish-Israeli lesbians refuse women's traditional role in their personal and national families, they see themselves as rupturing the social order. Yet Bar On cautions them to resist the offer of integration into a "new" Jewish-Israeli society, as this society will not redress their alienation and requires the continued exclusion of Palestinians to support its Zionist project.

And finally, *Diana Tietjens Meyers* urges us to discard a certain Freudian figuration. In the current controversy over recovered memory, the question has been whether women accusing their fathers of having sexually abused them when they were young are telling the truth. As this question is often unanswerable, Meyers suggests that we ask instead how the trope of sadistic incest—she dubs it the Freudian "family romance"—guides and shapes women's self-definition. Like other culturally appropriated tropes, sadistic incest can be literalized as a way of explaining a woman's unhappiness, but doing so does not seem likely to help women to lead more rewarding lives. Meyers offers a number of reasons for taking the family romance out of circulation and replacing it with figurations that support feminist emancipatory aims.

Here, then, are ideas that can be used to fill in the white spaces in books of feminist philosophy. Here is needed work on the relationship of families to theories of justice, political theory, duties to future generations, epistemology, queer theory, bioethics, theories of moral agency. Theory in these and other areas of philosophy is well served by adding families as a category of analysis, but it is also worthwhile to get better theory about families themselves, and several papers in this volume also contribute to that end. The collection thus supplies momentum on both fronts.

Feminism and Families owes its existence to Maureen MacGrogan, who suggested the project to me and has championed it enthusiastically at every stage. Linda J. Nicholson has provided savvy advice and warm encouragement, as has Diana Tietjens Meyers. To these three, many thanks. Thanks is also owed to the Department of Philosophy at the University of Tennessee, Knoxville, for its friendly colleagues and essential infrastructure. And finally, in the long tradition of acknowledgments in books of feminist theory, I express heartfelt thanks to my family, particularly Jim and our children, not only for what they have done for me but for who they are.

Part I

Histories

1

Families and Feminist Theory: Some Past and Present Issues

Susan Moller Okin

> Feminists have conducted a close scrutiny of the family in the last years and have seen how oppressive it can be for women. But undermining the family has costs, for women as well as men, in the form of isolation and the further deterioration of child raising, general unhappiness, social distrust, and solipsism; and sensitivity to these problems is also part of the feminist heritage.
>
> —Linda Gordon, in Thorne and Yalom 1982, 1992

The family has long been regarded by feminists as an important location where sexual equality must be won. Through centuries of English and American feminism, marriage and family have been amongst the foremost institutions critiqued. Yet most feminist critics are ambivalent about families. Barrie Thorne writes of "an ambivalence embedded in feminism since the nineteenth century and strongly evident today . . . between values of individualism and equality, . . . values that women have historically been denied and are now claiming; and values of nurturance and collectivity, which are historically associated with the family" (Thorne, in Thorne and Yalom 1982, p. 2). In this essay, I trace some of the history of this ambivalence and examine its contemporary manifestations. I then move on to address two related questions: How has the recent focus within feminism on differences among women affected feminist perceptions of families and their problems? Has this focus to some extent diffused feminist energies and weakened feminist responses to some of the major political debates of the late twentieth century, including the "family values" debate, the abortion debate, and the debate over welfare reform—debates to which past and present feminist analyses and critiques of families have much to contribute?

The reasons for feminist ambivalence about families are not difficult to discern. Feminists have found most forms of family prevalent in history and in the present to be destructive of women's equality both within the home and in all other spheres of life, and sometimes of their basic well-being. Due to assumptions about the family, women's child-rearing and other domestic labor and household management have been taken for granted and often not acknowledged to be work at all. Women's allegedly "natural" role within the family has been used for centuries to justify their exclusion from civil and political rights, as well as from many occupations—in effect, to make them publicly invisible. And women's economic dependence and subordinated position in the family have rendered them vulnerable to various forms of abuse—physical, sexual, and psychological. Thus, most feminists contend that women's public and private inequalities are closely linked, and have questioned the tendency in Western thought to dichotomize the two spheres (Pateman, Olsen). However, at the same time as they have critiqued existing family forms and divisions of labor, most feminists also think that a greatly changed conception of family—less exclusionary, much more egalitarian, and decidedly less idealized—could have an important place in a better future. And they argue that the achievement of such families will depend on substantial changes in all spheres of life.

Ambivalence about Families in the Feminist Past

Ambivalence about families goes far back in feminist thought. Mary Wollstonecraft, writing in the late eighteenth century largely in response to Rousseau's claims that women needed above all to be pleasing to men, criticized the unjust family relations she saw around her. She argued for greater equality within marriage, and for women's education and access to paid work. At the same time, one of her primary purposes in advocating the optimal development of women's reason was to make them better mothers and to strengthen families.

John Stuart Mill and Harriet Taylor, writing half a century later, denounced patriarchal power relations in families as Wollstonecraft had. They agreed with each other that women should have the right to vote and legal equality in marriage, as well as equal access to education and jobs. What they disagreed about was women's role within the family, with Taylor advocating married women's participation in the work force and Mill balking at this idea, preferring that wives and mothers devote their energies first and foremost to their families. Mill, however, was also one of the very earliest feminists to emphasize the potential of the family to be a school of moral development and to insist that without justice in families and particularly between husbands and wives, there could be no hope for justice in the larger spheres of social and political life.

The early Marxists, and other socialists too, were ambivalent about families. Engels found private property and men's subsequent need for heirs to be the cause of women's subjugation and exploitation within the patriarchal monogamous nuclear family—calling the overthrow of "mother right" the "world-historic defeat of the female sex" (Engels, p. 736). He thought that socialization of the means of production, the communalization of housework, and the entry of all women into the labor force would liberate women. But although he and Marx both ridiculed the bourgeois notion of monogamy as a proprietorial farce, Engels seems to have thought that genuine monogamy, founded in romantic love, would replace it. Thus, though he wanted to see many of the existing functions of families transformed, Engels did not foresee a future without families.

Similarly, George Bernard Shaw, the English Fabian socialist, deplored the economic dependence and restricted role of married women, but did not conclude that families were beyond repair. Rather, he proposed to make women and children economically independent within them by nationalizing industry, requiring that all adults work, and then distributing the profits equally to every child, woman, and man. Only then, he thought, would family ties truly be consensual.

Continuing this tradition of ambivalence, in the 1930s Virginia Woolf indicted the patriarchal English household as a prototype of fascism. Woolf attributed the tyranny of fathers to their economically based powers over their wives and children. She exposed the unity of the family purse as a fiction, and contrasted the actual situations in many households with the idealized vision of fathers as wielding power only in benign ways because their interests were at one with those of their families. Like Mill and Taylor, Woolf thought that the characteristics of families and larger political societies were "inseparably connected. . . . [T]he tyrannies and servilities of the one are the tyrannies and servilities of the other" (Woolf, p. 142). Thus violence and the abuse of power could not be eliminated from the public sphere until they were eliminated from the private one. But Woolf did not conclude that families should be abolished. Rather, she advocated wages for mothers, to free them from economic tyranny—adding that she thought fathers, too, could benefit from this change, by having more time to spend with their children.

Ambivalence about Families in Early Second-Wave Feminism

Contemporary feminists have continued to critique existing family forms, though in most cases, like feminists of the past, not giving up on families altogether. Second-wave feminism began in the United States with liberal feminism. Betty Friedan urged educated middle-class women to reject the myth of the "happy housewife," which, added to the actual tedium of most housework, was leading to frustration or neurosis in potentially creative women. Instead, she urged married women to engage in professional careers or other "meaningful work." She urged them to minimize, but not eschew, their family responsibilities. Subsequent early second-wave liberal feminism, less class-limited in its applicability, stressed the importance for women's equality in and out of the family, reproductive choice, maternity leave, job training for women in poverty, and subsidized child care, as well as an end to sex discrimination in employment ("National Organization for Women Bill of Rights," 1967, in Jaggar and Rothenberg, p. 159).

In England, Marxism was the predominant trend in early second-wave feminism. Juliet Mitchell and others extended the critique of the exploitation of workers under capitalism into a critique of the exploitative nature of the reproductive and household labor performed by women. They argued that women are doubly exploited under capitalism—for their paid labor in the workplace, and for their unpaid reproduction of the labor force in the family. But did women constitute a "class"? How might one account for the wives of capitalists, who seemed exploited as a sex even as they benefitted from class exploitation? Mitchell drew an analogy between their situation and that of the "rich peasants" in prerevolutionary China, since both groups were comparatively well-off members of a generally exploited class (Mitchell, p. 179). The family was clearly a major site of women's exploitation from this twentieth-century Marxist feminist point of view, though, like earlier Marxists, its critics did not explicitly seek to abolish it altogether.

In the late 1960s, radical feminists in the United States launched the harshest and least ambivalent critiques of the family to date: the "biological family"—a concept little informed by history or anthropology—was at the root of the "sex class" that constitutes women's oppression, and must be abolished. Some radical feminists, most notably Shulamith Firestone, viewed pregnancy and motherhood as in themselves oppressive, concluding that technological advances in reproduction would finally free women from the constraints of female biology. This was an unusual view. However, radical feminists frequently challenged the necessity of the family itself—not only its current structures and divisions of labor. Unlike Marxists, they saw patriarchy, rather than the relations of production, as the most fundamental of all oppressions. They found it in all societies, perpetuated by families, and at the root of other forms of oppression such as class and race. For many radical feminists, opting out of families and separatism from men were the only tolerable answers for women.

Socialist feminists synthesized the central approaches of Marxist feminism and radical feminism, also incorporating some of the insights of liberal feminism (Jaggar). They argued that both class analysis and an understanding of patriarchy were necessary for explaining the situation of women living in capitalist society. In developing explicitly socialist-feminist strategies for changing society, they addressed the intersecting and combined oppressions of capitalism and patriarchy, of which families and reproductive practices constituted a major part.

During the 1970s, some feminists approached the subject of the family from a psychoanalytic point of view. Both Nancy Chodorow and Dorothy Dinnerstein sought to understand inequality between the sexes, certain differences between the sexes, and misogyny as originating from prevailing child-rearing arrangements. Both argued, though in distinct ways, that the fact that women almost invariably raise small children deeply affects the psychological development of those children: girls can separate more gradually and less radically from the same-sex carer with whom they are initially psychologically fused, therefore developing less distinct ego-boundaries and a more relational sense of self; boys have to separate more distinctly, defining themselves as "not female," therefore devaluing what is defined as feminine and developing a more individuated sense of self. The logical conclusion of both Chodorow's and Dinnerstein's theories is that, were early child-raising to be more equally shared between men and women, boys and girls would develop more similar psychologies, misogyny would decrease, and the sexes would be more equal in all aspects of our lives. This was a powerful addition to other feminist arguments for the more equal allocation of family labor and wagework between men and women. It also represents another example of the prevailing feminist view that families, being neither all bad nor all good, need to be critiqued and reformed, rather than discarded.

Family Resemblances

The lines just drawn between liberal, Marxist, radical, socialist, and psychoanalytic feminisms have become less distinct since about 1980. To some extent, this may be attributable to the growing salience of other crosscutting distinctions—such as that between feminists who accentuate similarities and those who accentuate differences between the sexes, or that between feminists who stress differences (for example, those of race, class, or religion) amongst women and those who stress what women have in common. Endorsing the initially radical slogan "the personal is political," most current feminists are convinced of the multiple interconnections between women's status, roles within families, and their inequality and segregation in the workplace and the political realm, and between their socialization in gendered families and the psychological aspects of their oppression. Feminism has challenged the tendency to dichotomize public and private in at least three ways.

First, as some earlier feminists were clearly aware, what happens in domestic and private life is not immune from the dynamic of *power*, which has often been seen as definitive of politics. Power within families—whether of husbands over wives or of parents over children—has often not been recognized as such, because it has been perceived as natural or benign. But the notion that power even in its crudest form, physical violence, is not a factor in family life is a myth that has been increasingly exposed during the last century and especially during the last two decades. Largely because of the efforts of feminists, violence and sexual abuse in the home are now much less sanctioned or ignored as "private matters" than in the past; they are recognized as serious problems that society must act on. There is now no doubt that family violence and sexual abuse, as they affect both wives and children, are closely connected with differentials of power and dependency between the sexes. In addition, feminists have discerned and documented subtler, though no less important, modes of power that operate within families—such as spouses' different amounts of influence over important decisions, including the division of labor between them, and spouses' different anticipated costs in exiting the relationship. It is impossible to claim, in the light of current evidence, that families are nonpolitical in the sense that power is an insignificant factor in them.

Second, the very existence of a private sphere, its extent and limits, what is and is not acceptable behavior within it, and who can and cannot constitute a family have been and still are decided in the public sphere—directly in legislatures and courts, less directly in the workplace, media, and schools. Historically, the law defined marriage as a hierarchical as well as a heterosexual relationship, and excluded women not only from political rights but from most means of making a living wage. At present, public decisions—about the terms of marriage and divorce, about working hours, school hours, and the availability of child care, about wages, welfare payments, pensions, and taxes—all shape families and contribute to inequalities of private power. As Frances Olsen has written: "Because the state is deeply implicated in the formation and functioning of families, it is nonsense to talk about whether the state does or does not intervene in the family" (Olsen, p. 837). The question is not whether, but how it intervenes.

A third way in which the idea that public and private are autonomous realms breaks down is suggested in the psychoanalytic literature discussed above. Since domestic life is where most of our earliest and most formative socialization takes place, families are where, through gendered parenting, we *become* our gendered selves. Of course, this early gendering is reinforced in other social institutions, such as schools, workplaces, the media, and so on. In turn, the gendering of these other institutions helps to perpetuate and reinforce that within families: for example, women's typically lower pay reinforces the "rationality," in most two-parent families, of the mother's being the primary child-rearer, which continues the cycle of gender inequality between the sexes. Once we acknowledge that significant differences between women and men are created by existing divisions of labor within families, it becomes increasingly obvious how political family life is.

Family Differences

Much of the early second-wave feminist critique of families focused predominantly, if not exclusively, on relatively well-off, two-parent, heterosexual, white families. Subsequent feminist analyses have been critical of these earlier depictions of "the family" as insufficiently representative of the different forms that families take when class, race, and ethnicity, as well as sexual orientation, are considered seriously. African-American feminists, Latina and Asian feminists as well as those from other minority groups, lesbian feminists, those with a working-class perspective (as well as white, middle-class, heterosexual feminists writing in support of these perspectives) have pointed out that some of the problems found and some of the solutions arrived at in some earlier feminist discussions of "the family" do not apply in the case of all families.

Some aspects of earlier theories made them easy targets of such criticism. Most obviously, solutions to middle-class women's oppression, such as Friedan's in *The Feminine Mystique*, which rely on the employment of "help," cannot be solutions for those women whose race or class position makes them likely to constitute the "help" (hooks). Some other such critiques are equally telling: working-class and most Black mothers, for example, are unlikely to experience being a housewife as oppressive; rather, as mothers with no option but to work long double shifts—at work and at home—they may see it as an unattainable ideal. Black feminists are more likely to regard racism than men and sexism as Black women's foremost problem (hooks; Collins). Never-married mothers are far more likely to perceive poverty or time-poverty as pressing problems than to be directly concerned with the division of labor between the sexes (Zinn, in Thorne and Yalom 1992). Single mothers living in extended family situations may see the family more as a supportive than as an oppressive institution (Collins, in Thorne and Yalom 1992; Stack). Lesbians, who live in more egalitarian relationships than heterosexuals, are more obviously disadvantaged by the heterosexist norm of what constitutes a family than by the unequal division of labor between the sexes (Rich 1980; Weston).

Feminist work on families has been greatly affected by such critiques and the varied perspectives from which they are made. At the same time as we acknowledge this recognition of diversity as progress, though, it is important not to forget that some of the central insights of early second-wave feminism, in spite of its narrower initial focus of attention, still retain power in the context of more broadly focused attention. Some of its discoveries, arguments, and demands, even though they issued forth from a movement that was predominantly white, middle-class, and heterosexual, are extremely relevant to women (and sometimes to men) in very different life and family circumstances. It is therefore important that feminists not overreact to the challenge of differences among women by losing sight of their broadly relevant insights about families, their gendered division of labor, and its effect on sex inequality in all spheres of life. Unmasking the mythology of the public/private dichotomy, thereby challenging the division of labor between the sexes and the denial of women's domestic work as real work, seems not only, like Sisyphus with his rock, to be an unending struggle, it is a struggle that it is in many different women's and at least some men's interests to win.

Sometimes feminists of color have exaggerated the irrelevance of the work of white, middle-class, heterosexual feminists to their own different situations. Consider, for example, this introductory statement from a collection of writings of Black feminists: "Unlike some white feminists who have questioned, and at times rightfully rejected, the white patriarchal family, we want very much to retain our blood connections without sacrificing ourselves to rigid and demeaning sex roles" (Smith). This contrast between white and Black feminists is almost entirely imaginary, since as we have seen, except for a small radical fringe, all feminists, white as well as Black, want to retain the family but to reject its "rigid and demeaning sex roles." Sometimes, too, white middle-class feminists have overreacted to critiques of their work as "essentialist" and insensitive to differences. They are at times more apologetic than they need to be, proceeding on the basis of a larger-than-warranted concern about insufficient attention to differences among women and families.

Especially recently, there are signs that a healthy balance may be reached on this important issue. Some feminists who agree with the critique of earlier second-wave feminist theories of the family as insufficiently cognizant of or sensitive to issues of race, class, and sexual orientation are not reacting by dismissing such work out of hand. Instead, they take another, closer look at such theories. They ask: *Is* the theory relevant to situations and circumstances of women other than white, middle-class, heterosexual women, and if so, how? Denise Segura and Jennifer Pierce ask just this of Chodorow's theory about how "mothering" qualities are reproduced in girls in conditions of female primary parenting. Chodorow's work has been much faulted for its "essentialist" tendencies—for its attempt "to theorize in terms of a putatively unitary, primary, culturally universal type of activity associated with women" (Fraser and Nicholson, p. 29; see also Spelman, chap. 4). Segura and Pierce, however, respecting Chodorow's own recommendation that psychoanalytic method be employed in socially specific contexts, reexamine her theory in the context of Chicana/o families, only to discover its considerable relevance. They point out that, while features such as higher fertility, extended households, nonexclusive mothering, and parent/child sleeping arrangements tend to differentiate Chicana/o families from European-American ones, such differences do not render Chodorow's theory irrelevant to such families. They conclude, rather, that "Chodorow's theoretical framework is useful in understanding the acquisition of gender identity in Chicana/o families—families characterized by a unique constellation of features derived from their socially and historically specific context" (Segura and Pierce, p. 64).

There are obvious benefits to such reevaluations of earlier second-wave feminist theories about families that a decade or more of scholarship had been inclined to jettison as racist, classist, ethnocentric, or heterosexist. Indeed, when such theories are given a fair second chance rather than rejected as essentialist, they can sometimes be found to apply to or to have considerable relevance to those persons they had been thought to neglect and thereby to discriminate against. Let us look briefly at three more examples.

Gay men and lesbians are likely to benefit from the feminist challenge to gender roles in the heterosexual family. Why should this be? Because a great deal of the hostility that many people feel toward gay men and lesbians is related to their need to dichotomize the sexes. For them, gay men—whom they perceive as feminine—and lesbian women—whom they perceive as masculine—threaten to blur or undermine the gender roles that order their world. A number of sociological studies have demonstrated that respondents who strongly believe in a strict masculine-feminine sex role dichotomy devalue gay men and lesbians because they perceive them to be role deviants, while respondents who do not value sex roles do not share this negative attitude. Legal scholars, too, have discerned in the reasoning of judges this same stereotyping of and negative attitude toward gay men and lesbians, based in the same fear that homosexuality threatens the supposedly clear distinctions between the sexes. Such anxieties are surely not the only reason for homophobia in our society, but they are clearly a crucial component of it. Given this, it becomes apparent that feminist struggles to explain and challenge sex roles and to reduce the social salience of sex differences are also very likely to diminish hostility toward and discrimination against gay men and lesbians (Okin 1996 and references therein). It is especially clear that a yearning after distinct sex roles drives much of the hostility to gay and lesbian parents. Behind the intolerance for "deviant" sexuality in parents seems to lurk great discomfort with the idea that a child should have two mothers or two fathers. But if mothers and fathers were much more similar to each other than most are now in how they relate to children (and to each other), why should it matter whether a child in a two-parent family has two male parents, two female parents, or one of each sex?

Poor, single mothers—whether divorced or never married—are another part of the population that can clearly benefit from discoveries and arguments that were first made mostly by middle-class, educated, white women, thinking primarily in terms of two-parent families. The failure to recognize and valorize child care and housework as work continues to disadvantage women in many different family situations. To be sure, it affects negatively the divorcing middle-class mother who has spent twenty years raising children and supporting her husband's career, and who finds that the legal system gives her little economic recognition for any of this important work. But it also assails the welfare-dependent, single mother of small children. As the current attack on Aid to Families with Dependent Children has made clear, whatever her race (though especially if she is Black), her age, or her situation, a single mother asking for aid is accused of not "working" unless she takes a paid job. Unfortunately, little attention has been given to the obvious feminist response: she *is* working. She is doing some of the most important of society's work, albeit often under extremely difficult circumstances. Ironically, this expectation that poor women should "work," while their children are small, is expressed most vehemently by the same conservative politicians and pundits who insist most strongly that more affluent mothers, who are supported by a man, should stay home with their children. Apparently, they think the answer to the question, Does an infant or small child need its mother to stay home to take care of it? depends on the income of the child's parents (though they would be hard-pressed if required to defend this strange view of children's needs).

Finally, all women concerned with freedom of reproductive choice benefit from feminist arguments that child care and other family work is real, hard, and valuable work. For the conception of this work as not real work lends credibility to the antiabortion movement's depiction of a woman who is not willing to bear a child as a selfish murderess, rather than as a person who is responsible enough to know that raising a child in contemporary society is a complex, time-consuming, and stressful task she is not able or willing to take on. As Linda Gordon writes, "The abortion opponents today, like those of a hundred years ago, are afraid of a loss of mothering, in the symbolic sense.... the influence of nurturing women counteracting the completely egoistic principles of the economy" (Gordon, in Thorne and Yalom 1992, p. 152). It is most understandable why people would value mothering, including nurturance and altruism. The problem is that, being largely antifeminists, the opponents of abortion still want to be able to take this "mothering" for granted. Until there is a radical change in attitudes toward the work women have always performed without pay, "prolife" energy will be able to remain fixated on fetuses, rather than turning its focus toward building the infrastructure that society needs, now that many women have decided they are no longer going to take care of everybody else at the expense of their own well-being.

Families, the New Right and Other "Profamily" Fallacies, and the Feminist Agenda

Since the 1970s, there has been a strong resurgence of moralistic conservativism in the U.S. (and, perhaps to a lesser extent, in Britain). The New Right has taken on the defense of "family values" as one of its central aims, and is often overt in its antifeminism and its feminist-blaming (e.g., Bloom). Much of the agenda of the New Right is supposedly aimed at restoring the "traditional family": abortion should be illegal, divorce difficult, out-of-wedlock pregnancy punished, homosexuality discouraged and discriminated against and sex education nonexistent, children should pray at school—and "family values" will be restored to American society. Though libertarian on issues like taxation and (in the United States) the right to bear arms, the New Right wants to enforce its morality, especially on women and children. Rather than looking to alleviate the more preventable causes of teenage pregnancy and family breakups, such as poverty, unemployment, bad schools, and ignorance about sexuality, the New Right wants women and children back under the control of men. At the extreme, "traditional" marriage has been invoked to argue against both the legal recognition of rape within marriage and the provision of shelters for battered wives (Okin 1989, p. 42).

Family life, which not so long ago had to be placed on the political agenda by insistent feminists, has now become a central topic in political debate across the political spectrum. What is perhaps more surprising than the consciously antifeminist, profamily rhetoric of the New Right is the less intentional antifeminism of some closer to the political center. Iris Marion Young has recently written a strong critique of the profamily proposals of William Galston, author of *Liberal Purposes* and until recently the Clinton Administration's Chief Adviser on Domestic Policy (Young 1995). Galston, a liberal with communitarian leanings, recommends that the state encourage the two-parent family by restricting or delaying divorce when children are involved, because of its strong interest in maintaining such families as the best environment for rearing independent citizens. By "independence," Galston means "the disposition to care for, and take responsibility for, oneself and to avoid becoming needlessly dependent on others" (Galston, p. 222).

Young contests some of the evidence Galston looks to to establish the two-parent family as the best environment for raising children. But the main thrust of her argument is to reveal the antifeminist aspects of Galston's ostensibly gender-neutral depiction of families and of the civic virtue he so emphasizes—independence. As she demonstrates, by proceeding as if independence is equivalent to economic self-sufficiency, and by ignoring the gendered division of labor that persists in our society, Galston effectively restricts independence to those who do not need to be taken care of and whose labor market participation is not limited by others' demands for care. Thus the old, the young, the sick, and those, largely women, who are primary carers for any of the above cannot share in the citizenly virtue of independence. At the same time (though Young does not highlight this), Galston's assumptions about the care that takes place within families allow him not to see that even the minority of citizens he considers independent are not really so, for in important everyday ways (other than economic) they do not, of course, take care of themselves. Young shows that because of Galston's failure to attend to gender inequality within and outside families, his argument for the moral superiority of two-parent families amounts to this paradox:

> Mothers should subordinate themselves to and be dependent on men, even if they would rather parent on their own, for the sake of nurturing the independence of their children. Independence is a paragon virtue of liberal citizenship, but a mother's virtue entails dependence on a man. . . . [M]others are less than full citizens in the liberal society. (p. 544)

The strength of Young's persuasive argument is much enhanced by her clearheaded focus on the fact that, despite variations of class and race, women still provide the vast majority of the unpaid care in our society, and that the simultaneous assumption and neglect of this fact distorts many important things. Though Young has written elsewhere, eloquently and persuasively, about the "politics of difference" (Young 1990), the success of her critique of Galston is due largely to her putting differences aside to focus on what women and families have in common. In my view, only if we hold the fact of women's unrecognized work in focus, as Young does, will we be able to begin to resolve some of the most divisive issues our society faces—from abortion to divorce, from child abuse to the persistence of poverty and the increasing youth of perpetrators of violence. In the spirit of our feminist predecessors, we must continue to confront and challenge this neglected fact, and the injustices it embodies and leads to. Women have done and continue to do much of the crucial work of society without compensation or recognition, but their tolerance for this state of affairs has been approaching its limit for some time now. No longer able to assume and ignore the work that women do, society will have to face up to "rethinking the family."

Feminists are under no illusion that the "traditional family" either could or should be restored, for they have a starkly different view from those who idealize it of what it looked like and how it was experienced—to the extent that it existed at all. Feminists reject the New Right's and other similar solutions, not only as clearly unjust to women, but as likely to fail in a practical sense: the experience of other times and places suggests, for example, that rescinding abortion rights leads to dangerous illegal abortions, and that restricting divorce may result in (for lack of a better term) "common law bigamy" rather than restored monogamy, or in increased domestic abuse. Well aware of the extent to which feminist ideas as well as such changes as new reproductive technologies, easier access to divorce, women's greater financial independence, and the growing incidence of lesbian, gay, and single parenthood have challenged and altered previous notions of "family," feminists sometimes have differing views about the best directions law and public policy should take. But all are agreed that there is no return to a past in which, however "stable" it might look from a rapidly changing present, people were coerced into remaining within loveless or even violent marriages, women were defined out of citizenship and had their work taken for granted, and girls and boys were socialized into the constraining straitjackets of gender.

Families at Century's End

Many feminists are turning with renewed attention to the realm that has been seen for so long as paradigmatically not political. Ambivalent, as in the past, they value much of what families represent, but refuse to accept the continued reinforcement of women's subordination that for so long seemed almost synonymous with "family." They are responding to the multiple changes in family life that this *fin de siècle* has brought about— not so as to try to restore an overlauded and mythologized past, but so as to enable more egalitarian and more inclusive family forms and relations to develop in the future.

Thus most contemporary feminists, while critiquing the gender-structured family, have not rejected all forms of family. Many advocate that "family" be redefined so as to include any intimately connected and committed group, specifically endorsing same-sex marriage and parenthood; almost all, certainly, refuse to choose between accepting women's double burden and abolishing the family. Despite the evident difficulty of shifting the distribution of household tasks toward men as women have taken on more paid labor, feminists continue to refuse to accept the division of labor between the sexes as natural and unchangeable.

More and more, as the extent to which gender is a social construction has become understood, feminists have come to recognize how variable are the potential forms and practices of families. Families are in no way inevitably tied to the gender structures of the past, but until these are not only challenged but successfully undermined, nontraditional groupings are recognized, and equitable divisions of labor facilitated, there can be no hope of equality for women in either the domestic or the public sphere. Nor, as has been increasingly recognized in some nonfeminist as well as feminist circles in the last few decades, can there be hope of social well-being in general in a polity that neglects and takes for granted the nurturance of its citizens. Families are on the political agenda to stay.

Bibliography

Bloom, Allan, *The Closing of the American Mind* (New York: Simon and Schuster, 1987).

Chodorow, Nancy, *The Reproduction of Mothering: Psychoanalysis and the Sociology of Gender* (Berkeley: University of California Press, 1978).

———, "Family Structure and Feminine Personality," in M. Z. Rosaldo and L. Lamphere, eds. *Women, Culture, and Society* (Stanford: Stanford University Press, 1974).

Collins, Patricia Hill, *Black Feminist Thought: Knowledge, Consciousness, and the Politics of Empowerment* (New York: Routledge, 1991).

Dinnerstein, Dorothy, *The Mermaid and the Minotaur: Sexual Arrangements and Human Malaise* (New York: Harper and Row, 1976).

Engels, Frederick, *The Origin of the Family, Private Property, and the State*. Excerpted in Robert Tucker, ed., *The Marx-Engels Reader*, 2nd edition (New York: Norton, 1978).

Firestone, Shulamith, *The Dialectic of Sex: The Case For Feminist Revolution* (New York: Morrow, 1970).

Fraser, Nancy and Nicholson, Linda, *Feminism/Postmodernism* (New York: Routledge, 1990).

Friedan, Betty, *The Feminine Mystique* (New York: Dell, 1963).

Galston, William, *Liberal Purposes* (Cambridge: Cambridge University Press, 1991).

hooks, bell, *Feminist Theory: From Margin to Center* (Boston: South End Press, 1984).

Jaggar, Alison, *Feminist Politics and Human Nature* (Totowa, N.J.: Rowman and Littlefield, 1983).

——— and Rothenberg, Paula S., *Feminist Frameworks* (New York: McGraw-Hill, 1993).

Kymlicka, Will, "Rethinking the Family," *Philosophy and Public Affairs* 22 (1992).

Mill, John Stuart and Taylor, Harriet (1869), *Essays on Sex Equality*, ed. Alice Rossi (Chicago: University of Chicago Press, 1970).

Mitchell, Juliet, *Woman's Estate* (New York: Vintage, 1971).

Okin, Susan Moller, *Justice, Gender, and the Family* (New York: Basic Books, 1989).

———, "Sexual Orientation, Gender, and Families: Dichotomizing Differences," *Hypatia* 11, No. 1 (1996).

Olsen, Frances, "The Myth of State Intervention in the Family," *University of Michigan Journal of Law Reform*, 18, No. 4 (1985).

Pateman, Carole, "Feminist Critiques of the Public/Private Dichotomy," in *The Disorder of Women: Democracy, Feminism, and Political Theory*, ed. Pateman (Stanford: Stanford University Press, 1989).

Rich, Adrienne, "Compulsory Heterosexuality and Lesbian Existence," *Signs* 5, No. 4 (1980).

Ruddick, Sara, "Maternal Thinking," *Feminist Studies* 6, No. 2 (1980).

Segura, Denise A. and Pierce, Jennifer L., "Chicana/o Family Structure and Gender Personality: Chodorow, Familism, and Psychoanalytic Sociology Revisited," *Signs* 19, No. 1 (1993).

Shaw, George Bernard (1928), *The Intelligent Woman's Guide to Socialism and Capitalism*, ed. S. M. Okin (New Brunswick, N.J.: Transaction Books, 1984).

Smith, Barbara, ed., *Home Girls: A Black Feminist Anthology* (New York: Kitchen Table/Women of Color Press, 1983).

Spelman, Elizabeth V., *Inessential Woman: Problems of Exclusion in Feminist Thought* (Boston: Beacon, 1988).

Stack, Carole, *All Our Kin: Strategies for Survival in a Black Community* (New York: Harper and Row, 1974).

Thorne, Barrie with Marilyn Yalom, eds., *Rethinking the Family: Some Feminist Questions* (New York: Longman, 1982, also significantly revised edition, 1992).

Weston, Kath, *Families We Choose: Lesbians, Gays, Kinship* (New York: Columbia University Press, 1991).

Wollstonecraft, Mary (1792), *A Vindication of the Rights of Woman*, various editions, including Miriam Kramnick, ed. (New York: Penguin, 1975).

Woolf, Virginia, *Three Guineas* (London: Harcourt Brace, 1938).

Young, Iris Marion, *Justice and the Politics of Difference* (Princeton: Princeton University Press, 1990).

———, "Mothers, Citizenship, and Independence: A Critique of Pure Family Values," *Ethics* 105, No. 3 (1995).

2

The Myth of the Traditional Family

Linda Nicholson

The categories we have for sorting our world affect how we think about our present situation and possible alternatives. Unfortunately, the categories we have for organizing families—particularly the language that sorts them into "traditional" and "alternative" ones—make too many of us needlessly ashamed of the way we live. This dichotomy of possibilities leads many of us to think that the way we make our sexual, affective, and domestic arrangements is somewhat unusual and other than what it should be. Not only gays and lesbians but also heterosexuals living alone; unmarried heterosexuals living together; married couples with husbands at home caring for children or wives working outside of the home; and children living in single-parent, stepfamily, or alternating households are either "in the closet" or somewhat embarrassed about how they live.[1]

This shame is needless, for the language of the categories is duplicitous. The "traditional" family is not all that traditional, its most basic features emerging out of certain transformations in social life occurring in Western Europe and North America during the eighteenth and nineteenth centuries. While by the late nineteenth century such transformations had resulted in an ideal of family life in rough conformity with the version familiar today, it was only in the immediate post–World War II period that a specific form of this ideal became a mass phenomenon, particularly in the United States. The economic prosperity of the United States during the postwar period, an enormous housing boom coming out of the overcrowding and lack of housing construction of the 1930s and 1940s, and an increasing view of the family as *not* including grandparents, aunts, uncles, and cousins contributed to very large numbers of people constructing lives in conformity with a relatively new and very specific ideal of family life. But as the 1950s model family was made possible by certain historically specific factors, so too did other historical factors—such as the growing participation of married women in the paid labor force, rising divorce rates, and the creation of homosexual communities—lead to the emergence of new family types. Such family types are no more "alternative" to what had preceded them than had been the 1950s type to its historical predecessors.

But not only does the "traditional" family possess no more claims to "naturality" or historical universality than do "alternative" families; it is also that what constitutes "traditionality" itself keeps changing. Thus, if one compares the "traditional" family of the 1950s to the one of the 1990s, they are not the same. Such historical observations lead me to the next stage of my argument: that the distinction between the "traditional" and "alternative" family functions not descriptively but normatively, legitimizing certain family types over others on the basis of dubious historical assumptions.

The question then arises as to the basis for the privileging function of this distinction, independent of its historical claims. Here I wish to make two arguments. First I want to claim that the specific type of privileging we today give to the "traditional" family—in either its 1950s or 1990s form—has morally dubious origins, being strongly associated with the post–World War II period's racism and tendencies to marginalize poverty and to classify as "un-American" modes of life which did not conform to "middle-class" life. Certainly, it has not only been the post–World War II period that has privileged certain family types over others. But I will argue that the specific form this privileging assumed in this period must be related to certain specific features of the period, many of which are morally problematic.

Secondly I will argue that abandoning the distinction between "traditional" and "alternative" does not leave us, as some critics have suggested, with an "anything goes" attitude towards family types. We can still make evaluations of family types or specific features of family types on the basis of their consequences on people's lives and in relation to the contexts of their functioning. Whether a type of family provides economic and emotional sustenance to its members, with special attention to children, given the resources at its disposal and the demands it must face, should constitute the primary criteria by which it is evaluated. The distinction between "traditional" and "alternative" families gets in the way of our being able to make such considered evaluations.

The "Traditional" Family

When present-day English-language speakers use the word "family," they can mean one of two things by it. They can refer to the relatively small unit composed of people related by marriage or blood who live together; however, there is another sense of "family," where "family" refers to all those people with whom one is related. Grandmothers, even very great ones, get counted here as well as distant cousins, aunts, and so on. This latter meaning of "family" makes "family" synonymous with "kin."

Insofar as "family" is equated with "kinship," a good case can be made for thinking of "family" as ranging over most, if not all, human societies. However, when conservatives claim that "the family" is under attack, their concern is not with the preservation of "family" in this sense. Rather, the kind of "family" they are typically referring to is that captured by the first sense above, that is, the unit of parents with children who live together. However, this concern is typically justified with the argument that what is being destroyed is "universal." In other words, there is a slippage in the use of language so that the universality of one type of institution becomes claimed about another only because the two institutions share the same name, that is, "the family."

To be sure, many people recognize the family form of only parents with children as somewhat recent. However, they tend to think of this institution—typically referred to as "the nuclear family"—as only a slightly modified version of "the extended family." Indeed, "the extended family" is frequently thought of as a nuclear family with some extra relatives attached. And since it is widely believed that this "extended family" is in fact universal, its underlying similarity with the nuclear family makes it appear appropriate to think of "the nuclear family" as basically universal, even if somewhat shrunken in size in recent times.

This commonsense view of family history is, however, mythical. While there is a good deal of debate within the field of family history about how far back the nuclear family extends and about what type of family form immediately preceded it, no one credits any family form as universal. Too much anthropological literature exists which documents the variability of kinship systems, living arrangements, and the ways in which these combine across cultures. Indeed, when conservatives claim that we need to hang on to "the traditional family," I am often tempted to retort that a true enactment of such would have us all organized into tribes or into those forms of living arrangements in which very early human beings actually lived.

To be sure, the rejoinder might be made that even if the nuclear or extended family does not encompass *all* of human history, this basic family type extends far enough back to provide good enough grounds for calling it "traditional." To ascertain the validity of this claim we need to do a bit of family history. We need to determine what family history tells us about the origins of what many of us understand by "the family."

Family history, a relatively new subfield of the discipline of history, has evidenced a great deal of controversy within its short life. Part of the problem here is that this branch of history, like other branches, yields different types of stories depending on the questions asked and the methods used for answering them. One of the studies which became prominent early in the development of this subfield was carried out by Peter Laslett and his colleagues at Cambridge University.[2] The Cambridge group wished to debunk the thesis of extended family structures in preindustrial Europe. Through the examination of various records they demonstrated that the average size of coresident groups in the West dating back at least as far as the seventeenth century and extending to the early twentieth century was approximately 4.75 persons per household. These figures were taken to show that the nuclear family unit extended much further back in Western history and was a more stable family type than many had previously thought.

The work of the Cambridge group was soon, however, called into question. Part of the problem was the utility of using average size to demonstrate anything. As Wally Seccombe points out, a focus on a mean or average size discounts the possibility that some households may be very large and others very small.

> By fixating on mean household size, the Cambridge paradigm disregards the elementary fact that more people live in large households than in small ones. Given this asymmetry, the average size of households is a deceptive index; the more illuminating measure is the proportion of the population living in households of a certain size. In fact (as Laslett himself acknowledged), when the average size of households was 4.75 persons, *5.3 per cent of the population lived in households of six or more people*. (Seccombe, p. 121)

A focus on mean or average size also ignores the question of how household members view each other, whatever their number. Are all members of a household counted as family? Does family go beyond household? In short, is family coextensive with household? To answer these kinds of questions one needs some answers to the question of how the word "family" itself has been defined over time. Jean-Louis Flandrin has done much of the influential work in this branch of family history. In his work, *Families in Former Times*, Flandrin argues that in Western Europe prior to the nineteenth century, the word "family" has two meanings, neither of which is "relatives who live together." One of its meanings includes an extended kinship network who do not coreside, similar to one of our contemporary meanings. But even here the meaning is not quite identical. In earlier periods, this meaning of family tends to be applied only to extended kinship networks of some wealth, though wealth of a certain sort. It tends to be a term more widely used of the bourgeoisie rather than of the aristocracy, the latter more typically referring to themselves as of a given "house."

There is a second meaning of "family" also prevalent during this period. This meaning refers to those who live together, those related through kinship as well as those who are not. This meaning is reflected in Samuel

Pepy's opening section of his Diary, where he states: "I lived in Axe Yard, having my wife, and servant Jane, and no more in family than us three" (Flandrin, p. 5). This meaning of "family" tends in fact to be the prominent meaning of "family" of this period, being listed first or principally in many English and French dictionaries of the seventeenth and eighteenth centuries, though becoming less important in France during the course of the eighteenth century (Flandrin, p. 5).

What was the context, then, for the emergence of that meaning of "family" which made it neither synonymous with extended kinship nor with household membership but referred to that collection of close kinship members who reside together? The context seems a wide variety of factors taking place in Western Europe and North America from the sixteenth century on, but which began to coalesce in a certain form during the eighteenth and nineteenth centuries. To skim over the surface of a great deal of detailed work that has been done on the history of the modern family, one can identify certain very broad trends. For one among those of property, there occurs very early in the modern period a diminishment in the importance of the ties of the extended kinship network and a greater sense that one's fortune is tied to one's more closely related kin. Lawrence Stone, in depicting what he calls "The Restricted Patriarchal Nuclear Family" of England of the period 1550 to 1700, emphasizes the increasing tightness of the bonds between parents and children in this period over earlier times. (Stone 1979). As Natalie Zemon Davis notes, this change signifies an increasing sense of the nuclear family unit as a type of planning unit oriented to the future welfare of its members (Davis 1977).

But it is not only that the ties which bind close kin to a more extended kinship network become increasingly diminished for those of property beginning in the early modern period; there also emerges a sense of what constitutes the character and meaning of household life that begins to change, particularly in the eighteenth century. Prior to about the middle of this century, households of property appear strongly organized around relations of authority where the status of servants is not all that different in kind from that of wives, younger siblings, or children. During the course of the eighteenth century, such relations of authority appear to give way to relations of greater equality and affection among members related by kinship and to more contractual-type relations between servants and heads of household.

What we mean by "the traditional family" is an institution that begins to emerge for the upper classes during the eighteenth century. It is typified by a strong sense of the separation of the unit of parents and children from both a more extended kinship network and from such non–kin-related persons as servants. It is marked by a norm of partnership between husband and wife and by the special role of the mother in shaping the character of her children.[3] In brief, it represents an institution less organized around relationships of authority and more geared to relations of affection as the household becomes less a unit focused on production and more on sexuality, intimacy, and consumption.

Among the lower classes, relations among family members appear more egalitarian than among those of property, even in the earlier period.[4] But that pre-eighteenth-century peasant households were governed less by principles of patriarchal authority than were the households of the aristocracy does not mean that they resembled the later domestic model either. Rather, here the transformation—taking place more predominantly in the nineteenth than the eighteenth century—seems to be from a household whose members are more allied to their respective peers in the village than they are to each other, to one where conjugal ties take precedence over external ones. In other words, if domesticity arose in the upper classes in the eighteenth century in relation to a certain model of patriarchal authority, in the lower classes it arose in the nineteenth century in relation to a distinctive model of village life. It appears that by the late nineteenth and early twentieth century, working class households both did and did not exemplify the new ideal of domesticity developed by the aristocracy and bourgeoisie in the second half of the eighteenth century. Certainly with the decline of the strength of village constraints, there had developed for the poor the notion that marriage was something chosen by the couple rather than organized by external authorities. And there was a similar idea of the conjugal couple with children as an autonomous unit within a hostile world. But there were also many aspects of the new norm of domesticity that were unattainable for the poor. Households require a certain amount of economic resources for even minimal maintenance. For the poor, achieving such resources often required the creation of living arrangements not quite in keeping with the new form. Thus in working class households there was often the presence of "boarders" or families sharing lodging (Coontz, p. 136).

If one turns to the United States context, the content of much of the social reform movements of the late nineteenth and early twentieth centuries appears aimed at strengthening the new ideal. In the late nineteenth century, campaigns directed at making poor and immigrant families conform to the new ideal of domesticity were often spearheaded by private charity organizations; however, often the actions of such groups led to the actual breakup of poor families whose behavior did not conform to the norms the ideal demanded. Reformers during the Progressive Era not only turned from private organizations to the federal government for promulgating the ideal but also worked for legislation which would keep more families intact.[5] The goals were clear: households where husbands worked, wives stayed home, children went to school, and no one other than these lived within the home. Child labor legislation, protective labor legislation for women, the creation of Mother's Pensions, and federally supervised arbitration aimed at ensuring male heads of households "a family wage," all were geared to furthering these ends.

The notion of "proper" family life that spearheaded much of the social legislation of the Progressive Era did not die during the 1930s and 1940s. However, the Great Depression and World War II placed strong limits on the degree to which it could be lived out by large numbers of people. It was not until the post–World War II period that the ideal became a real possibility for the masses. Most basically, the great economic boom of the 1950s made for an increase in real wages. It also made possible substantial amounts of government spending: on the GI Bill, on sewer and highway construction, and on extensive subsidization of home mortgages. These factors, combined with the savings that many Americans had been able to generate during the war years, contributed to massive housing construction and the creation of suburbia. During the period of the depression and World War II, many Americans had lived with relatives or strangers in crowded housing conditions; the idea of a "home of one's own" containing only one's spouse and children came to seem highly desirable to many.[6]

As Stephanie Coontz points out, the 1950s family was experienced by most people of the time as something new. Many of the films and television plays of the period dealt with people trying to negotiate ties to a larger kin network with ties to the nuclear family. Invariably, the "happy" ending meant that ties to the nuclear family won out. She notes how many commentators urged young couples to "adopt a 'modern' stance and strike out on their own" (Coontz, p. 26).

What was new was not only that wide segments of the population were coming to believe in the desirability of living only with spouse and children; also new were many of the expectations people held about what such a family was to be about. While the Victorian ideal of domesticity included wife and mother at home, it portrayed her household activities in very different ways from the ideal of the 1950s. A notion of woman as moral guardian of the hearth who left her more practical tasks to servants gave way to an ideal of woman who was morally and psychologically fulfilled through housework and child-rearing. The family became seen as the site of leisure and consumption where, ideally, leisure activities were carried out together (Coontz, pp. 27–28).

Changes in the class structure in the United States and the emergence of a large middle class in this period can be significantly related to the emergence of the idea that the ideal family of the 1950s constituted the "traditional" family. Let me explain. The economic boom of the 1950s was a strange phenomenon. On the one hand, a significant percentage of the population prospered. Kenneth Jackson has claimed that the post–World War II United States represented the first society in the history of the world where the distribution of wealth did not reflect the shape of a pyramid or tree (Jackson, pp. 290–291). On the other hand, the economic expansion of the 1950s left out a large number of people; unemployment rates, for example, remained significantly high (Lekachman, p. 190; Harrington, pp. 31–32). This meant that while the boom changed the economic circumstances of most, it also left unaffected the lives of many. As Robert Lekachman noted: "Thus, most Americans have never had it so good; possibly 15 to 20 percent of Americans have had it as bad as ever" (Lekachman, p. 190).[7]

Two factors contributed to which group one was in: (1) whether one was in the right place at the right time with the right skills and (2) racism. Both factors led to a growing correlation between being African American and being poor.[8] The economic expansion of the 1950s was not an industrial one. Rather, the period witnessed a decline in industrial jobs as the service and professional sector of the economy expanded (Harrington, p. 31). The families of many European-American immigrants had already been in urban settings long enough to have acquired the types of education and skills that were necessary to flourish in this new type of economy. This was not the case for the families of many African Americans, whose emigration to Northern cities occured primarily later in the century. This factor, combined with the strong racism that prevailed in the United States during the 1950s, meant that many African Americans were excluded from the expansion of the 1950s.

During the 1950s, the family types of African Americans were not as different from those of European Americans as later became the case. Differences in types of family formation between African and European Americans only gradually began to emerge after 1940, intensifying after the 1970s in conjunction with the economic downturn beginning then and the growing exclusion of African-American men from the workforce (Walker, 1988; Coontz, pp. 242–243). But during the 1950s, African Americans, as well as other poor European Americans, were more likely than those who were becoming prosperous to possess features of family life that were associated with economic hardship: "extra" relatives in a household, a greater likelihood that a household would be female-headed, the presence of boarders, and so on.

But this meant that family type could serve, along with other factors, as indicator of whether one had made it into the new middle class. The nuclear family with wife at home became as much a symbol of middle-class life as a house in the suburbs. To be sure, this was not the first time in United States history that family type served as a class indicator. It had long been the case that the ability to keep a wife outside the workforce signaled a man's class status. The difference, however, was that now a certain type of family life was becoming a mass possibility as entrance into the new middle class was becoming available to large numbers of people.

The mass nature of the new economic prosperity meant that many in the United States could think of their country as possessing "one great middle class." Since many of those who were not considered part of this class were African Americans and increasingly lived in areas physically isolated from middle-class European Americans, the poor could become marginalized in the consciousness of those who had "made it." As Michael Harrington brilliantly noted, by the early 1960s the poor in the United States had become invisible, constituting what he called "The other America." Being poor, being African American, not living within the Ozzie and Harriet type of family came to mean for many not really being "American." The racism that had long existed in the United States, combined with the homogeneity of class that was coming to dominate much of the consciousness of the period, created a new belief in the universality and/or superiority of a certain narrow conception of family life.

"Alternative" Families

However, even as a certain ideal of family was coming to define "the American way of life," such trends as a rising divorce rate, increasing participation of married women in the paid labor force, and the growth of female-headed households were making this way of life increasingly atypical. In all cases, such trends preceded the 1950s. That by the 1950s these trends were confined to relatively small percentages of the population, and within the general population tended to be more true of those who were poor or from negatively viewed ethnic and racial groups, made it possible for the ideal to come to appear during the 1950s as both indomitable and as "natural." It has only been recently, as such trends have continued to accelerate, that it has become easier to see the fragility of the 1950s ideal.

Yet a version of the 1950s ideal is still thought of as "natural." The irony, however, is that what is today understood as the "traditional" family is not the same as the 1950s version. Certain features of the older ideal—which earlier had been viewed as both essential to the ideal and as expressing what was "natural" about it—are now seen as having been less crucial all along.

A striking example is changing perceptions about married women in the paid labor force. Married women have entered the paid labor force in ever greater percentages over the course of the twentieth century. In 1890 in the United States, only 4.6% of married women were in the paid labor force. By 1950 the figure had climbed to 23.8%. By 1970 it was 40.8% and by 1985 it was 54.2% (Davis, p. 67).

Today, not only do a very high percentage of married women work in the paid labor force, but this is even true of married women with small children. Consequently, very few people think of married women working as "unnatural." Similarly, as long as both partners are heterosexual, the families of working wives are considered "traditional." The criteria defining a "traditional" family have changed.

Families constituted by second marriages are also interesting in the light they shed on changing criteria of "traditionality." As with married women's participation in the paid labor force, divorce rates have steadily increased over the twentieth century.

> Despite fluctuations associated with wars and depression, the increase in the U.S. divorce rate was remarkably consistent from the 1860s (the first years for which information is readily available) until the 1980s. In 1983 the rate was 18 times what it had been in 1860, and 2.4 times what it had been in 1940. (Davis, p. 79)

One result of the growing incidence of divorce is that families where one or both of the adult partners have been previously married are increasingly being allowed to count as "traditional families" to the degree they appear at a given moment similar to the old-style family. The 1950s "traditional" family was associated with strict rules about the timing of marriages and the timing and spacing of children. The increase of the divorce rate has undermined those rules. People have reconciled older notions of a "traditional" family with the rising divorce rate by discounting the importance of prior marital history or means by which children have been acquired. Without such discounting, too few contemporary families would be "traditional" and the label itself would become dangerously irrelevant.

Gays and lesbians have made use of this tendency to discount some of the old rules by describing the households they create as families.[9] They point to the similarities between their households and those of heterosexuals, with adults making long-term financial and emotional commitments to each other comparable to heterosexuals. They note that their households also sometimes include children, who relate to adults in the same kinds of ways as do children in heterosexual households. An emphasis on such similarities makes it easier to isolate only one factor, the same gender of the adult partners, as differentiating gay and lesbian households from heterosexual ones.

An obstacle which gays and lesbians face is that the same gender of adult partners makes gay and lesbian households appear different from heterosexual ones in visual terms. And while there has been a general tendency for people to discount prior history and to focus on contemporary arrangements, they have tended to do so to the degree to which current arrangements "look like" the older model. Many of the changes which have taken place since the 1950s, such as the rising divorce rate, rising rates of heterosexuals living together outside of marriage, or rising rates of children born outside of marriage are not changes that appear on the surface in interactions with strangers. Since family forms created within these new contexts tend often to "look like" the 1950s model, it is easier for many to assimilate them to that model and thus think of them as "traditional."

The converse of this point is that family forms which are not traditional but "look so" on the surface reinforce ideas about the pervasiveness of the "traditional" family. Many people today who appear related in traditional ways are, upon closer examination, related in very untraditional ways: gay men and heterosexual women who socialize together, older men and women who live together but are not married, married couples with children having a complex premarital history, and so on. In the eyes of strangers, such relationships are perceived as "traditional" and reinforce a sense of the pervasiveness of the "traditional" family.

These ways in which "traditionality" is superimposed intersect with cultural ideologies of race, class, and age. Thus a well-dressed, young, white woman alone with a baby will not be perceived as an "unwed mother," whereas an African-American woman from a range of classes may very well be. An older heterosexual couple of any race or class will be perceived as married, whereas class and race may influence whether a younger heterosexual couple is so perceived. Thus the ways in which "traditionality" is imposed are heavily influenced by ideologies of race, class, and age. In general, however, the belief in the "traditional" family has been sustained, even in the context of widespread changes, because of the surface invisibility of many of the changes. This surface invisibility allows people to impose "traditionality" even where it does not exist. This factor, combined with a general cultural tendency to allow "traditionality" to apply to families with known histories of divorce or of nonstandard ways of acquiring children, particularly to the extent such families otherwise "look like" the 1950s model, has helped maintain the idea of "traditionality" even in the context of widespread change.

Evaluating Families

Sometimes those who criticize the idea of the "traditional" family are regarded as allowing for an "anything goes" attitude towards family forms. To attack the distinction between "traditional" and "alternative" families is seen as allowing for no distinction between families at all. However, this does not follow. We can evaluate family forms even when discarding this distinction. To be sure, when we attack the idea of the naturality or historical universality of the "traditional" family and describe all family types as historically specific adaptations to particular contexts, this does suggest a certain tolerance for all types of family forms. And indeed, such tolerance is in many cases warranted; when new family types emerge on a wide scale, there are probably good reasons for their emergence. But to say that does not entail that tolerance is always warranted or warranted to include all specifics. In some contexts one might want to intervene in the circumstances which make the creation of the new family type reasonable; in others, one might want to bring about more localized changes to affect specific elements of the type under question. In all cases, however, what seems most appropriate is to examine the specific consequences of family types on people's lives, rather than to base our judgments on historically dubious references to "traditionality."

Let me illustrate this argument by focusing on two contemporary family types: the family type described by Carol Stack in her important work *All Our Kin* and the "traditional" family of the 1990s, that is, a two-parent household with children, with both parents working. Stack spent several years becoming close with members of a poor Black community in a Midwestern city in the late 1960s. From her observations of the way in which this community operated, she described a family type very different from what is taken as the "traditional" nuclear family. Her claim was that this family type was both a reaction to and a necessary adaptation to the poverty and economic instability members of this community faced.[10]

Individuals in this community depend upon a wide network of relationships, constituted by both "real" and "assumed" kinship ties to meet economic needs. Among members of a personal kindred there is continuous and extensive exchanging: of money, furniture, clothes, services, children, food stamps, and so on. The norms of the community demand that when an individual requests something from another member of her or his personal kindred, such as a sofa, the request is granted when it is possible to do so. The recipient is then in debt to the giver for goods and services of an equivalent value repayable at a later time. Individual households have elastic boundaries; they "expand or contract with the loss of a job, a death in the family, the beginning or end of a sexual relationship, or the end of a friendship" (Stack, p. 91). Ties over three generations are often strong and extend over a lifetime. Households are frequently female-headed with men, such as boyfriends, brothers, and husbands, circulating over time.

The advantage of this family structure is that it provides a social insurance system for those with barely enough economic resources to survive. Yet within such a system, it is impossible to accumulate the kind of resources necessary to move into middle-class life. Stack tells the story of a couple, Calvin and Magnolia Waters, who inherited $1500 on the death of an uncle who had recently sold an old farm in Mississippi. Their first thought was to use the money as a down payment on a home. However, the welfare office immediately cut off benefits to Magnolia's children upon hearing of the inheritance. Within the next few weeks, when family emergencies arose, such as an ill sister being threatened with eviction, a former boyfriend of Magnolia's dying and needing a burial, children and grandchildren needing coats, hats, and shoes, it was to Magnolia and Calvin that people turned. Within a month and a half, the money was gone (Stack, pp. 106–107).

This family structure also discourages marriages or overriding commitments to a romantic partner. Other members of one's personal kindred tend to view such commitments as threats to one's ability or willingness to share resources. Given the job instability of many Black men, women, not surprisingly, will tend to see their personal kinship network as a more reliable source of support than that potentially available from any one man. But instability in heterosexual relationships also means that children frequently experience instability in relationships with father figures. At the end of a romantic relationship, while some men do continue relationships with children, both with those they have created as well as those they have helped raise, and grandfathers and uncles often provide long-term meaningful relationships, children frequently do not have the type of long-term relationships with father figures which is taken as normative within middle-class households.

In short, we see a family type with both advantages and disadvantages for its members. But the same can be said of the 1990s "traditional" family. As earlier noted, because of declining real wages over the past forty-year period, both adults participate in the paid labor force in most middle-class families. Contrary to some conservative discourse, this is not because such families seek "luxuries," but because it is necessary to maintain a middle-class existence. When there are only two adults in a household, and both work at full-time jobs outside the home, tremendous time pressures are placed on the adults in combining such work with the tasks of running a household and raising children. As most studies indicate, this pressure falls disproportionately on women.[11] Moreover, because many of our current institutions, such as schools, are geared to there being an adult at home able to take care of children during the summer, after school, and when children become sick, time conflicts between child-rearing and paid labor demands are intensified.

The small size of the 1990s "traditional" family also places heavy emotional and psychological burdens on its members. For children, it means that if one or both of their parents are emotionally or physically abusive, there is little recourse to other adults to mitigate the abuse. For the adult members, heavy expectations are placed on the other partner to satisfy needs for companionship and love. When work often takes people in different directions from their spouses, fulfilling those needs for companionship can become difficult. The conflict between twentieth-century expectations that marriage be based on companionship and passion and the real-life factors which mitigate against either lasting over time certainly accounts for a significant portion of the rising divorce rate throughout the century. And when divorce does occur, the small economic base of the nuclear family often means that one or both of the households subsequently created will lose access to many of the accoutrements of middle-class life. Finally, this family type is restricted to those adults who desire companionship and passion with someone of the "opposite" sex. The 1990s "traditional" family still requires heterosexuality of its adult members.

All of this does not mean that this family type has no advantages for some. While its small size places heavy psychological burdens on its members to provide companionship and love for each other, when they do this family type can be very satisfying. The small size works towards an intimacy among members. Because this family type is associated with the institution of marriage and the expectation that the obligations of all members to each other are lifelong, it also can bring with it very long-term connections. Moreover, the economic insulation of this family type from the demands of extended family or community means that it sometimes can stockpile resources for such purchases as buying a house or sending children to college.

Thus neither of these family types is without benefits and liabilities. In both cases we need to be attentive to the specific features as well as the factors which appear to cause them, which make each family type both advantageous and disadvantageous to the people they serve. The distinction between "traditional" and "alternative" has little to contribute to such attentiveness.

As I have argued, the distinction between the "traditional" and the "alternative" family is dubious, historically and morally. Historically, it attributes a sense of false universality to a family type which is of relatively recent creation and continuously in change. This false historical attribution is then used to give legitimacy to certain family types and not others, independent of the specific consequences of each on the lives of the people they serve. Thus on both historical and moral grounds the distinction is problematic.

But the distinction is also politically problematic. While there is a growing tolerance towards some new family forms, the 1950s model of family life still structures many of our institutions. Moreover, while such tolerance has encouraged changing understandings of "traditionality," older understandings based on the 1950s model linger on. But most people today live out large portions of their lives in family types which clash either with that model or with the 1990s model in some respect or other: the adult partners are gay or lesbian; one of the adult partners has children living in a different household with whom she or he is trying to maintain a loving relationship; the fact of both partners working makes summer or after-school hours a real source of problems, and so on. The distinction between "traditional" and "alternative" families encourages those who experience such clashes to think of them as the relatively isolated effects of living a slightly "deviant" life. We need fully to acknowledge that in relation to many contemporary conceptions of "traditionality," most of us are "deviants." Having done that, we can begin mobilizing the political power necessary to make our present institutions conform more adequately to our needs. But acknowledging that most of us are "deviants" means recognizing that the distinction between "traditional" and "alternative" families no longer has meaning.

Acknowledgments

For their generous and insightful help with this article, I would like to thank Nancy Fraser, Hilde Nelson, Philip Nicholson, Steve Seidman, and Eli Zaretsky.

Notes

1. The categories we have for sorting families include more than "traditional" and "alternative." There are also categories such as "deviant" and "unnatural." Indeed, the category "alternative" represents a more tolerant attitude towards non-"traditional" families than do the latter categories. I use the category "alternative" instead of these more derogatory categories as the contrast category to "traditional" only because I can thereby illustrate more clearly some of the privileging which is still accorded "traditional" families even in the context of the increased acceptance of non-"traditional" ones.

2. See Peter Laslett, *The World We Have Lost* (New York: Scribner's, 1965) and Peter Laslett, ed., *Household and Family in Past Time* (Cambridge: Cambridge University Press, 1972).

3. Alan MacFarlane, in *Marriage and Love in England: Modes of Reproduction 1300–1800* (Oxford: Basil Blackwell, 1986), pp. 174–208, cites literature which documents the importance of love and the tying of love to marriage as far back as the time of Chaucer. Even if MacFarlane is right, this would not invalidate the thesis of the transformation among the upper classes from a patriarchal to a more egalitarian notion of marriage, for love does not entail either equality or partnership.

4. Trumbach argues that this is because it was the aristocracy who primarily adopted patrilineal kinship structures around the period of the tenth century. Other groups continued with more ancient forms of cognatic kinship principles, relating children to kinspeople on both the mother and father's side. Trumbach argues that such principles tend to promote greater equality between women and men. See Trumbach, p. 16.

5. Stephanie Coontz elaborates on this point in Chapter Six of *The Way We Never Were: American Families and the Nostalgia Trap* (New York: Basic Books, 1992), pp. 130–137.

6. For an elaboration of those factors that made the creation of a certain ideal of family life possible for many in the '50s, see Coontz, *The Way We Never Were*, pp. 23–41.

7. This quote by Lekachman was first brought to my attention by Arlene Skolnick in *Embattled Paradise: The American Family in the Age of Uncertainty* (New York: Basic, 1991), p. 55.

8. Obviously, many nonblacks in this period were also poor and most blacks prior to this period had been poor. What made this period unique, however, is that many nonblacks who had been poor, unlike many blacks, were now able to become not poor.

9. For an excellent discussion of this movement by gays and lesbians and of how it has opposed prior trends to place gays and lesbians outside of kinship, see Kath Weston, *Families We Choose: Lesbians, Gays, Kinship* (New York: Columbia University Press, 1991).

10. It should be emphasized that Stack's study is of a particular community at a particular point in time. The degree to which her study was generalizable to other poor Black communities in the late 1960s, and the degree to which it can be found within any community today are open questions.

11. For an excellent study of this issue see Arlie Hochschild with Anne Machung, *The Second Shift: Working Parents and the Revolution at Home* (New York: Viking, 1989).

Bibliography

Coontz, Stephanie, *The Way We Never Were: American Families and the Nostalgia Trap* (New York: Basic, 1992).

Davis, Natalie Zemon, "Ghosts, Kin, and Progeny: Some Features of Family Life in Early Modern France," *Daedalus* 106 (Spring 1977), pp. 87–91.

Flandrin, Jean-Louis, *Families in Former Times: Kinship, Household and Sexuality*, trans. Richard Southern (Cambridge: Cambridge University Press, 1979).

Harrington, Michael, *The Other America* (New York: The Macmillan Co., 1962).

Laslett, Peter, *The World We Have Lost* (New York: Scribner's, 1965).

———, ed., *Household and Family in Past Time* (Cambridge: Cambridge University Press, 1972).

Seccombe, Wally, *A Millennium of Family Change: Feudalism to Capitalism in Northwestern Europe* (London: Verso, 1992).

Stack, Carol B., *All Our Kin: Strategies for Survival in a Black Community* (New York: Harper and Row, 1974).

Stone, Lawrence, *Family, Sex, and Marriage in England, 1500–1800* (New York: Harper and Row, 1979).

Trumbach, Randolph, *The Rise of the Egalitarian Family: Aristocratic Kinship and Domestic Relations in Eighteenth-Century England* (New York: Academic Press, 1978).

Walker, Henry A., "Black-White Differences in Marriage and Family Patterns," in Dornbusch, Sanford M. and Myra H. Strober, eds., *Feminism, Children and the New Families* (New York: The Guilford Press, 1988), pp. 87–112.

3

"The Family" and Radical Family Theory

Naomi Zack

By trading on the general sense of "the family," conventional philosophers have been able to write about the family as though all readers (and perhaps everyone else, as well) shared the same meaning of "the family," experienced the same kind of family life, and strove for the same family values. They have written about "the family" as though an unstated specific form of it were a universal, natural phenomenon. As a result, radical philosophers who have critiqued social structures that give rise to, support, and are in turn supported by the specific form of the family to which particular conventional philosophers intend their use of "the family" to refer, have been accused of wanting to "destroy the family." Feminist critics of patriarchal family forms that restrict women's autonomy and development as human beings present an attractive target for such accusation, although they are not the only target. The problem posed by the accusation of being antifamily is that practically everyone, including feminists and other radical philosophers, share the intuition that "the family," on the vague, universal level, is necessary and valuable to all human beings. The widespread intuition is thereby used to condemn all criticism or implied criticism of the family, including criticism that is not against "the family" in the universal sense.

The purpose of this chapter is to clarify methods that radical philosophers can use to criticize conventional uses of "the family" without being antifamily. In Part I, I examine examples in the history of political philosophy in which a specific form of family is concealed under an advocacy of "the family" in general to support a particular form of government, the specific family form itself, or the interests of a particular social class. Part II is a discussion of family politics and empirical aspects of the family. My general plan is to learn from the apparent critical naiveté about the family in the history of philosophy, so as to bring to the surface normative ideas about the family as well as broader structures of social and political power. Once the normative assumptions are identified, it should be possible to reconceptualize "the family" more inclusively, in a way that allows for diverse forms of the family and family values.

I. Conventional Philosophical Argument and "the Family"

Some conventional philosophers have drawn on common intuitions about the goodness of the family in general and used that approval to add weight to an argument for a form of government that depends on and gives rise to a specific form of the family. The specific form of the family, not fully revealed in the course of such political argument, has, in modern Western philosophy, been a patriarchal family form. The equivocation between the family in the general and specific senses goes through by assuming that: (1) what is good for "the family" is good, and (2) any form of government which is inextricably linked to "the family" is good. The specific form of government the philosopher wants to advocate is shown to be good for "the family" when in fact it is only good for some specific form of the family (which is the conventional philosopher's unstated meaning of the term "the family"). This device can be seen at work in Aristotle's criticism of Plato and Locke's theory of the family.

A more direct advocacy of the patriarchal family assumes that: (1) the family is good, and (2) the term "the family" means "the patriarchal family." From (1) and (2) it can be deduced that anything which furthers the patriarchal family is good and anything which attacks it is bad. This kind of reasoning is at work in Hume's analysis of female modesty and in criticism of feminist critiques of the patriarchal family.

The most complex argument for a specific form of the family occurs in normative theories of family life that not only focus on a particular family form but provide a blueprint for the reproduction of that form in order to further the interests of the social class which that form of the family represents. This strategy is evident in Locke's theory of childhood education.

Plato and His Critics

Plato's endorsement of community property in order to preserve a primary loyalty to the state within the guardian class has two radical consequences. First, knowledge of who one's parents and children are becomes a state secret, and second, ruling-class women are freed from private domestic duties—to the extent that their talents and energies can be mobilized in athletics, statecraft, and war.[1] For many of Plato's critics, this represents an antifamily dystopia, both in terms of female equality and through unknown parentage. However, as Susan Moller Okin points out, Plato's primary motive here is the abolition of private property among the ruling class.[2] That Plato advocated the dissolution of the family in *The Republic*—the traditional interpretation—rests on a definition of the family as a private group with a male leader (or owner). But if "the family" is read more broadly, then Plato can be interpreted as offering an alternative form of the family because he extends parent-child, child-parent, and sibling ties across the entire ruling class.[3]

When Aristotle endorsed a form of aristocratic government with democratic structures within the aristocracy, his proposals, unlike Plato's, were closer to known forms of government in Greek city states at that time. Aristotle "naturalistically" worked from the assumption that prosperous private households or extended patriarchal families were the basic civic unit. It was from the perspective of the goodness of such households, based on a general methodology in normative theory of not straying too far from empirical reality (that is, a conventional perspective), that Aristotle upheld what he called a natural propensity for husbands and fathers to value their "own" wives and children. On that basis, he found Plato's proposal for a communal form of the family unnatural and unlikely to succeed.[4] Since the upper-class, prosperous, private, patriarchal household was the dominant form of the family in Aristotle's historical period, his location of the basic component of civic society in that form of the family, and his assumption that the patriarchs of such households are the natural rulers of the entire state, justified the advantaged status of upper-class, Greek, male heads of household. As a result, those who did not belong to such families or occupy dominant positions within them would "naturally" have disadvantaged political status.

Locke and the Economic and Political Importance of the Family

Locke also universalized a restricted form of "the family." Locke projected the model of a married couple, united for the sake of procreation, onto a pregovernmental state of nature. According to Locke, men and women remained together after children were conceived because a first child and its mother were known to require protection and care from its father. Since a second child could be conceived before the first child was independent of paternal care, humans, unlike other mammals, "naturally" required extended relationships between parents.[5] The social complexities of paternal obligation (which, as we shall soon see, included paternal control over child-rearing) were in effect declared instinctive by Locke. As Linda Nicholson has interpreted Locke's distinction between family relations and political relations, Locke reified and universalized the emerging seventeenth-century *nuclear* family, and he privatized it during a historical period when industrial change favored that form of the family among the rising bourgeoisie.[6]

Those who owned the new factors of production, that is, early capitalists, had the most to gain from seventeenth-century mercantile political policies and parliamentary representation. Locke justifies all government on the grounds that it is a more efficient and just way to protect private property than measures agreed to in a state of nature. His *Second Treatise* arguments for representative government, which was at the time understood to be limited to representing property owners only, were supported by a form of the family that in itself had little economic importance, because economically significant work moved outside private residences during the seventeenth century.[7]

Hume on Female Modesty

Hume paid more attention than Locke to the artificial nature of the social and civic virtues, and he did not attempt to derive them from a hypothetical or historical state of nature. Nevertheless, Hume assumed that patrilinear descent and patriarchy were unquestionable values. This assumption is implicit in his claim that the artificial virtue of modesty was valued in women because immodest behavior might be an early accompaniment to infidelity, and modesty prevented the expression of (natural) sexual impulses in women. Infidelity needed to be discouraged because men, insofar as they were required to work for the maintenance of their wives' children, were entitled to assurance that they were, in biological fact, the fathers of their wives' children.

Since Hume did not think it was necessary to justify existing custom by proving it was based on nature as opposed to culture and long-standing tradition, his analysis begins to suggest how the dominant form of "the family" in turn supports culture and tradition.[8] For Hume, tradition and convention are simply accepted as social goods worthy of preservation and conformity. His almost-complete obliviousness to the reality that entrenched social rules have to be accepted and reproduced in the present in order to retain their social force allows him to endorse tradition without serious question. Hume does not really need an assumption about the goodness of the family in a general sense in order to sneak in an endorsement of the patriarchal family. He need only note, as he must have done, that the patriarchal family is the dominant family form in his culture, accept its goodness on those grounds, and transfer that goodness to mores and social virtues that support the patriarchal family.

Locke on Education and Class Interests

The conventional, patriarchal concept of "the family," besides its implicit endorsement of the subordination of women to men, also contains an idea of the rights of parents—that is, fathers, primarily—to control child-rearing. The purpose of this control is not so much the kind of fantasized protection and survival that can be projected onto an imagined state of nature in the distant past, but social reproduction in the present. Patriarchal fathers expect the sons they rear to occupy the same positions in society that they do. Childhood education was recognized as a basic tool of social engineering by Plato and Aristotle, who were concerned with how the ruling class ought to be educated in order to rule best—they not only wrote about the education of that class, but took an active role in teaching princes. Something similar can be said of Locke, who combined an early modern recognition of childhood as a distinct formative state with an answer to the question of how gentlemen's sons might best be reared.

Locke's gentlemen were men like his patron, Lord Shaftesbury, and his relative, Peter Clarke, the correspondent to whom he first drafted his program for the home education of the heirs of the ascendant bourgeois class.[9] In *Some Thoughts Concerning Education*, Locke added content to the "natural" care of sons by fathers alluded to in the *Second Treatise on Government*. On the basis of his well-known *tabula rasa* characterization of the human mind at birth, he began the *Education* with a consideration of its civic importance, "for if those of that Rank are by their education once set right they will quickly bring all the rest into Order." Locke believed that "to be Emminent and useful in his Country according to his Station" was part of "a Gentleman's Calling."[10]

Locke's program for the education of gentlemen's sons consisted of a spartan physical regimen and a kindly but manipulative program of home tutelage in the virtues of self-restraint. Character was to be developed by training, with paternal approval as a reward and the threat of public shame as a punishment.[11] There was no plan to encourage the child's independent understanding and ability to make informed choices. The liberality of Locke's views on childhood education stands out in the seventeenth-century historical context, when corporal punishment was an integral part of teaching in schools. However, even though Locke rejected corporal punishment and thought that learning ought to be incorporated into the natural play of children, his main use for play was that it provided parents with an opportunity to observe those "crooks" in their children's temperaments that would need to be bent "the other way."[12]

II. Radical Philosophy and Family Theory

From a feminist perspective, the male-centered and class-centered forms of "the family" that conventional philosophers have drawn upon through the vague sense of the term cannot be the final pronouncements on "the family." We are all biological creatures, thus far born of women, and we all have particular genealogies whether we are familiar with their details or not. Human genealogy is the kind of process that is identified by proper names in all of its individual occurrences. This is a naturalistic sense of "the family" shared by everyone, which has two characteristics that the patriarchal family form deployed by conventional philosophers lacks. First, this genealogical sense of "the family" has matrilinear lines of descent that are easier to track than patrilinear lines of descent (as Hume was aware).[13] Second, all of the particular genealogical families in human history fully instantiate the concept of "family" or "families" insofar as that concept refers to biological generation. In contrast to "family," the abstract concept, "the family" has an impoverished empirical base. Therefore, in order to balance or rectify "the family" in its general abstract sense, family theory is needed as a space for discussion in which different political, empirical, and normative meanings of "family" can be assessed.

Family and Politics

Politically, it should be possible to noncontroversially identify a description of a particular kind of family which is implicit in a certain use of "the family," when the naturalness and goodness of the family, in a general sense, is being used to support an argument for a particular kind of government, social structure, or public policy. The political form in question may turn out not to be good for all families once the nature of the families it is good for is examined. Many traditional philosophical uses of "the family" would be clarified by this kind of analysis, as the examples in the first part of this paper begin to suggest. The use of "the family" in the history of political philosophy to support specific political structures suggests that the political structures in question might not have been justifiable without rhetoric that drew on the widespread approval associated with "the family." Therefore, in political theory, all references to "the family," and even to "family" in an empirical sense, ought to be scrutinized.

While familial metaphors may be positively associated with utopian governments in the distant past or future, there is no solid reason to revise Locke's general conceptual separation of government from family. In Locke's time, that separation was a liberal advance over Robert Filmer's argument for the divine, patriarchal, rights and powers of kings. Locke himself did not take the separation seriously enough because he spoke from the interests of a particular social class. Perhaps "the family" as an institution within an inegalitarian society can never be completely separated from public political issues. In that case, radical philosophers ought to be anarchists about "the family."

Indeed, the political nature of families in oppressive societies is itself an important critical topic. Children learn how to conform to oppressive social structures in their families, even and perhaps especially when they will grow up to be members of oppressed groups. Parents police the boundaries of race and gender by imposing macrocultural norms on their children. For example, according to the American rule of *hypodescent* for black inheritance, mixed black and white individuals are identified as black in the macroculture. Since this identification does not make sense biologically, it has to be taught to mixed-raced children in their families. And insofar as the macroculture defines racial whiteness as pure whiteness, white families cannot have nonwhite members.[14] Categories of gender that are considered appropriate in the macroculture are analogously taught in families: heterosexuality; female submissiveness and skill at domestic chores; male protectiveness and skill at mechanical chores; and so on.

In contemporary society, families are primary units of economic consumption, as well as political indoctrination. The premodern family produced goods for itself and, as one unit added to the units of other families, made up the total economy. The modern and postmodern family consumes the end products of the macroeconomy by buying them (this is why housing starts and major appliance purchases are "key economic indicators"). Children must be taught to grow up motivated to do the kind of work that will enable them to purchase the kind of products consumed in their families. They must also be taught to respect private property and obey social rules "in the home" in order to be good citizens.

These public services performed within families suggest that the privacy and autonomy attributed to families in the traditional rhetoric about "the family" may sometimes be a smoke screen around interests that ultimately have nothing to do with family values as most people understand them, even vaguely. They also support the accounts of many women, poor people, and nonwhites of having to rebel against what their older relatives taught them in order to develop beyond the oppressed social categories that they were first sorted into through family membership. These are justifiable grounds for being "antifamily" in some radical critical contexts and they suggest that politics within families may require a revolutionary approach in order to change public oppressive conditions.

Family and Empiricism

In empirical studies of families, it may be desirable to balance objective criteria for the existence of families against personal testimony, so as not to prejudge the goodness, wellness, or existence of those families that do not meet the criteria. For example, since the turn of the century, American social scientists have used the symbol of an owner-occupied house to stand for a home in the sense of the morally good and materially sustaining aspects of family life. When the expected members of a family do not live together in the same house, the home—and thereby the family—is referred to as "broken." House ownership—called home ownership—may be a convenient demographic tool for identifying coresidence. But as a primary criterion for identifying a family, it valorizes wealth and stability and may pathologize poverty, homelessness, and physical separation to the point where such "unfortunate" characteristics of a family block recognition of the existence of that family. Insofar as they do not live in houses with both biological parents, children whose parents are divorced or unmarried, and the adults they do live with, may fail to qualify as families simply because the dominant family type does not value this kind of family structure.

In ways resulting from their cultural disadvantage and difference, racial minority families may also fail to "measure up" to demographic criteria for family identification. Black American families, for example, are not only less likely to own houses than white American families, but they are also less likely to conform to other norms of white patriarchy due to economic and status discrimination against black males. The cultural problems faced by black males may in turn be blamed on black family life by white cultural critics who fail to understand that norms for family life that are generalizations of family life for advantaged groups in society are not appropriate norms for disadvantaged groups, because those groups cannot fulfill them with the same ease.

There are factors besides racial bias and economic conditions that may prevent some family types from "measuring up." Families may apportion family functions differently from the norm, for varied reasons. For example, nurturance of children by their biological mothers is not universal, and neither are biological mothers the only satisfactory nurturers of children. Patricia Hill Collins discusses the importance of "othermothers" in black communities. Other mothers are important not only because biological mothers have to work outside of their homes but because in the West African cultures from which American black culture partly derives, children were considered to be the responsibility of neighbors, aunts, and grandmothers as well as biological mothers.[15]

The difference in family form that results from race, social class, and cultural and individual psychological differences suggests that what constitutes a family or a good, well, or intact family may be impossible to determine before the fact. Families ought to be able to self-identify as families, and self-diagnose their ills. Radical philosophers, especially, ought to be tolerant about what counts as a family, and precise, universal definition is probably impossible. Family theory needs the empirical base of all human families. Although human genealogy has a biological foundation, whether that foundation is recorded through matrilinear or patrilinear descent is a cultural variable, as are all forms of family structure and family relationships. The endless possibilities and results of individual personality and choice and the effect of unpredictable biological and cultural events and conditions add an indeterminacy to the empirical base of family theory.

Returning to my initial plan to learn from the misuses of "the family" in the history of political philosophy, the lesson is that family theory ought to be general enough to include patriarchal, nonpatriarchal, nuclear, and extended family forms. The idea of an indeterminate empirical base of existing families, which allows for self-assertion of family existence, gives rise to acceptance of an unpredictable diversity of family values. This diversity and subjective nature of family values preclude universal normative judgment of specific family values, although they do not block moral and legal criticism (and censure) of harmful interactions among family members.

Notes

1. Plato, *The Republic*, Desmond Lee, trans. (New York: Penguin, 1987), Part IV, Book V, 1 and 2, pp. 225–253.

2. Susan Moller Okin, "Philosopher Queens and Private Wives: Plato on Women and the Family," in *Feminist Interpretations and Political Theory*, Mary Lyndon Shanley and Carol Pateman, eds. (University Park: Pennsylvania State University Press, 1991), pp. 32–52.

3. Plato, *Republic*, Part IV, Book V, 2, p. 243.

4. Aristotle, *The Politics*, ed. Trevor J. Saunders (London: Penguin, 1981). On his naturalistic derivation of the state, see Book I, ii, 1252a24–1253a29, pp. 55–61; on his argument against communal family life, see Book II, iii, 1262a1, p. 108.

5. John Locke, *Two Treatises of Government*, Peter Laslett, ed. (Cambridge: Cambridge University Press, 1967), II, VII, Sec. 79–80, pp. 319–320.

6. Linda Nicholson, *Gender and History* (New York: Columbia University Press, 1986), pp. 137–138.

7. For further discussion on the connections between Locke's political, economic and family theories, see Naomi Zack, *Bachelors of Science: Seventeenth Century Identity, Then and Now* (Philadelphia: Temple University Press, 1996), chaps. 5 and 14.

8. David Hume, *A Treatise of Human Nature*, Book III, Part II, Sec. XII, in *Political Writings*, Stuart D. Warner and Donald W. Livingston, eds. (Indianapolis: Hackett, 1994), pp. 76–79.

9. John Locke, *Some Thoughts Concerning Education* in *The Educational Writings of John Locke*, James A. Axtell, ed. (Cambridge: Cambridge University Press, 1968). See pp. 3–18 for an account of the development of this work.

10. Ibid. pp. 112–113.

11. Ibid. Sec. 41–54, pp. 142–158. For more discussion of the manipulative aspect of Locke's *Education*, see Zack, *Bachelors of Science*, chap. 10.

12. Ibid. pp. 7–8.

13. Hume, *Treatise*, p. 77.

14. For discussion of the racism inherent in racial categories of black and white in the United States, see Naomi Zack, *Race and Mixed Race* (Philadelphia: Temple University Press, 1993), Chaps. 2, 3, 4, 19. Without the bias of white norms, black families, for example, may appear less pathological to social scientists. For a bibliographic review of studies of black families that have been redone taking black cultural norms into account, see Wade W. Nobles and Lawford L. Goddard, *Understanding the Black Family* (Oakland, CA: The Institute for the Advanced Study of Black Family Life and Culture, 1984). See also Zack, *Race and Mixed Race*, chap. 5, for a discussion of this issue in terms of Black family identity.

15. Patricia Hill Collins, *Black Feminist Thought* (New York: Routledge, 1991), pp. 10, 19–22.

Part II

The Breakdown
of the Family

4

Are Families Out of Date?

Mary Midgley and Judith Hughes

The perceived "breakdown of the family" has provoked a good deal of moral panic on both sides of the Atlantic. In the United Kingdom in particular, the widely publicized doctrine of "communitarianism" has recently provided both a new impetus for this panic and a new hope of resolution. Communitarianism has been seized on by politicians of all parties as a welcome antidote to the selfish individualism of the 1980s. Those of us who for several decades have been criticizing individualist excesses will naturally hope that this is a significant step in the right direction. Any way of thinking, talking and acting which stresses our connections with, rather than our separation from, the world around us deserves our attention.

What, however, is communitarianism? It is not just a general call to love and sociability. At its heart is the belief that the welfare state is not sustainable in its present form. The state should be the last rather than the first port of call for solving problems. These should be tackled first at the individual level, then through the family, then through the local neighborhood, resorting to the state only when all these have been progressively tried and found wanting.

This principle may seem a somewhat strange one. It is not easy to see how it could work in a world where life is already so complex that people are profoundly interdependent, so that many individual troubles flow from existing large-scale arrangements in the first place. However, that oddity is not our first business here. Communitarians recognize that traditional family structures and local neighborhood communities are not as supportive as they used to be or (at least) as they are thought once to have been. It is therefore a priority to restore these structures through an active program of rewards and penalties.

This practical approach, which is surely welcome so far as it goes, is combined with a more theoretical one; namely with the belief that in the pursuance of our rights, we have failed to give due attention to our duties, and that this failure is a cause of the breakdown of these communities of family and neighborhood. This view is encapsulated in the demand for a return to family values and community spirit, or, as it was described in Britain, "back to basics." However, communitarianism brings problems of its own.

The most obvious of these is the tendency of right-wing politicians to seize on its central tenets to justify promptly cutting benefits to single mothers. The thinking involved here seems to be that we need to force people into larger units ("communities") by making it impossible for them to survive in smaller ones. The most obvious difficulty about this is that for many people there simply is no larger unit available. They do not have a viable background family that can help and support them. That means that the other object of the exercise, which is certainly to save money, cannot be achieved in this way. It would seem, too, that there must be better ways of saving money than by making the poorest families even more desperate.

If however—as sometimes appears—the main aim is rather to punish them for having got into this situation in the first place, it is not altogether clear what offense they are supposed to have committed. Here, as so often happens, the urge to "teach people a lesson" by punishing them is impractical and unhelpful. Something rather subtler than the experimental psychologist's apparatus of sticks and carrots, food pellets and electric shocks is going to be needed. These people's children have been born already. Present mothers, like the already contributing fathers targeted by the British Child Support Agency, are of course sitting ducks who can easily be identified and penalized. But they are not criminals. Unlike the moonlighter on benefits, or the affluent father who refuses to pay maintenance at all, they are not defrauding or treating anyone with contempt. They are simply in need.

Fathers—Who Wants Them?

When this is recognized, the next suggestion is often to try and force the fathers back to take responsibility for their children. There has been no shortage of suggestions for how this could be done. One move in Britain was the setting up of the discredited Child Support Agency, which was supposed to extract maintenance from married and unmarried fathers for their children. The problem is that many fathers are in no position to support themselves, let alone anybody else. We should also note that, in present-day Britain, it is the increasing number of economically inactive men of working age who are the greatest consumers of the welfare budget, not single mothers.

Another suggestion is that the tendency of young males to reproduce outside of marriage should be actively discouraged by advantageous taxation for the married. But once again, this hardly seems a genuine incentive for the unemployed. Forcing them to marry would not, by itself, reduce the welfare burden at all.

When financial arguments lose the day, it is not unusual for moral pressure to take over. Recently, discussions of family "breakdown" have mainly treated the absence of fathers as the central cause. In particular, apparent increases in the criminality and irresponsibility of young males have been attributed to the absence of their fathers. The existence and strength of this particular causal link are at present much disputed, and, unfortunately, ideological commitments on both sides make considerable caution necessary in interpreting the evidence.[1] But it is not the case that the absence of the father is always the choice of the father himself. It begins to seem that substantial numbers of mothers do now seem to be choosing to be lone parents, rather than relying on the support of a man. We need to ask why they should make this choice.

In the economic climate of industrialized countries today, we have already mentioned the obvious answer; high unemployment means that many men are simply unable to provide financial support. And the kind of unemployment now prevailing, in which low-paid, insecure, part-time jobs for women replace full-time ones for men, has an evident tendency to break up families. But it seems that more is at stake than money. After all, men and women have always lived together in situations of extreme poverty and deprivation. Women do not refuse to live with men simply because they are poor. The reasons they are now giving have more to do with the attitudes of the men themselves than with their inability to be providers.

One young woman interviewed on a British television program in September 1993 described how the father of her child occasionally came round to visit, stayed a while, and then went off to his mother's house when he felt like it. She complained that he had no sense of responsibility and just wanted to do as he pleased. She was clear that he did not play a significant part in her life or the life of her child. She did not seem to think this a desirable situation, but rather a sorry fact. And no doubt she had reason to be sorry. When the two-parent arrangement does work it has obvious great advantages. Effort and worry can then be divided, the partners can support each other, and the children can get two satisfactory role models. But when it does not work, all this fails to happen, and then it is difficult indeed to see what advantage accrues to a woman who has to be both the provider and the nurturer for the man as well as the children.

Does the young male's inability to be a financial provider somehow deprive him of that sense of responsibility in any walk of life which comes with having a real role to play in the family? This surely cannot be inevitable. Many men have learnt to take on other responsibilities in the family than that of breadwinner. But here, justice demands that we tread very carefully indeed. Is role-reversal a real option?

Given that an increasing number of women are the principal wage earners in one- or two-parent families, is there anything other than men's arrogance and self-importance which prevents them from learning the business? Perhaps not, but that does not entail that we should recommend it. Women know only too well that a life of nothing but domesticity suits very few of them for very long. The reasons are both economic and personal. But we should not forget that many women want to work, for the money, for the company, and for their own satisfaction. There is nothing wrong with that. They may choose domesticity for certain periods of their lives; some who can afford to, may choose it on a permanent basis; but the women's movement, the liberation of women, the drive towards equality were not just the fantasy of a few deranged malcontents. There seems no good reason to think that men would be content with what so many women rejected. It is not role-reversal we need, but role-reform, and for that we have to have the options open to everyone.

Young Men's Responsibilities

Is it the case that young men are irresponsible about their family obligations in a way which previous generations would find incomprehensible? Do we, as a society, demand much less of our young men or are we demanding considerably more of them than previous ages did? Is it that they simply do not or cannot meet those demands?

There was perhaps some common sense behind Aristotle's recommendation that a man should marry and begin to produce children at the age of thirty-seven while a woman should do so at eighteen.[2] Aristotle may have been wrong to think that these respective ages indicated the physical peak of the two sexes, but his suggestion that men need to mature—in other words, grow up—before taking on family responsibilities is one which is echoed through the ages. It has appeared in many forms. When men were obliged to soldier or to save or to learn before they were in a position to support a family, they married at a suitably late age. The need to delay starting a family became celebrated and tied to a notion of carefree bachelorhood which was tolerantly regarded as a necessary period of "sowing wild oats."

Obviously, a great deal of hypocrisy surrounded these attitudes. Men were not expected to do without sexual activity during this period and they were not legally obliged to provide for the children that they then fathered. But what was recognized, in the case of men, was that sexual proclivity and readiness to discharge family obligations do not necessarily go hand in hand. Neither, perhaps, do they with women, and the concern about teenage pregnancies and motherhood is sometimes tied to a concern that fourteen- or fifteen-year-old girls are not psychologically or practically fitted to motherhood.

Modern Western society adds a special difficulty here for both sexes in its remarkable segregation of different age groups, which tends to keep current teenagers more ignorant than they are in most societies about what child-rearing will actually involve. Girls as well as boys now confront this problem, but they seem to manage their responsibilities better and at an earlier age than men do. They do not, on the whole, choose to give up their children for adoption or abandon them, nor to abuse them. Nor do these young single mothers produce an undue proportion of criminals or psychopaths.

It seems then, that the demand made on young men to marry or to provide for their offspring outside marriage is stronger in our society than it has ever been. That does not mean that it is an unreasonable demand but it is not a diminished one.

Nearly Everybody Wants Children

At this point, the next option proposed is to stem the reproductive tide by putting pressure on people not to have children unless they can afford them. But pressure of this kind is not known to have succeeded in any culture.

In China, which is probably alone at present in attempting to control births by law, that policy is imposing alarming strains. Such a strategy would, too, embody a very different set of values from those which its advocates profess to recommend. Making children a luxury item, a status symbol, is a strange way to think about children and no way at all to help to restore community spirit and mutual support.

Altogether, then, that side of communitarianism which aims to cure individualism by forcing detached individuals to regroup themselves into standard families does not look very realistic. In particular, its punitive element seems misplaced. It is not helpful to approach this problem in the spirit of Lady Catherine de Bourgh, who, "whenever any of the cottagers were disposed to be quarrelsome, discontented or too poor, sallied forth into the village to settle their differences, silence their complaints, and scold them into harmony and plenty."[3] The business of government is not to punish those who are already in bad situations for having got there. It is not to blame them for the existence of the pits into which they fall. It is to make a more decent way of life possible. The taking on of family responsibilities ought to be a real option for all, not merely a luxury for the middle classes. Sooner or later, almost everybody wants children.

That said, the communitarian aim is surely still worth considering. It is surely better than the suggested means. Can we find a better way to think about these things? Is there a path by which the emphasis on sociability and cooperation, which is the welcome side of the communitarian message, can be followed through without involving harsh and unrealistic attempts to dragoon people's private lives?

In this paper we will discuss that possibility. In the first section we will start by looking at the ambiguities which surround the notion of a return to "family values." This is one of those phrases which is used as though we all knew and agreed what it means. Yet the current debates about single mothers and the welfare state, the responsibility of men to provide for their offspring, young mothers and adoption, all display deep confusions over both the content of such subjects and the reasons why we are concerned about them.

What Are Families For?

It has been widely noticed that the so-called "traditional" family structure has changed dramatically, not least because of biotechnological techniques. Attempts have been made to redefine "the family" using old and new concepts (for instance, nuclear and extended families, genetic, birth or nurturing mothers, and so on). Social scientists have paid much attention to the changing shape of families and have debated about the limits of the relationships which can properly be said to constitute a family. But surprisingly little attention has been paid to the different concepts involved in the notion of *family* when it is used in different contexts.

It seems to be assumed that "the family" is a definable entity, a functional unit, comparable perhaps to an army or a company, and that the problems are about its margins, about the limits of inclusion and exclusion. But is this true? Perhaps the attempts to "redefine" the family founder not just because of new and confusing familial patterns but because "the family" was never a simple, functional concept in the first place. What we mean by a family has always varied, not just in different cultures or different periods of history, but according to what we want from it—to the different needs felt in the various contexts in which we use the idea.

In a political context, the family is thought of as the fundamental building block of society. It must therefore, above all, be solid. This building block always includes certain individuals united by blood and marriage, but in many societies it has also included other dependants such as servants and slaves. The family in Greek and Roman society was that web of individuals over which power was exercised by the *paterfamilias*. It could include slaves whom he never saw. The bonds uniting it were not necessarily bonds of affection, and in certain circumstances could easily be broken. Slaves could always be sold. Indeed, Cato the Elder, in his treatise on domestic management, particularly warned householders against the sentimental tendency to keep weak and aging slaves who were merely a burden on family finances. Officially, the family was essentially a power nexus, a productive and military unit that could be relied on to help in the defense of the country.

In reality however, this political setup was not so simple. Family members in these cultures did—especially in earlier times—undoubtedly feel a deep loyalty to their house, a corporate unity within it, which could often carry them through profound self-sacrifice. Membership of family and clan provided a corporate identity which was a central part of the meaning of life, and which, when things went well, was felt as continuous with the wider loyalty to one's city. Even retainers and slaves clearly often shared this sense of a family bond, which was something independent of personal affection.

This powerful kind of social and domestic glue undoubtedly did help to maintain social standards, though of course when families were at odds with each other or with the state it could also do a great deal of harm. Montagues and Capulets, Krays and Corleones are not ideal social units from the political point of view, though they certainly do achieve solidarity and embody some striking family values.

This kind of glue has, in any case, become much harder to procure in the enormous, mobile states where we live today, as we shall shortly notice. There are indeed still some families in our present culture which preserve such a corporate tradition—for instance, ones that are united by the practice of a particular art or craft, which may range from organized crime to music. But in general, the long continuity which is needed to build up the force of these traditions has become rare in our present way of living. It is no accident that this kind of bond was often felt as loyalty to "the house"—an entity which included the actual building and place in which people passed their whole lives. Not many of us live like that today.

This political aspect of the family, this pattern of firm, balanced, stable power is, then, what is most visible from above, from the angle of politicians and administrators. Closely allied to it is an economic aspect in which families are meant to be self-supporting units, able, willing and expected to take care of their own most of the time, though they may sometimes need outside help in times of crisis. From this angle, the central concept of power gives way to that of financial responsibility, but, again, these bonds have no necessary basis of affection. Without affection, people who are asked to be financially responsible for those over whom they do not have power are liable to get resentful. For instance, in Germany young peoples' earnings can be attached to pay for care for an elderly relative—an arrangement which sounds startling to British or American ears, particularly where that relative is not a parent or a grandparent.

But of course politics and economics are not all. To the individual, the family is that network of individuals to whom, for better or for worse, one is most closely bound by personal and emotional ties. These ties are based on commitments which do sometimes result from blood relationship, but not always. The recent development of the nuclear family in the West has drastically restricted the number of people commonly involved in these commitments, but it has also made them less dependent on formal relationships than they used to be. Many cohabiting but unmarried couples of the same or different sex regard themselves as forming close and united families. So do other small groups who are not cohabiting but just get on well together.

All this means that "the family" is a slippery concept, because the interests of politicians and social reformers and those of individual members of society are not the same. The point is not that these people favor different values from the same perspective, but that their aims are different.

The administrator, looking down with a political and economic eye, wants a society composed of stable unions which can be self-supporting and self-regulating. The individual, looking around with a personal and emotional eye, looks for loving, supportive relationships wherever they can be found. The politician sees the family as the political and economic unit and sees value above all in the permanence of that unit itself, never mind what is going on inside it. The individual thinks of the family as an emotional and supportive network and sees value in that love and support. He or she probably does in general also wish for permanence. But that wish is often in conflict with other motives which can powerfully call for change. This means that both what the family is and where family values lie can look quite different from these two perspectives.

Individuals Still Matter

What we have here, in fact, is one more case of the large problem that arises in so many contexts for liberal democracies, a problem which always has to be dealt with by careful compromise. Individual interests really do clash with social interests, and this clash is not just an external one. It occurs within one and the same person, depending upon which perspective he or she is taking. It should not, then, surprise us if some politicians who espouse family values in the public sphere also conduct steamy extra-marital relationships in private. The hypocrisy does not lie in being moved by these two motives at the same time but in being ready to condemn and punish others who are experiencing the same conflicts.

It is not uncommon for those whose marriages have broken down to be at once relieved that an unloving relationship has come to an end and also full of regret that successful marriages seem few and far between. Individual and communal ideals cannot simply fight a war here. Most of us recognize both of them. While we agree that the concept of common good has been submerged in the unseemly scramble for individual fulfillment, we cannot cure this trouble by simply eradicating the concern with individual good.

For example, it has taken a great deal of time, effort and argument to get rape seen for what it is, a crime against individual women, rather than simply as an affront to public morality or an attack on the status of families and husbands. This is an important achievement. The problem is not to get rid of one aspect or the other but to find new ways of trying to reconcile them, to achieve a balance between them which does justice to both kinds of need.

If the notion of a family is itself ambiguous, it should not surprise us if the notion of family values also produces confusion. And if the restoration of families is indeed as powerful a medicine as current theorists seem to suggest, we may wonder why that institution has been allowed to become so eroded in recent times. What has gone wrong with it?

Living in Flux

The sense of loss here is undoubtedly real. People do not only feel that the state is being sapped politically by the weakening of its units; they also feel a loss of that personal closeness and emotional security, that sense of *belonging* that families everywhere have usually conveyed. But if we ask what has loosened that closeness, we see at once that the change grew from much wider causes than the behavior of family members. Though the personal may be political, the political is not always personal. Much larger factors than private vices and virtues have been at work here. Huge shifts in the world during the last two centuries were bound to weaken family bonds.

Before the industrial revolution, nearly all human beings spent their lives with a single set of people. Though some traders and travellers and administrators knew about matters at a distance, most people neither saw nor envisaged any other way of life than that of their parents and grandparents. Now, most people in the wealthier nations feel mobile from the very start of their lives. They see many alternative ways of life and meet any number of strangers. They are brought up knowing that they may go anywhere, and also that customs in their own lands are constantly changing.

No doubt this mobility provides much welcome freedom. But of course people do not move just for pleasure. They often have to move because they cannot support themselves where they are. Employment constantly sucks them from place to place, dropping them at its own convenience, not theirs. Workless people drift into big towns. And the sheer numbers who are swirling around in this way are constantly growing. Neighborhoods, which used to back and strengthen family bonds, are weakened and replaced by crowds of strangers. As communitarians have quite rightly pointed out, networks of various sizes, both formal and informal, that used to structure life in clans, villages, churches, schools, clubs, societies, political parties, and other groupings have become weaker, more transient, harder to maintain. The turnover of workers in every workplace is increasingly rapid.

As all these wider patterns shift around, families tend to be left as the last remaining unit that is available to maintain some stability. This naturally puts great strain on personal affection, which is often left to do, in isolation, the connective work that used to be shared over a whole social network. In such a situation, it seems strange to blame the most exposed people, the ones who have been stranded by this retreat of a wider society, for not managing to do its work on their own.

What Is It to Be Mine or Yours?

The dilemma about families is, then, a real one. Close personal relations do involve ambivalence. They make possible the worst as well as the best in human life. People brought near to each other do collide and often hurt one another gravely. R.D. Laing and the campaigners against child abuse are right to stress the risks involved in individual parenting. The difficulty is that no one has ever found a real alternative, an infallible, impartial, nonintimate way of rearing babies.

Can the concept of intimacy be cleared of its connection with the notion of *possession*? Plato thought that it was all right to think of other people as belonging to one—as "mine"—provided that this was done unanimously throughout the community. His attack on families was aimed simply to avoid partiality, to make sure that all citizens regarded each other equally as family members. William Godwin, by contrast, suggested that there was something hopelessly corrupting about the idea of using the pronoun "my" for people at all. "Pure, unadulterated justice," said Godwin, ought to make someone save from a burning building a gifted benefactor of mankind, such as Archbishop Fénélon, rather than his chambermaid, even if that chambermaid happened to be his own wife or mother. Godwin asks:

> What magic is there in the pronoun "my" to overturn the decision of everlasting truth? My wife or my mother may be a fool or a prostitute, malicious, lying or dishonest. If they be, of what consequence is it that they are mine?[4]

Many people have been unhappy about this argument, and indeed Godwin himself later became doubtful about it. Yet this contempt for natural ties is a part of Enlightenment thinking which is still active in our culture. Is it justified? Is there indeed something wrong with the whole concept of "belonging" when it is applied to people?

Certainly owning or possessing people can sound wrong. Yet nobody willingly consents to be "disowned," or to belong nowhere. The trouble seems to be that this idea of possession or belonging covers an enormously wide spectrum. Possessive pronouns such as "mine" range from unalarming uses such as *my shoes* and *my cup*, through *my house*, *my trees* and *my land* to much more mysterious cases like *my cat*, *my colleagues*, *my friends*, *my mother*, *my children*, and *my country*. At one end, there seems to be a simple property relation based on contract, a relation that gives total control and no duties. At the other end lies a set of most complex personal relations involving deep respect and responsibility. And these relations unavoidably bind us to the wider community.

But even at the narrow end—the apparently neutral relation with shoes and cups—matters are not really so simple. Attachment comes in and plays its part. A small child who does not learn to care for its belongings, a child who is encouraged to treat them with casual contempt, misses something vital. Our shoes and cups are not just items that we have bought by contract so that we can smash them when we feel like it. They link us with the wider community. Perhaps Kant was wrong to rule that respect belongs only to persons, not to things. Things have meaning. They are tokens binding us into our culture, and also into the wider realm of nature. Contempt for things has in fact played a great part in our recent destruction of the environment. Perhaps the whole notion of belonging is one that we—the heirs of the Enlightenment—should learn to treat more seriously.

Bonds Are Not Just Fetters

Individualism is certainly here to stay, and we have reason to be thankful for that. When individuals are harmed, by their families or anything else, we do need to insist that they matter, that they should not be sacrificed to an ideal, however lofty, that their freedom is indeed a precious thing for which it is worth struggling. For those who are oppressed, freedom comes first, because without it nothing else seems possible. But there are other goods to consider as well as freedom. "Bonds" are not just fetters; they are also lifelines. Enlightenment thinking has tended to ignore the deep human need to balance freedom by love and cooperation, independence by sociability. In particular, a number of philosophers, themselves celibate, have been disastrously blind to the intense, specific social needs of small children—and indeed of their parents too.[5]

Many Western societies, including Britain and the United States, seem now to have reached a stage where many people fear the evils of loneliness and emotional insecurity more than the pains of traditional constraint. Philosophers need to help in articulating this feeling, in rephrasing individualism in more human, less antisocial terms. This responsibility falls above all on philosophers who aim to be realistic—philosophers whose aim is to understand the world as it is rather than simply to contradict their colleagues or to build an elegant and dignified abstract system. And this group, surely, ought to include all philosophers who think of themselves as feminists.

In an age when loneliness is so pressing, we need to talk less about freedom in the abstract and more about the balance between particular freedoms, the relation between the various evils from which people need to be free. In our view, that is perhaps the main philosophical issue emerging from this topic. The idea that life would be better without close, lasting attachments such as those that arise in families seems a foolish one. But how can people today organize the individualistic world in a less isolating way? How can we control our civilization's current fluidity so as to leave pockets of refuge in which people can safely bring up their children?

Practical Angles

At an everyday level, various suggestions seem to surface as important. For instance, since children do make these intense demands for stable support, we surely need to help adolescents who cannot yet provide that support to avoid having their children too early. Unwanted teenage pregnancies are a real and serious evil. So it seems to us that the duty of making contraception, and an understanding of it, freely available to the young ought to rank high among the duties of a responsible government. It is extremely unfortunate that, in some countries, governments have tried to do this in a heavy-handed and overbearing manner which has discredited the whole project. But there are also countries, such as Mexico, where family planning campaigns conducted by local people have proved both popular and effective. Their example should surely be followed.

For older people who already have children, the question is, rather, whether the parents will stay together. Here again, the conventions that used to enforce this stability undoubtedly caused a good deal of misery. It is neither possible nor desirable to revive them. Even within those conventions, however, it was not necessarily thought that upbringing by a mother alone— say, a widow or a sailor's wife—must be disastrous, though it was always recognized that her work was hard and she would need outside support.

The reformers who made divorce and separation easier evidently thought that children would do better if the parents parted than if they stayed together while quarrelling. And it does seem that what upsets children most is not so much absence as discord. Unfortunately, however, current arrangements tend to provide both these things, since separated parents tend to go on quarrelling over the difficulties of disentangling their lives, and particularly over the children themselves. The importance of conciliation services seems now to be being recognized, along with the danger of letting adversarial lawyers inflame disputes. Family courts, devoted to resolving difficulties rather than allotting blame, are now being established. All this is surely a step in the right direction. It emerges indeed that great care will be needed to design these services in a way which prevents the more powerful party from simply talking down the weaker or less articulate. But once the importance of this is clearly understood, that can surely be done.

Undoubtedly, however, there is still a general dilemma here. At many points we today, in all kinds of societies, have to ask which we want more, secure social bonding or complete individual freedom? How shall we balance these ideals? It is not a single black or white choice between going into moral decline and returning to old ways. Instead, each society has a range of problems, some much harder than others, concerned with finding ways in which people can live together. Those ways will not necessarily produce familiar patterns. In many countries, family arrangements have changed a great deal over the ages, and they can very well change again.

A Moral Matter

Whatever may eventually be done about these things, it seems clear that for some considerable time many children in Britain and similar countries will be being brought up in one-parent families—or in what has been described as "the mother-state-child family."[6] It will not do, therefore, to dismiss their predicament as somehow provisional, temporary and not quite real. We need to find ways of making life tolerable for these small families, for whom outside support is in fact more necessary than it is for the familiar larger units. We also need to find ways of helping parents to stay together. Everything that tends to revive neighborhoods, to reintegrate social contexts, to provide some sort of permanence within which these networks can grow and prosper, is urgently called for. Communitarianism is right to emphasize these things, but wrong to suggest that they are rewards which will be offered only to deserving traditional families.

This kind of support is not just a pragmatic, economic need, a device for keeping down crime, disease and protest. It is needed morally. The sort of provision that a society makes for its families is indeed a moral matter, an aspect of its structure of ideals. If some kind of social Darwinist belief in the universal value of competition leads us to treat families as just one kind of unit among many, a unit that will survive or not according as it is fit to do so, then we shall be handing on an unbalanced, absurdly individualistic morality to our children.

If, too, that kind of competitive ethic leads us to treat the interests of men and women as necessarily in competition then we shall fail to look for ways in which they can be reconciled and can live harmoniously together. But living together is something absolutely essential for humans. It has to be made possible for the two sexes, just as it does across every other division where people often find it hard to understand one another. It is surely open to us to look for a more balanced form of individualism, a more human kind of freedom, that can make this possible.

Acknowledgments

Some parts of this article overlap with parts of our article "Trouble with Families?" to be found in *Introducing Applied Ethics*, ed. Brenda Almond (Oxford: Blackwell, 1995). We are grateful to the editor and publishers of that volume for allowing us to use them here.

Notes

1. See Berger et al., *The Family: Is It Just Another Lifestyle Choice?* and Norman Dennis, *Rising Crime and the Dismembered Family* (both London: Institute of Economic Affairs, 1993).

2. Aristotle, *Politics*, Book VI, chap. 16, 1335a.

3. Jane Austen, *Pride and Prejudice*, Vol. II, chap. 6.

4. William Godwin, *Enquiry Concerning Political Justice*, ed. K. Cadell Carter (Oxford: Clarendon Press, 1971), Book II, chap. 2, p. 71. In his second edition, Godwin altered this passage to refer to Fénélon's valet, who might be "my brother," thus opening further vistas of extraordinary speculations on class and gender which we cannot pursue here.

5. See Judith Hughes, "The Philosopher's Child," in *Feminist Perspectives in Philosophy*, eds. Morwenna Griffiths and Margaret Whitford (London: Macmillan 1988). Also Susan Moller Okin, *Women in Western Political Thought* (London: Virago, 1980) index, s.v. "Child-Rearing."

6. See Berger et al., p. 45.

5

Babystrike!

Laura M. Purdy

One of the hallmarks of early second-wave feminism was its critique of marriage and the family. There was, of course, a good deal of apparently outrageous and unreasoning expression of hatred for men; however, there was also a series of well-reasoned objections to contemporary norms. The popular mind, conflating the two, rejected feminism.

In the last ten or fifteen years, feminism has gone on to emphasize other issues, such as sexual harassment, workplace equity, and pornography. Indeed, the critiques of marriage and family seem almost forgotten as feminists, like society at large, now seem generally to assume that all women—including lesbians—will pair up and have children. Those for whom the old critiques are still vivid seem a bit old-fashioned, a bit stuck on tired, worn-out issues. Yet, as I watch friends struggle to accommodate both family and work in their lives, as I watch the economic situation deteriorate for most women, cutting their reserves to the bone, I wonder whether contemporary feminism truly represents a new, more mature theory, or whether it simply buries those fundamental issues that are so threatening to society at large.

The Problem

There was no shortage of naked rage at men and at family arrangements in those early days. Betty Friedan recalls the temper of the time in her 1981 call for a second stage of cooperation with men: "The popular (and un-popular) image of the modern feminist was that of a career 'superwoman' hellbent on beating men at their own game, or of a young 'Ms. Libber' agitating against marriage, motherhood, the family, sexual intimacy with men and any and all of the traits with which women in the past pleased or attracted men."[1] She goes on to quote comments by SCUM,[2] Mary Daly, Kate Millett, TiGrace Atkinson, and Shulamith Firestone.[3] Friedan concedes that such rhetoric "distorted the main thrust of the women's movement for equality and gave its enemies a powerful weapon. For it played into the fears and violated the feelings and needs of a great many women, and men, who still look to the family for security, love, roots in life."[4] This feminism seemed so far out that most women could not identify with it.

Friedan rightly concluded that feminism needed to move beyond such rhetoric if it were to appeal to a wider audience. But, despite media distortions, this outrage was never the heart of the feminist critique of marriage and the family. The important center was the reasoned work of such writers as Jessie Bernard, Ann Oakley, and Ellen Peck, and the essays collected by Robin Morgan, Vivian Gornick and Barbara K. Moran, Ellen Malos, and Ellen Peck and Judith Senderowitz.[5] This body of work provided solid evidence that, on the one hand, women are subjected to intense pressure to marry and have children, and, on the other, that benefits and burdens in marriage and child-rearing are unfairly allocated. Underlying these claims were two assumptions. The first was that women and men have many interests in common, including an interest in determining how they shall live. The second was that the belief that women's biology is destiny is often propagated by those who benefit unfairly from the status quo.

Has anything changed since the '70s? It seems to me that the ethos of having it all has, if anything, intensified the pressures described by these critics. It is true that some changes have taken place that could increase women's choices. For example, most young women now realize that they must prepare to work most of their lives; larger numbers of women are entering some professions, such as medicine. Also, the salaries of young professional women are now more comparable with those of men. These changes encourage women to be financially independent and thus less in need of a husband to help them maintain a decent standard of living. However, many women cannot aspire to these relatively high-paying jobs and still need a second salary to live at all well. And when even feminists seem to take it for granted that having children is a normal part of life, where do girls and young women hear that life might be fully satisfying—or perhaps even more satisfying—without children? Nowhere. Nowhere do they hear that some people shouldn't have children, either because they don't really want them, because they are not able to care for them well, or because they have other projects that are incompatible with good child-rearing. On the contrary, the most common response to couples who choose not to have children is still that they are selfish.[6] These pressures are reflected in the way those who buck the trend and ultimately decide against motherhood describe their path.[7]

Whether human happiness, or women's happiness, requires procreation and child-rearing is an interesting question that feminism has yet to address fully. I believe that there is good reason for thinking that having children is not essential to a happy life, and that, indeed, child-rearing in contemporary circumstances may well lead to more suffering than satisfaction.[8] However, further exploration of this most fundamental question must be left for another day; instead I want to examine here only the more limited question of how feminism should approach having children now.

First and foremost, feminism should obviously be countering pronatalism because it leads to so many women's having children they really do not want or cannot care for adequately. It should do so by a variety of measures, including showing young girls splendid examples of women who have led satisfying lives doing things other than child-rearing. Society's attitude toward children also needs to become a major topic of public discussion. Although there are political risks in open discussion about the value of children, and of responsibility for them, the risks of continuing to avoid such discussion now seem even greater, for I think that Martha E. Gimenez's assertion that "motherhood, if conceived as a taken-for-granted dimension of women's normal adult role, becomes one of the key sources of women's oppression" is true.[9] On the one hand, women are expected to cope, often single-handedly, with the demands of child-rearing that are met in most other societies by means of community support. In addition, they may well be completely unprepared for the demands of motherhood in this society.[10] On the other, those demands make it difficult or impossible for women individually and as a class to advance toward genuine equality.

Because public life is still so male-centered, there is little social recognition of what it means to become a mother. Laurence Tribe puts it beautifully: "Pregnancy does not merely 'inconvenience' the woman for a time; it gradually turns her into a mother and makes her one for all time."[11] In fact,

> having a child is a permanent commitment. . . . A child becomes part of a woman's life forever. To be a mother is a lifelong task. The decision to become a mother is fraught with implications. . . . In many ways, to have or not have a child will be the deciding factor in hundreds, perhaps thousands, of other little decisions down the road—what job you'll take, what house you'll buy, what neighborhood you live in, how you spend your days, your money, your weekends, holidays, vacations, where and when you'll travel, who your friends are, who's in your kinship network, and so on.[12]

For poor women, of course, having children has still more far-reaching consequences, as former Surgeon General Joycelyn Elders notes.[13]

The financial cost of children is suggestive of the demands of child-rearing. According to the U.S. Dept. of Agriculture, raising a "no-frills" kid to the age of eighteen costs some $100,000; college adds another $100,000.[14] Middle-class children cost more still, and neither of these figures includes opportunity costs for women who choose to be housewives.[15] Other costs are equally substantial. Studies show that married women without children have three months more discretionary time a year than do mothers, months of twelve-hour, five-day weeks. Husbands average twenty percent of the domestic work, and while this is up from eight percent in 1965,[16] there is still a huge imbalance in the child-related work done by women and by men. Worse yet, despite women's burden, many children are suffering because of insufficient adult attention.[17]

Women often become mothers unaware of the demands having children will make on them:

> Young women are rarely prepared for the sleepless nights, the noise, exhaustion, worry, and responsibility that come with children. Louis Genevie and Eva Margolies, authors of *The Motherhood Report* and researchers who looked at 1,100 mothers of all ages, found mothers frazzled, frustrated, and furious by the day-to-day grind of raising children. . . . [Some mothers said:] "This is not what I bargained for." "Your life is not yours. You have to put your children first. Your emotions and needs come last."[18]

One woman said: "There are times I feel like a 'prisoner' in my home—really tied down—unappreciated. I often feel that I am losing myself—my own time no longer exists. I did not realize how my whole life would center around the children."[19]

None of this is to say that women should never have children. Many women strongly desire a close, nurturing relationship with a child, as well as to continue their family line. It is to say that girls and women need to be fully informed of the costs and trade-offs involved in having children, costs and trade-offs that pronatalism conspires to hide from them. It is also to suggest that girls and women need to be encouraged to think about whether they want children, rather than assuming that there is no other path in life. At present, I fear that these conditions are rarely met before women conceive.

A Solution

It seems clear that as long as women continue routinely to have children—especially when they are young and poor—the prospects for progress toward equality for women are bleak. How can women energetically fight the entrenched sexism in society and pursue positions of power and prestige if their time and energy is mostly taken up with children's needs, needs that cannot and ought not to be ignored? After all, most decent jobs *still* presume that a housewife will meet the earner's personal needs so he can concentrate on his job; women are unlikely to be fully successful in them if they have domestic duties. Only superwomen have a chance of success in the public arena if they are doing a good job of child-rearing.

Can women look to others to fight on their behalf? Husbands allegedly love their wives but they seem mostly to be part of the problem.[20] The progressive Left, although theoretically in favor of women's rights, has been in reality relatively unhelpful in fighting for the practical changes that women need. It is still quite male-dominated and it seems unlikely that it will push for measures that reduce, or seem to reduce, men's power. In any case, the progressive Left is, like the liberal middle, fairly powerless at present in the face of a militant and extreme right with its philosophy of "family values" that sees women primarily as biologically determined nurturers.

If women themselves are hobbled in the fight for equality by the demands of child-rearing, and no other group will take up the fight, it seems to follow that equality for women is doomed unless women temporarily refrain from child-rearing so that they can devote themselves to changing the situation. What would happen if they did that? I think we could expect extremely intense pressure to get them to reproduce, by force if necessary.[21] I suspect that this development would open women's eyes to the fact that society wants babies, but that it prefers women to think that producing them is both naturally women's lot and that doing so is an individual decision. After all, in those circumstances society owes women no help in bringing up new generations. If women stopped having babies, the resulting pressures would unmask this reality.

A babystrike wouldn't be a huge sacrifice for middle-class white women. But what about the unfortunate young women who are so deprived that they see early childbearing as a source of love and satisfaction? It seems fairly clear that such childbearing is no real solution for their difficulties, since it generally renders both them and their offspring worse off in the long run. The practical difficulties in getting them to join a babystrike are daunting.[22] It is plausible to believe that the girls and women in question will not refrain from early childbearing until society offers them both realistic alternative visions and the means to achieve them. Doing so would undoubtedly require additional social programs, as well as a truly meritocratic system that rewarded talent and hard work no matter what the personal characteristics of the worker. No such plans are on the horizon; on the contrary, in 1996 we are waging a losing battle to retain already existing programs. It follows that the relevant communities would need somehow to motivate themselves to participate in a babystrike. This is probably especially difficult since such participation might be seen as caving in to the aims of the Right, aims adopted for elitist and racist reasons rather than the welfare of girls and women and their children. However, it is reasonable to act prudently and morally, even if others want you to do the same things for the wrong reasons. Also, it's quite possible that limited participation on the part of the poor wouldn't really matter, given the powerful elitist and racist view that equates only the failure of middle-class white women to reproduce with the collapse of civilization.

My suggestion will probably be laughed off as utopian or simply ridiculous. But I challenge others to find a more viable approach to achieving women's equality: the clear, cold light of reason seems to me to show no other feasible alternative. A babystrike would be both difficult and risky, for it might be unsuccessful, or even leave us worse off than before—images of Margaret Atwood's *Handmaid's Tale* haunt me here. However, any bad outcome short of that one would lead women to forego child-rearing far more often than is now the case. If so, the aim of the babystrike might well be achieved, even if more slowly and indirectly. It's just possible, of course, that the babystrike could be successful. . . .

Notes

1. Betty Friedan, *The Second Stage* (New York: Dell Publishing, 1981), p. 32.
2. Society for Cutting Up Men.
3. Friedan, *The Second Stage*, p. 36.
4. Ibid.
5. See Jessie Bernard, *The Future of Marriage* (New York: World Publishing, 1972) and *The Future of Motherhood* (New York: The Dial Press, 1974); Ann Oakley, *Women's Work* (New York: Vintage Books, 1974); Ellen Peck, *The Baby Trap* (New York: Pinnacle Books, 1971); Robin Morgan, *Sisterhood Is Powerful* (New York: Vintage Books, 1970); Vivian Gornick and Barbara K. Moran, *Woman in Sexist Society* (New York: Basic Books, 1971); Ellen Malos, *The Politics of Housework* (London: Allison & Busby Limited, 1980); and Ellen Peck & Judith Senderowitz, *Pronatalism: The Myth of Mom & Apple Pie* (New York: Thomas Y. Crowell Company, 1974).
6. See, for example, letter to Ann Landers, *The Ithaca Journal*, October 14, 1995, by "Childless by Choice."
7. See studies of childless women in Mardy S. Ireland, *Reconceiving Women: Separating Motherhood from Female Identity* (New York: The Guilford Press, 1993) and Susan S. Lang, *Women Without Children: The Reasons, the Rewards, The Regrets* (New York: Pharos Books, 1991).
8. I believe that there is probably little or no biological component in the desire for children (as opposed to having sexual intercourse) and that in a nonsexist and non-pronatalist society women as a group would desire children just in the way and to the extent that men as a group desire them. Undoubtedly there would be significant individual differences, and different societies would probably have different ranges and frequencies of desire for children.
9. Martha E. Gimenez, "Feminism, Pronatalism, and Motherhood," in *Mothering*, ed. Joyce Trebilcot (Totowa, N.J.: Rowman and Allenheld, 1984), p. 287.
10. It is also important to remember that women often become pregnant not out of a desire for motherhood but because they have not used contraception or because abortion is not available to them.
11. Laurence H. Tribe, *Abortion: The Clash of Absolutes* (New York: Norton, 1990), p. 104.

12. Lang, *Women Without Children*, pp. 3–4. She goes on to point out that studies show that "parenthood . . . tends to wreak havoc on a marriage. . . . Study after study confirms that the negative impact of children on marital happiness is pervasive, regardless of race, religion, education, and wives' employment" (p. 81).

13. " . . . if you're poor and ignorant, with a child, you're a slave. Meaning that you're never going to get out of it. These women are in bondage to a kind of slavery that the 13th Amendment just didn't deal with. . . . You can't control your life." Quoted in "Joycelyn Elders Toughs It Out," *New York Times Magazine*, January 30, 1994.

14. Lang, *Women Without Children*, p. 206. In its most recent report, the Department of Agriculture breaks the figures down as follows: for a family with an annual income under $32,000, raising a child to the age of 18 will cost some $100,000. For a family with an income between $32,800 and $55,500, the cost will rise to $136,000, and for a family with an income over $55,500, it will be $198,000. (See *The Ithaca Journal*, October 14, 1995.)

15. Lang, *Women Without Children*, p. 207.

16. Lang, *Women Without Children*, pp. 208–209.

17. See my *In Their Best Interest? The Case Against Equal Rights for Children* (Ithaca: Cornell University Press, 1992). I believe that many children are suffering from insufficient individual attention from adults and that if one knows that one will be unable to meet a child's needs here, one ought to seriously rethink the decision to have children.

18. Lang, *Women Without Children*, p. 81.

19. Lang, *Women Without Children*, p. 82.

20. There are, of course, many wonderful exceptions.

21. Some people, like the manufacturers of disposable diapers, benefit directly from the existence of babies. In addition, most people probably want us to continue to exist as a species and would become deeply demoralized if that were in doubt. Consider the entirely plausible picture drawn by P.D. James in her novel *The Children of Men* (New York: Alfred Knopf, 1993) where women suddenly become infertile.

22. The problem is complicated by our society's contradictory and obsessive views about sex, contraception, and abortion. There are no easy solutions here, but better parenting, education, social programs, and commonsensical substitutes like puppies might help them act more consistently in their own interest. For a useful discussion of these issues, see Myra and David Sadker, *Failing at Fairness: How America's Schools Cheat Girls* (New York: Charles Scribner's Sons, 1994), p. 115ff.

6

Feminism by Any Other Name

Michele M. Moody-Adams

A claim that emerges repeatedly in popular political discussion, and even in some scholarly settings, is that feminism is fundamentally "antifamily." Shortly before the 1995 United Nations Conference on Women, for instance, conservative critics insisted that it would be wrong for First Lady Hillary Clinton to attend the conference because of the allegedly antifamily agenda of its feminist organizers. Even feminists themselves have sometimes suggested that central feminist ideals are too closely linked with opposition to the existence of family life. Thus, in *The Second Stage* (1981), Betty Friedan chastises feminists for their "blind spot about the family"—as expressed, she adds, in "our own extreme reaction against that wife-mother role."[1] Other critics who are reluctant to charge feminism in general with hostility to family life nonetheless hold, with Mary Anne Glendon, that feminist ideas are irrelevant to the concerns of real women seeking "a decent family life" in the current uncertain economic climate.[2] All such views share the notion that acceptance of central feminist values is incompatible with any serious commitment to the importance of family life.

Yet much recent feminist thought could hardly be deemed antifamily, nor even properly be thought to have a "blind spot" about family life. Contemporary feminist moral theories, for instance, often take the personal relationships formed in families to be fundamental to the nature and identity of the self, and they treat an understanding of the moral dimensions of family life as crucial to the development of moral maturity.[3] Even more important, many feminist critiques of the division of labor between the sexes are expressly concerned with the most desirable ways to transform the institutions and practices of modern family life—not to eradicate them.[4] Some of these critiques aim to show how changes in the social and political institutions of the societies from which they have emerged—typically liberal democracies—might help create and protect families that more fully realize deeply held political ideals.[5] Many changes urged by such views, including equality of obligations in matters such as child-rearing and housework, concern the internal workings of individual families.[6] But some feminists hold that there is also a social responsibility to create a context in which equality of obligations within families might flourish. Indeed some feminists argue that although principles basic to liberal democracies entrust certain elements of care for children to individual families, it is consistent with—perhaps even required by—those same principles that the well-being of families be treated as both a public and a private concern. Practices most likely to embody that concern include the restructuring of work to make child care leaves and flexible schedules more widely accessible, public support for affordable and competent day care, and income supports for at least some families with children.[7] To be sure, other feminist critiques link their accounts of family life with skepticism about the political and economic ideals of existing societies—especially of liberal democracies.[8] But even for those who may reject their underlying skepticisms, these critiques nonetheless allow useful scrutiny of the links between the institutions of family life and the division of labor between the sexes. A wide array of feminist treatments of the family can thus serve as constructive aids to the socially beneficial transformation of family life. Any facile association of feminism with opposition to the existence of families is at best a caricature.

Why, then, has the linking of feminism with fundamental opposition to family life become so widespread, and so powerful a component of much contemporary political rhetoric? First of all, feminism's critics have seized upon an important element of some feminist thought. Many feminist critics of institutions that underwrite the division of labor between the sexes have doubted whether commitment to women's autonomy and equality could be compatible with a concern to preserve and protect family life. I argue in Section I, however, that a reflective feminism can take such doubts seriously, and yet defend the relevance of some feminist ideals to the constructive transformation of family life. But the unreflective association of feminism with fundamentally "antifamily" sentiments has a second, even more problematic, source. Feminism's unsympathetic critics have exploited the insecurities of many women to persuade them that to embrace the label "feminism"—and actively to celebrate any of its central ideals—is to reject their "essential" womanhood, along with all the institutions, practices, and prerogatives attached to it. Central among such institutions and practices, of course, are those bound up with family life; according to unsympathetic critics, feminist ideals and aims are simply antithetical to the stability and security of family life. Yet I show in Section II that this antifeminist stance fails to make sense of real women's lives. If one examines the substance of those lives, even (perhaps especially) in circumstances where women confront great economic instability, a woman's commitment to the preservation of her family is often inseparable from an equally strong commitment to women's autonomy and equal rights of self-determination. It is not unimportant, of course, that the demonization of feminist ideals has successfully persuaded many women to avoid describing their feminist ideals for what they are. But I show that, far from being a fundamental betrayal of "family values," feminism—by any name—can often be indispensable to the preservation of families. In the final section of the paper, I show that many feminists have failed to appreciate the powerful link between feminism and the genuine valuing of families. I show, moreover, how feminist thinking might benefit by greater attention to the ways in which everyday women embody feminist ideals in their efforts to cope with the burdens of family life while preserving and enhancing its rewards.

I. A Familiar Caricature

I claimed at the outset that the simple linking of feminism and hostility to families is a caricature, yet a caricature can be effective as a tool of persuasion if it is widely perceived successfully to exaggerate some pre-existing characteristics of its subject. The caricature of feminism as fundamentally antifamily is effective in so many contexts because it exaggerates certain tendencies of "second-wave" feminist theories that—unlike recent feminist celebrations of the nurturing learned in families—often take direct critical aim at institutions central to family life.

Second-wave feminism highlighted the tensions between the unreconstructed institutions of family life, on one hand, and, on the other, feminist conceptions of what social life would have to be like in order to realize equality and self-determination for women. Unlike first-wave feminists, who emphasized the need for equal political (and sometimes economic) rights, second-wave feminists typically argued that women's equality required that women gain control of institutions and practices associated with female sexuality—especially those bound up with reproduction.[9] For this reason, second-wave feminism (and many more recent views influenced by it) may appear to involve radical departures from feminism's "traditional" concerns. Attacks on these apparent departures sometimes proceed from avowedly sympathetic critics of feminism. One such critic has recently charged that contemporary "gender feminists"—who trace their intellectual lineage most directly to second-wave feminism—have "stolen" feminism from the "moderate, unpretentious" mainstream of "equity feminists."[10] But all such charges overlook a crucial fact: the underlying concern of second-wave feminists (as of their "gender" feminist descendants) continues to be equality for women. To be sure, the social and political effects of many contemporary feminist views often include the very anger and resentment derided by some recent critics.[11] But this fact would not distinguish feminist-inspired political discourse from the rhetoric of contemporary commentators who summarily demonize feminists as "feminazis." This rhetoric plays into socially constructed fears that feminists are so authoritarian and socially dangerous that they cannot be "real" women.

What most unsettles feminism's critics is that feminist theorizing about the family tends to efface allegedly clear-cut distinctions between the "personal" and "political," and to treat as socially constructed and changeable domains of experience that others take to be "natural" and fixed. The resulting critiques target institutions and practices that are intimately connected with the unscrutinized dimensions of people's fundamental self-conceptions—institutions and practices thought by many to be properly immune from theoretical scrutiny. This is one of the principal reasons that feminist views on family life have been so uniformly dismissed as antifamily—without reflection on the content of any particular feminist account. It is easier to demonize the theorist who demands scrutiny of institutions deemed immune from scrutiny, rather than examine the potential reasonableness of the disturbing substance of those demands. It is true that some feminist theories are overtly opposed to the very idea of families, as socially separate units charged with the care and nurturing of the vulnerable—as well as to conceptions of motherhood and childhood linked with that notion.[12] But the many feminists who reject such stances must try to reclaim feminism's potential as a force for beneficial social change in families.

In order to do this, they must combat the caricatures and facile identifications of feminism and antifamily thought that have come to dominate political discourse about feminism. Theorists who wish to show the social and political importance of feminist thought for families must display the richness and complexity of feminism's varied stands on the family. But this project must begin with a clear-eyed appraisal of the actual content of influential feminist views. Portions of *The Feminine Mystique* (1963), for instance, simply strain credulity: at one point, Betty Friedan compares the life of the 1950s suburban American housewife with the horrific experience of prisoners in Nazi concentration camps.[13] This kind of hyperbole is little more than fodder for feminism's most vocal—and most unsympathetic—critics, and in more recent accounts Friedan herself has been rightly critical of the "extreme reaction" embodied in such claims.[14] Friedan's rejection of such hyperbole, moreover, has allowed her to pursue compelling replies to feminism's unsympathetic critics. Thus she has recently argued that to charge the women's movement with having undermined the stability of families simply diverts attention from other, more fundamental, causes of family instability—in particular powerful forces leading to global economic upheaval.[15]

Yet despite its occasional hyperbole, many readers today might find *The Feminine Mystique* to be a relatively tame account of the conflict between women's autonomy and "that wife-mother role." In the concluding chapter of that work, for instance, Friedan contends (perhaps unexpectedly) that:

> In actual fact, it is not as difficult as the feminine mystique implies, to combine marriage and motherhood and even the kind of lifelong personal purpose that once was called "career." It merely takes a new life plan—in terms of one's whole life as a woman.[16]

Friedan was always certain, that is, that it would be possible to combine "the love and children and home that have defined femininity in the past with the work toward a greater purpose that shapes the future."[17]

Shulamith Firestone's *The Dialectic of Sex* (1970) attacks the compatibility of motherhood with autonomous womanhood more insistently than virtually any other feminist text of the period. Yet according to Anne Snitow, *The Dialectic of Sex* is not an attack on motherhood itself, but simply on the patriarchical organization of motherhood.[18] However, this reading is difficult to square with much of what Firestone actually says, especially her blunt expressions of distaste for the pregnant female body. She argues, for instance, that while some women think a belief that pregnancy is "not beautiful" is merely a "cultural perversion,"

> The child's first response, "What's wrong with that Fat Lady?"; the husband's guilty waning of sexual desire; the woman's tears in front of the mirror at eight months—are all gut reactions, not to be dismissed as cultural habits. Pregnancy is the temporary deformation of the body of the individual for the sake of the species.[19]

In addition to its unsupportable claim that every culture demeans pregnant women, the revulsion Firestone expresses seems as deeply influenced by patriarchal attitudes toward a woman's body as any attitudes Firestone herself attacks. Further, in her zeal for developments in "artificial reproduction" that might eventually "free women . . . from their biology," Firestone never considers that motherhood (in any and all of its biological and social dimensions) might sometimes be a healthy, autonomous choice for a woman.[20]

More recent feminist critics of "pronatalism" attempt to build on Firestone's views, charging that "mainstream" feminists are insufficiently critical of the "compulsory nature of motherhood."[21] But while it is true, as such critics maintain, that few societies recognize any "legitimate or socially rewarded alternatives to the performance of parental roles," even in circumstances where motherhood may be the only valued role for women to assume, it is nonetheless possible to make an autonomous and intrinsically valuable decision to become a mother.[22] As Jean Elshtain has argued, "However shakily and imperfectly," family life helps to preserve an alternative to the impersonal and often "brutal" values that tend to dominate social and economic institutions external to it.[23] A woman may certainly make an autonomous choice to promote the respect, trust, and care that are possible only in the close personal relationships found in families. Participation in the institutions of motherhood and family life may even provide an important means of developing a depth of personality and moral character that enrich the life of the individual woman—in addition to promoting socially beneficial values. One need not deny the possibility (and the reasonableness) of such choices in order to celebrate the worth of decisions not to mother. Feminists who think otherwise have as constricted a view of authentic womanhood as any of the views they typically attack.

Yet even the feminist thinker who rejects Firestone's skepticism about the possibility of an autonomous motherhood may find much of value in attempting to meet the concerns that underlie it. The claim that motherhood and family life require women to sacrifice their autonomy and relinquish hopes for social, political, and economic equality is a view that forces reflection on the need to reform those elements of family life that unduly confine and oppress women—and perhaps also to reject those that cannot be reformed. Moreover, efforts to counter unduly narrow conceptions of the possibilities of motherhood may yield richer understandings of the benefits (as well as the burdens) of family life for women than would otherwise be likely. On this interpretation, then, even actively "antifamily" feminist thought can yield lessons that are useful in the effort to beneficially transform family life. The task of the thinker who would glean those lessons is to try to distinguish those institutions and practices of family life which can be appropriately reformed and reconstructed from those which cannot and hence may need to be jettisoned.

II. 'Tis But Thy Name That Is My Enemy

But even if such a task might be carried out, feminist reflection on the beneficial transformation of family life still confronts an important difficulty. Most feminists consider feminist social and political theory more capable than most such theory of bridging the gap between theory and practice; feminist theorists, that is, typically view their theories as genuinely useful contributions to practical efforts to transform real women's lives. Yet some of feminism's most vehement—and most influential—critics object that feminism seeks to liberate women (in Marilyn Quayle's phrase at the 1992 Republican National Convention) "from their essential natures." These critics predict that feminism will inevitably fail in its efforts to transform social life because, in their view, most women accept a conception of their "nature" that is antithetical to virtually everything that feminism (broadly construed) entails. On this antifeminist conception, they continue, women are best suited by nature to be partners to husbands engaged in full-time paid labor outside the home, and to be mothers for whom full-time care of their children is their only rightful occupation.

These critics do acknowledge that some women *cannot* conform to this familiar conception of a woman's "nature." Some women must engage in full-time paid labor, or will fail to find suitable marriage partners, or will prove unable to have children. But even most of these women, antifeminists contend, never fully relinquish the nonfeminist conception of womanhood. Those women who think they have, the argument goes, are self-deceived. Proponents of this view take as the prime example of such self-deception the woman who for years pursues security in a demanding profession only to eventually lament the expiration of her "biological clock." Although these critics concede that some women will successfully reject nonfeminist ideals, such women, they contend, are anomalous and socially dangerous, pursuing personal fulfillment at the expense of institutions (like "the family") that have historically underwritten the flourishing of Western civilization. Feminism, these critics continue, is really addressed to women with just such anomalous desires. They conclude that this is why so many women are reluctant to accept the label "feminist," and they treat this reluctance as palpable evidence that most women ultimately reject feminist concerns as antithetical to their deepest aims and desires.

But this analysis fails to explain why—to adapt a phrase of Shakespeare's Juliet—it is so often merely the word *feminism*, and not the content of specific feminist aims, that women actually take to be their "enemy." The lives of many women who expressly eschew the label *feminist* nonetheless embody many of the preoccupations and assumptions that have long fuelled feminist theory and practice. Unsympathetic insistence on feminism's alleged distance from the concerns of most women simply cannot account for this striking fact. Consider the example of women in Appalachian Kentucky of the 1990s, struggling to cope with long-term structural decline in their region's economy. The Appalachian economy was for a long time based primarily on mining and logging, but increasing automation and decreasing supplies of coal and wood have gradually led to a high rate of unemployment among men in the region. Familiar ways for local women to supplement family incomes (principally, part-time work on small family farms) no longer remedy the serious economic hardships resulting from male unemployment. As a consequence, many women in the region have responded by seeking new job skills, engaging in full-time paid labor outside the home, and relying on day care and baby-sitters to care for their children while they do so.[24] These responses all presuppose social and economic changes that would be impossible but for the influence of feminist ideals. Moreover, in accepting the changes which make their choices possible, many women of Appalachian Kentucky have implicitly embraced at least some feminist aims and goals.

Feminism's unsympathetic critics might be heartened to learn that virtually all the women interviewed for a lengthy article on economic change in the region were reluctant to accept that their choices, and the self-conceptions that emerged along with those choices, might be deemed "feminist." But the fact remains that these choices required the deliberate—and often difficult—rejection of the local tradition of "breadwinner" husband and "homemaker" wife.[25] For example, one thirty-eight-year-old woman who had been married at thirteen, and had borne her five children by the time she was twenty, insisted that her husband would simply have to accept her textbooks and her job and "deal with me being a grown-up." Another woman declared that she started making her own decisions when emergency room treatment for a miscarriage left her (uninsured) family with a large unpaid hospital bill. The upshot of those decisions was a demanding schedule of paid employment outside the home, and a simultaneous effort to become a social worker by taking extension courses at a local university. Though worried that she and her husband might be "growing apart"—because of his fear of her newfound assertiveness—she was steadfast in her conviction that she was doing the right thing: "Right now, I'm in the ball park and I'm going to throw the ball." Her commitment to a woman's right of self-determination is inextricably linked with feminist ideals. Yet she was especially vehement in her insistence that she was "not a women's libber."

Feminist thinkers who would reassert feminism's socially transformative potential must provide a plausible explanation of such vehemence. But the elements of such an explanation emerge fairly clearly from reflection on the striking ironies in the experiences and choices of the women in my example. Unsympathetic critics insist, as I have noted, that feminism ultimately *requires* a commitment to "antifamily" ideals. Many would insist, further, that while the economic dimensions of feminist ideals may be of use to the highly ambitious, upwardly mobile woman seeking, say, to head a Fortune 500 company, they are not particularly useful to the "average" woman concerned about the economic stability and security of her family. Yet neither of these claims is borne out by the facts of my example. Indeed that example reveals, in a particularly striking way, that commitment to feminist ideals can sometimes be most useful to women trying to negotiate their way—and that of their families—through periods of great economic hardship.

To be sure, there is reason for concern, as some critics of feminism contend, about the class-bound character of some elements of feminism. It may be impossible to separate an Appalachian woman's resistance to being aligned with feminist ideals from her perception of feminism as a largely middle-class phenomenon. In this respect, moreover, such class-based suspicion of American feminism bears important similarities to widespread resistance among African-American women, for whom racism—often combined with economic oppression—long constituted its own kind of exclusion from some feminist concerns.

But the perceptions which underlie such responses to feminism may not tell the whole story: many important dimensions of the feminine mystique have always been part of the experience of women in a variety of social and economic settings. Women of all classes may struggle, for instance, with the thought that a wife's economic assertiveness in her family might cause serious disruptions of her family life. Whenever a woman's worth is supposed to be linked with her ability to perform the "woman's work" of the domestic household, a man's worth will be linked to his ability to be "a good provider" for his family. In such a setting, a man's economic frustrations—and their resultant blow to his self-conception—may make a woman's effort to contribute to a family's economic well-being seem like an assault on the husband's self-respect as well as a challenge to socially accepted norms. The woman of modest means who insists that her husband simply accept her as a "grown-up," and as entitled to make important decisions about the economic well-being of her family fights against the feminine mystique—and against the accompanying socially constructed patterns of self-respect shaping her spouse's self-conception—as much as any middle-class suburban housewife of the 1950s. Moreover, the stakes in the struggles of the woman of modest means will tend to be more closely linked with the very possibility of survival than are the struggles of middle-class American housewives for personal fulfillment and meaningful engagement in life outside the home. Many contemporary women—unlike most middle-class suburban housewives of the '50s—must make choices about work and family in contexts where acquiescence in any demand to go home and take care of "women's work" might well lead to the destruction of their families.

In this regard, even the middle-class American wife of the 1990s has more in common with the working-class women in my contemporary example than with the middle-class housewife of the 1950s. Some social critics charge that women's pursuit of outside income for their families is a function of uncontrolled individualism, or the excessive materialism of families in industrialized nations. They even suggest that social struggles with deepening unemployment and job insecurity would abate if only women who are currently in the workforce would go home again. But structural economic changes endemic to industrialized nations in the late twentieth century have made the two-income family less a matter of anybody's wishes to promote personal fulfillment than of economic necessity. Further, the upheaval caused by economic dislocations is a major source of the changes in family life that unsympathetic critics attribute to the influence of feminism.[26] Increasing automation and continual advances in technology have led to a corresponding increase in low-paying service jobs. Moreover, increased demands for quick profits in global financial markets have made corporations reluctant to invest in long-term economic development and all too ready to "downsize" as a means of increasing productivity. In the midst of such developments, feminist support of women's autonomy and self-determination serves to offer women—especially women in families with children—new ways of negotiating unfamiliar economic terrain. In such a climate of economic upheaval, ironically, opposition to feminism is more profoundly "antifamily" than feminism itself.

Yet there is no simple reason why some of feminism's critics find it easier to attack feminism's alleged threats to family life than to recognize that developments in economic institutions pose genuinely fundamental threats to the family.[27] Many of these critics believe that the family is in some way a "natural" institution—and that there is a fixed, natural boundary between the domestic household (the home) and the economic institutions from which the domestic household allegedly provides a secure haven (the market). This belief stands in marked contrast to the stance assumed by influential feminist treatments of the family. At least since the second wave of feminist thought, most feminists have defended some version of the "social constructionist" thesis about families—the thesis that the family is principally a social institution, and that particular forms of family life are primarily products of the conventions of particular societies.[28] On such a view, it is difficult to support the notion that there is some fixed, natural boundary between the institutions and practices that constitute the domestic household and the institutions and practices that constitute the "market." In fact, for a social constructionist view of the family, economic institutions and practices are among the most important social conventions working to preserve and protect particular organizations of family life.

Feminist thinkers have offered several distinctive versions of the view that particular family forms tend to emerge in association with particular economic institutions. Especially familiar are feminist challenges to the idea that the model of breadwinner husband/homemaker wife might represent some timeless essence of authentic family life.[29] Nearly as familiar are feminist concerns about family leave and child care, equal pay for equal work, and the persistent undervaluing of work connected with the care of children, the sick, and the elderly. Such concerns subtly challenge the notion that there is a fixed or natural boundary between the domestic household and the market. They do so by challenging the notion that there is a fixed, natural boundary between "women's work" and every other kind of work—between domestic goods and services that are beyond economic valuation, and goods and services exchanged on the market where value is measured by relative price.[30] Those who believe that families are primarily natural, not social, institutions will be bound to reject even many "moderate" feminisms as "enemies" of the family. But what these critics overlook, as I have argued, is the extent to which some feminist views might provide both women and men with new insight about how to preserve families in the face of an increasingly hostile economic environment. Feminists who would develop this insight should examine the practice of everyday women who implicitly recognize the value of feminist ideals—despite their resistance to a label so effectively demonized by those critics who have managed to monopolize debate about the worth of feminist thought. Such an examination should not merely seek to diagnose the causes of their resistance, but to reveal the feminist ideals that underlie their practice and thus show that a feminism by any other name can be useful in securing the well-being of the modern family.

III. Motherhood beyond Mystique

I have suggested that a reflective feminism about families must take seriously the practice of women whose lives embody feminist ideals independent of any readiness to explicitly acknowledge allegiance to those ideals. One insight that would be central to such a view is suggested by a striking passage from a 1983 essay by Betty Friedan, in which she remarks on many women's persistent desire to have a child when, in her view, "women no longer need to have a child to define themselves as women, to have status, economic support, and identity in society." Friedan argues that the persistence of the desire suggests that feminism "has liberated an exultant motherhood, beyond mystique."[31] The claim is important to a reflective feminism about families for several reasons. First, it provides a promising alternative to the view that a woman's desire to have a child is always evidence of allegiance to some nonfeminist conception of a woman's "essential nature." It also suggests that familiar fears that the social ascendancy of feminist views might make women unwilling to have children are unfounded, at best. Indeed, if Friedan is right it is feminism itself—or, more precisely, certain feminist ideals—which helps make possible and sustain an autonomous choice to become a mother. Friedan was perhaps unduly confident, in *The Feminine Mystique*, about the ease of composing a "life plan" that might allow women who wished to do so to combine motherhood and family life with the demands of paid employment outside their homes. Or perhaps she was unduly confident about feminism's capacity to change social institutions as quickly as it was able to influence women's self-understandings. This kind of confidence may even be at the root of some women's apparent feeling that they have been "betrayed" by feminists who have championed the kinds of choices about work and family that require as yet uncompleted changes in social and economic institutions. Yet feminists who remain skeptical about the possibility that motherhood is compatible with women's autonomy are simply inattentive to the power of many feminist ideals. A woman who does not need to link her self-worth with the capacity to mother—and who can make choices about reproduction in an appropriate social context—is then free to desire motherhood for her own reasons. This fact is crucial, even though the freedom to desire a motherhood beyond mystique does not guarantee that choices made on the basis of such desires will be easy.

But how might a reflective feminism emphasize those kinds of social support that would make motherhood beyond mystique more uniformly accessible? Just as many feminist views have challenged the idea that there is a fixed, natural boundary between the domestic household and the market, it is also important to challenge the idea that there is a fixed, natural boundary between the domestic household and what some social theorists call the "public household." By "public household" I mean, following Daniel Bell, the public political means by which state revenues and expenditures are used to provide for public needs and wants.[32] A reflective feminism about families would insist that care for the vulnerable in families—especially children—is a concern of the public household, as central to the stability and health of a society as national defense or public highways. Such a view would point out to antifeminist critics that one can acknowledge the importance of the benefits that individual families provide its members, while accepting that the provision of care for vulnerable members of families is an important and fundamental public concern.

But it is the lives of real women trying to reap the benefits of a motherhood beyond mystique—and bearing the burdens of doing so in a social climate which is too often hostile to their efforts—which are likely to offer the best lessons about how to express that concern. The single most important lesson to be gleaned from their experience is that a reflective feminism is not merely compatible with, but indispensable to, serious concern for the stability and well-being of modern family life. A reflective feminism need not overlook the value of the lives of those women who do not choose motherhood and family life. As Friedan reminds us, in liberating a motherhood beyond mystique feminism has also liberated women "to be generative in other ways, without . . . feeling like freaks."[33] But any feminism worthy of the name should recognize the value of choices to be generative in the more literal sense, and help make sense of those social and economic institutions most likely to make such choices compatible with women's equality.

Notes

1. Betty Friedan, *The Second Stage* (New York: Summit Books, 1981), p. 203.
2. Mary Anne Glendon, quoted in Fox Butterfield, "U.N. Women's Forum is a Test for Pope's Advocate," *New York Times* (August 29, 1995).
3. See, for instance, Carol Gilligan, *In a Different Voice* (Harvard: Cambridge University Press, 1982); Nel Noddings, *Caring: A Feminine Approach to Ethics and Moral Education* (Berkeley: University of California Press, 1984); Virginia Held, *Feminist Morality* (Chicago: University of Chicago Press, 1993); and the essays in Eva Feder Kittay and Diana T. Meyers, eds., *Women and Moral Theory* (Totowa, N.J.: Rowman and Littlefield, 1987).
4. Some important examples of these critiques include Held, *Feminist Morality*; Susan Moller Okin, *Justice, Gender and the Family* (New York: Basic Books, 1989); Nancy Chodorow *The Reproduction of Mothering* (Berkeley: University of California Press, 1978).
5. See, in particular, Okin, *Justice, Gender and the Family*, and Held, *Feminist Morality*.

6. Several of the essays in Treblicot, ed., *Mothering*, discuss these issues. See, especially, Virgina Held, "The Obligations of Mothers and Fathers," pp. 7–20; and Diane Ehrensat "When Women and Men Mother" pp. 41–61.

7. This point is made quite forcefully in Zillah Eisenstein, "The Sexual Politics of the New Right: Understanding the 'Crisis of Liberalism' for the 1980s," [1982] rpt. in Nancy Tuana and Rosemary Tong, eds., *Feminism and Philosophy: Essential Readings in Theory, Reinterpretation and Application* (Boulder: Westview Press, 1995), pp.10–26.

8. See, for instance, Heidi Hartmann, "The Family as the Locus of Gender, Class, and Political Struggle: The Example of Housework," in Tuana and Tong, eds., *Feminism and Philosophy*, pp. 104–128; and Nancy C. M. Harstock, "The Feminist Standpoint: Developing the Ground for a Specifically Feminist Historical Materialism," pp. 69–90 in Tuana and Tong, eds., *Feminism and Philosophy*.

9. A useful survey of these issues appears in Maggie Humm, ed., *Modern Feminisms: Political, Literary, and Cultural* (New York: Columbia University Press, 1992).

10. Christina Hoff Sommers, *Who Stole Feminism? How Women Have Betrayed Women* (New York: Simon and Schuster, 1994), p. 51; cf. pp. 16–18.

11. Sommers, *Who Stole Feminism?*

12. Shulamith Firestone, *The Dialectic of Sex: The Case For Feminist Revolution* (New York: Quill Books, 1970).

13. Friedan, *The Feminine Mystique*, pp. 395–399.

14. Friedan, *The Second Stage*, p. 203.

15. Friedan, *The Second Stage*, p. 204.

16. Friedan, *The Feminine Mystique*, p. 342.

17. Friedan, *The Feminine Mystique*, p. 338.

18. Anne Snitow, "Feminism and Motherhood: An American Reading," *Feminist Review* 40 (Spring 1992), p. 36.

19. Firestone, *The Dialectic of Sex*, p. 188.

20. For the relevant passages from Firestone, see *The Dialectic of Sex*, pp. 190–194.

21. Several of the essays in Treblicot, ed., *Mothering*, attempt to build on Firestone's suspicions about motherhood. See especially Martha E. Gimenez, "Feminism, Pronatalism, and Motherhood," pp. 287–314; and Jeffner Allen, "The Annihilation of Women," pp. 315–330.

22. See, e.g., Gimenez, "Feminism, Pronatalism, and Motherhood," p. 288, on the absence of socially rewarded alternatives to motherhood.

23. Jean Elshtain, "Feminists Against the Family," *The Nation* (November 17, 1989).

24. Peter Kilborn, "In Appalachia, From Homemaker to Wage Earner," *New York Times*, July 7, 1991.

25. Kilborn, "In Appalachia, From Homemaker to Wage Earner."

26. Eisenstein, "The Sexual Politics of the New Right"; Friedan, *The Second Stage*, p. 204.

27. Friedan, *The Second Stage*, p. 204.

28. Jane Collier, Michelle Z. Rosaldo, and Sylvia Yanagisako, "Is There a Family? New Anthropological Views," in Thorne and Yalom, eds., *Rethinking the Family: Some Feminist Questions*, pp. 31–48.

29. Collier, Rosaldo, and Yanagisako, "Is There a Family?"
30. Okin, *Justice, Gender, and the Family*; Alice Abel Kemp, *Women's Work: Devalued and Degraded* (Englewood Cliffs, N.J.: Prentice Hall, 1994).
31. Friedan, "Twenty Years After," in rev. 1983 ed. *The Feminine Mystique.*
32. Daniel Bell, *The Cultural Contradictions of Capitalism* (New York: Basic Books, 1976), pp. 220–227. Bell does not, however, defend the view of the role of the public household defended here.
33. Friedan, "Twenty Years After," p. xiv.

7

Fluid Families:
The Role of Children
in Custody Arrangements

*Elise L.E. Robinson, Hilde Lindemann Nelson,
and James Lindemann Nelson*

Having lived in a postdivorce family for more than a decade, the three of us have had a practical reason to be intensely interested in the question of what is best for children when their parents no longer share the same household. In this essay we express and try to motivate our unease with how Americans think about and make postdivorce child custody arrangements—beginning with a certain discomfort at the use of the word *custody* in this context at all. After exploring three problems with the reigning conception of postdivorce arrangements, we offer an alternative vision of what families are about that can in turn help us understand what we should be seeking as we all—children and parents alike—sort out how to respond to this deep change in our affective lives.

In abbreviated form, the complaint we want to level at standard ways of thinking and acting about child custody is this: custody decisions mistakenly tend to try to reproduce an ideal of family life that has dominated the American imagination for about 150 years—the ideal that has been called the "sentimental family." The family as conceived on the sentimental model is a private, patriarchal "haven from a heartless world," whose structure supplies its members with intimacy and emotional fulfillment. It consists of a heterosexual couple and their helpless and incompetent children, around whose needs the family's activities revolve.[1] Divorce, on this view, shatters the family.

In postdivorce custody decision-making, the impulse to "put things back"—to rearrange life so that it returns as nearly as possible to the sentimental ideal—expresses itself most particularly in the following four norms. First, as "private spaces," family reconfigurations should be to the extent possible protected from social scrutiny and control. Second, the distribution of familial obligations should track gender roles, with women taking their responsibilities for continual engagement and nurturing of their children much more seriously, on average, than men do. Third, the power to name reality—particularly, to name what arrangement of people will constitute the children's family—properly belongs to the parents rather than the children. And fourth, "minor" children are to be regarded as incompetents who lack moral agency and therefore need to be "in custody."

As we see it, the aim to approximate the sentimental family in post-divorce arrangements is badly misguided, as it is based on mistaken views about both the perils and the promises presented by family reconfiguration. We seek to show that the goods derived from involvement in families do not depend on the existence of one particular family structure; indeed, the inability to acknowledge that other structures might serve as well has contributed not a little to the trauma associated with divorce. We are going to argue that family life after divorce may hold the promise of distinctive benefits for children, and we'll wind up by offering a vision of what post-divorce families might look like if they were no longer held captive by the sentimental picture.

To begin, then, let's look carefully at how custody decisions in the U.S. have in fact been made in the last ten years or so, and say a little about the valuative commitments that seem to be embodied in these decisions.

What Does (Typically) Happen to the Kids

Who "Gets" the Children

At the present time, the law in nearly every state insists that in deciding who should have sole physical or legal custody of their child, no preference should be given to either parent simply on the basis of gender: mothers and fathers are said to stand on a level platform before the law.

What actually happens, though, suggests that the parental platform is tilted at a rakish angle indeed. In a recent, large-scale California study conducted by Eleanor E. Maccoby and Robert H. Mnookin (hereafter referred to as "M & M"),[2] it was found that three months after divorce papers were filed (which was also typically six months after the parents separated), the large majority of both boys and girls—67.6 percent—lived with their mothers only, while 15 percent lived in both their mother's and their father's households, and 9.6 percent lived solely with their fathers. Infants and toddlers (whose need for care is pronounced and prolonged) almost always lived with their mothers. Three years after divorce, the pattern was remarkably similar: 66.3 percent lived with their mother only, 16.8 percent were in dual residence, and 11.7 percent lived with their father.

The preference for mother residence does not seem to rest on the fact of the mother's having more time available to take care of the children. In the M & M study, four-fifths of the mothers with primary residence worked outside the home, and most worked full time. Indeed, mothers who were working over forty hours a week were no less likely to have the children living with them than were mothers who had a lighter work schedule.

When they explained why their custody arrangements so often assigned mothers the brunt of the child care, parents did not explicitly endorse traditional gendered lines of responsibility for children. The most common reasons offered had to do with logistics: how much driving was involved in taking children to school, who had time to chauffeur children to after-school activities, who could be home when school let out. M & M point out that in families where *no* divorce has occurred, working wives are:

> much more likely than their husbands to have chosen jobs in which the work demands are compatible with child-rearing. This need not mean that they work part time—it can mean that they work closer to home or school, or that they take jobs in which they do not need to travel or work overtime on short notice. In so doing, they have accepted jobs which are often at a lower level than the jobs they would be qualified for and could get if they did not have children. Thus most mothers, before the separation, have already made the adjustments in their work schedules that enable them to work while carrying the major responsibility for child-rearing. Fathers, by and large, have not done so. (p. 96)

How Are Arrangements Achieved?

Joint legal—as opposed to physical—custody appears to be assuming the status of most favored on-paper arrangement. In the 1979 California divorce decrees, only 25 percent of the judgments provided for any form of joint custody. In 1981, the year in which California became the first state to adopt joint custody legislation, 37 percent of the final decrees provided for some form of joint custody. By way of comparison, in the M & M sample, where the divorces became final between 1985 and 1989, 79 percent of the decrees provided for joint legal custody, although joint physical custody was awarded in only 15 percent of cases.

Before divorce, fathers in most families in the study had assumed primary responsibility for the financial support of the children. After divorce, custodial mothers became the primary source of support, even though on average they earned only half as much as the fathers. Child support usually represented only a small fraction of the custodial mother's total postdivorce household income.

When conflict over custody escalates to levels that require judicial intervention—which according to the M & M study occurs in only 20 percent of cases—judges tend to play the role of Solomon to the hilt, cleaving not exactly the children, but their homes, by awarding joint physical custody to the contending parents. Many critics of joint physical custody, in fact, have expressed concern that this strategy is too often being used to resolve custody conflicts, and M & M's study provides some support for this worry. Where divorce was uncontested, 70 percent of cases resulted in mother physical custody and fewer than 15 percent in joint physical custody. Where judges had to decide, 40 percent of cases resulted in joint physical custody, as compared to 44 percent in mother custody. While the judicial intervention may seem to promote gender equity, we want to point out that it also upholds the idea that families are private places: by falling back on a procedural fifty-fifty split, the judge avoids the need to inquire too particularly into the parents' personal affairs.

And Three Years Later?

In examining where kids end up—and how long they stay put—M & M checked in on their sample at three temporally distinct points—the first at three months, the second at two years, and the third at three years after the divorce papers were filed. By Time 3, some parents were able to create and sustain cooperative coparenting. Others were still in conflict. The most common pattern of coparenting, however, was parental disengagement. Most parents did not try to establish the same rules for the children at both households, or even consult with each other about the children. "It appears," M & M observe, "that parents can manage to share the residential time of their children even though they are not talking to each other or trying to coordinate the child-rearing environments of the two households" (p. 292). What went on between parent and child in one home was generally not considered to be the business of the outside parent unless there was flagrant abuse.

At Time 3, nearly two-thirds of the children who were living with their mothers were still seeing their fathers during regular portions of the school year. An even larger proportion of children who were living with their fathers were visiting their mothers. Although children under twelve looked forward to these visits, for older children they seemed to be regarded as a necessary part of their lives but not something they would actively choose to do.

Custody and What We Value

What are we to make of all this? The little that philosophers have had to say about divorce in marriages in which there are children suggests that divorce is a very bad thing indeed. Bertrand Russell, a man well experienced in these matters, regarded "the family as a reason for stable marriage."[3] Jeffrey Blustein, in his pioneering *Parents and Children: The Ethics of the Family*, wrote that divorce and remarriage undermine the stability in children's relations with their parents and leave children vulnerable to "jealousies and conflicts of loyalty not found in traditional families." Children of divorce, Blustein claimed, are "no longer part of a functioning family unit."[4]

The M & M data, however, suggest that maybe the outlook is not quite so dire. From the data we may infer that parents generally get what they want, that the kids adjust, that kids' contact with the noncustodial parent often continues. The ills of custody, one might well be excused for thinking, are really a matter of fine-tuning the details, not tampering with the basic structure or its goals.

However, as we suggested at the outset, the three of us are not so willing to accommodate what is generally taken to be the basic aims and structures of custody. Divorce and subsequent custody arrangements, as we see them, systematically tend to favor the powerful over the less powerful, and they also tend to close off important avenues of access to the goods of family life.

As the M & M data suggest, the values expressed by our customary custody arrangements are these:

1. *the privacy of the family* is assured by a no-fault, "split the difference" perspective toward divorce that takes what has actually gone on within the family to be no business of the court, and by parental disengagement that seals the child's two households off from each other;
2. *the gendered division of responsibility* and labor within families is upheld, and even reinforced;
3. *the perspective of parents* on what constitutes a family is determinative;
4. *the fragility of children* is protected by keeping them away from the process of reconfiguring their family.

Taken together, these values of privacy, gendered division of labor, the privileged parental perspective, and the view of children as helpless objects to be "kept" in "custody" bear a suspicious resemblance to the sentimental model of the family with which we began. But this is a model that is not necessary, fair, nor good for people who have experienced divorce. It is not necessary, because the goods that familial intimacy aims at do not require a family that is structured on the sentimental model. It is not fair, because not only does the sentimental model require women to do vastly disproportionate amounts of caregiving and so prevents them from equal access to rewarding jobs, money, and the other goods of society, but it also fails to take children seriously as moral agents. And it is not good, because in attempting to recreate itself, the sentimental model forecloses the possibility of allowing the postdivorce family to be a source of special benefits for children—it keeps children from experiencing the sense that their family goes on despite structural disruptions, it denies them a sense of their own power, it interferes with their ability to enjoy the advantages of living in two different worlds, and it prevents them from gaining useful ways of thinking about the families they will form in their adult lives. Let's examine these claims one at a time.

Our first claim is that *the goods at which families aim do not require the structure of the sentimental family*. A good part of the stigma still attached to divorce involving children, we hazard, is a result of illicitly associating the *benefits* of family life with the family *structure* that fits our normative ideal. In rehearsing the liabilities of the sentimental model we don't mean to imply that it has no strengths; there is much to be said for having father and mother in one household, centered together on the children, enjoying a respite from the demands of business and civic life and enjoying as well the order and security that comes from preestablished familial roles. We would simply like to suggest that this is not the only structure through which the benefits of family life may be delivered.

In their book, *Child Custody*, James C. Black and Donald J. Cantor observe that a healthy family is one in which a child's emotional needs are cared for, where their personality and sexuality are nurtured, and where they learn to control their impulses and develop a moral worldview.[5] In *Maternal Thinking*, Sara Ruddick provides a not dissimilar conception: mothering work (which is not limited to one gender) involves keeping children physically safe, helping them grow, and socializing them (by teaching them impulse control, among other things); hence to be a mother is "to be committed to meeting these demands by works of preservative love, nurturance, and training."[6]

We suggest that these benefits can usefully be seen as contributing to *identity formation*. We might note that identity formation is an ongoing process: our identities are continuously shifting and changing as we are affected by various events and people. So although theorists tend to focus on the impact parents have on their children's identity formation, there is as much impact in the other direction, as any parent knows. Intersibling relationships and relationships among adults in the family also contribute to the process of forming its members' identities. It is important to recognize that families often contain a multitude of interdependent relationships, and the welfare of a family depends on the constant flow of benefits among the different family members.[7]

A particular aspect of identity formation deserves explicit consideration for reasons that will appear shortly. We'll call it *agency formation*, by which we mean acquiring a sense of oneself as a person with the power to act, to shape reality. Where much of what we associate with identity formation might be seen as inward looking (Who am I? What is most important to me? What characterizes me as a distinct individual?), the notion of agency suggests an outward orientation (What is my impact on the world around me? How do my actions affect me and others? How am I empowered to make changes in my relationship to my environs?).

Agency formation, like identity formation in general, crucially depends upon practices that arise within interfamilial relationships. A child learns to trust others by participating in relationships with trustworthy intimates, to refrain from cruelty because others install norms of conduct in her through the family's systems of rewards and punishments, to make music because those with whom she is in relationship all sing or play an instrument. But note that in learning to exercise her agency, the child (or adult) need not inhabit the familial structure we have been calling sentimental. Children in loving single-parent families, gay or lesbian families, or families made up of three generations also develop a sense of their own agency in the world. It is the child's relationships with intimate others, not residence in a sentimental household, that conveys this and the other benefits of family life.

Our second claim is that *custody arrangements exploit women and fail to take children's perspectives seriously.* Although mothers' overwhelming preference to have physical custody of their children is well served by the current system, it is certainly open to question whether that preference well serves mothers, other women, and children. At the very least, it contributes to a lowered standard of living for children in postdivorce households (even given financial support from fathers), and at most it reinforces as "natural" something that we should be vigorously questioning: that giving birth to children should be assimilated to special responsibility for nurturing them.[8] As M & M point out, many women, even in making career decisions, are influenced by considerations of staying available to their children, in ways that men are not. Standard assumptions about gender and child-rearing responsibility are, if anything, intensified by our customary practices after divorce, with a corresponding diminution of women's agency.

These points about the impact of postdivorce practices on women's agency have been made before. What has been less frequently examined, perhaps, is the impact of postdivorce practices on the agency of children. To explain what we mean, let's think for a moment about the act of reconceptualizing the family after divorce—an act that can be understood as naming the postdivorce reality. Most accounts suggest that either two new families are formed, with the children being a part of one or both, or that one new, single-parent family is formed, made up of the children, the residential parent, and (perhaps) any new partner the residential parent may come to have, but not including the outside parent. But whichever account is adopted, it should be clear that it privileges the parents' view of the matter.

From the child's point of view, however, things can look very different. As *she* sees it, both parents (and, for that matter, both sets of grandparents and other extended family members) may still be members of her family. If one were to honor the child's own conceptualization of her relationships, one would say she is not so much a part of two families, but of one.

We can illustrate this point from our own experience. Elise's mother is married to Jim. Her father is married to Carol. Jim and Hilde are not inclined to think of Tim and Carol as members of their family in any sense, and Tim and Carol are similarly disinclined. But in Elise's living room there is a hinged picture frame, holding a picture of Jim and Hilde on one side and a picture of Tim and Carol on the other. Whatever view Jim and Hilde or Tim and Carol may take of the matter, all four of her parents are, from Elise's perspective, a part of her immediate family. And, we may point out, she owns the picture frame.

Most kids, however, don't own their own frame. When the parental perspective is taken to be the only one that counts, children have very little power to construct their own meaning of the changes that take place in their families after divorce. But denying children's agency in this crucial respect cuts off possibilities for how their lives will now be lived. How the *parents* understand the postdivorce reconfiguration, and how they act on what they understand, will largely determine how all the affected parties go on.

Here we see another way in which the model of the sentimental family makes itself felt, as it emphasizes children's fragility and passivity and denies that children are competent moral agents. Many philosophers have concurred, explaining that the primary constitutive condition of moral free agency is that the agent has the ability to control or regulate her conduct, that children lack this ability, and that children are therefore not free agents. Something like this contention prompts Harry Frankfurt, for instance, to classify young children as "wantons" and Peter Strawson to claim that we adopt an objective attitude toward children rather than the attitude of interpersonal participation and involvement we extend to responsible adults.[9]

As Paul Benson has pointed out, however, children do not lack the regulative control which on this view is requisite for freedom. A five-year-old boy who has been warned not to tease his baby sister is not necessarily driven by desires he cannot help acting out; he may be fully able to stop teasing if he wants to.

It is not absence of control that keeps the five-year-old's agency from being less than fully free, Benson argues[10]; it is rather that in an ordinary moral context his actions cannot adequately express who he is as a person. His behavior lacks "normative self-disclosure" (p. 53). That is, others who observe him cannot infer from his nastiness to his sister that he is a nasty person. He may be perfectly aware that teasing his sister makes her unhappy. He may know full well that his mother doesn't want him to do it. He may even have developed a belief of his own that teasing his sister is wrong. But what he cannot yet do is appreciate how other members of the wider moral community evaluate the kind of action in which he is engaged, nor does he have much of a basis for judging the worth and correctness of the standards they use for this evaluation.

Johnny's inability to understand how ordinary people will react to his teasing affects how well his acts reveal who he is, and, therefore, affects his freedom. One can see this quite clearly with adults. To the extent that a grown person is unaware of, or finds it difficult to appreciate, standards that operate in the normal moral context, the person will be perceived as morally underdeveloped and irresponsible, and treated accordingly. Free agency, according to Benson, thus requires *normative competence*—"an array of abilities to be aware of applicable normative standards, to appreciate those standards, and to bring them competently to bear in one's evaluations of open courses of action" (p. 54). Our actions are free when they reveal who we are, both to ourselves and to others, in the normal moral context in which these actions are judged.

Benson's analysis yields two observations about children's moral agency, both of which will be useful as we think about children's role in reconfiguring the postdivorce family. First, because normative competence can be incomplete and admit of degrees, there is reason to suppose that even very small children can exercise limited amounts of moral agency.

Second, because we can distinguish (although Benson does not) between ordinary moral contexts and special contexts, we have a reason to believe that a child's agency is freer inside his family than elsewhere. Here we return to the idea that the child's relationships with his parents, grandparents, siblings, and other intimates *make him who he is*. Within these relationships of identity formation his self becomes visible even when his actions don't yet reveal who he is to strangers. The familial relationships that constitute him create a special moral context, different from the one in which adults ordinarily operate. In this special context his exercise of agency can be judged more lovingly: those who form him can, better than other morally competent people, interpret what his actions say about who he is. They can express his self for him.

Here is a story that illustrates what we mean. When a little girl named Louisa was in first grade, her widowed father got a call from the school principal. Louisa had deliberately knocked the playground supervisor down at recess and was refusing to apologize or even explain why she had done it. The principal was sorry, but under the circumstances Louisa would have to be suspended from school. On the drive home, Louisa only glowered when her father said, "I know you had a good reason." But once they entered the kitchen and sat down with Louisa's four-year-old sister over a companionable cookie or two, the tale gradually emerged. While Louisa and her classmates were at recess, Louisa's friend Harry, who has Down's Syndrome, suddenly needed to go to the bathroom. He asked the supervisor for permission, but understanding his speech required patience and the supervisor was fresh out. She demanded that he stop pestering her and finally marched him to the sidelines, telling him to stand there until recess was over. It was when he wet his pants that Louisa ran halfway across the yard and butted the teacher as hard as she could. The next morning, Louisa, her sister, her father, even an aunt were all in the principal's office.

When the family had finished explaining and expostulating, it was the principal who apologized.[11]

As this story reveals, those who inhabit the normal moral context may not always recognize a child's moral agency when they see it in action. Correctly understanding what Louisa was doing in butting the teacher required a loving eye and the enriched moral context of the child's intimate relationships. Louisa had not yet developed the competence that would allow her to justify her deed or articulate the wrong done to her friend, but her family could interpret and express on her behalf what her behavior said about who Louisa was. This ability of families to provide a special moral context for their children takes on a crucial importance when arangements are being made regarding how and where children will live after a divorce.

Our third claim is that *standard custody arrangements foreclose the possibility of seeing the postdivorce family as a source of special benefits for children*. Standard arrangements, predicated as they are on the belief that the sentimental family structure is best equipped to provide its members with the benefits of family life, are bound to come up wanting, as, on their own terms, they are an inferior deviation from the sentimental model. They are always second best. And because the sentimental model has such a firm hold on the collective social imagination, children living in custody learn to think of their "second-best" postdivorce families as broken, dysfunctional, inadequate.

That in itself is bad. But what is worse, we suggest, is that when people believe that the best structure for conveying the goods of family life will never again be theirs, they cannot easily create better alternatives for themselves. As we have argued, the sentimental ideal does not in any case deserve the devotion we as a society have bestowed on it, and when it becomes an impediment to careful thinking about living well after divorce, the harm is doubled. If we can tear our eyes away from the sentimental picture, we will see that postdivorce families actually have goods to offer children that the sentimental family offers less well—among them, the sense that the child's important relationships will continue no matter what the family looks like, affirmation of the child's sense of herself as an agent, the advantages of living in two worlds, and useful strategies for thinking about the families they will form when they themselves become adults.

An Alternative Vision: "Fluid Families, Committed Parents"

The advantages to a model of fluid families and committed parents are many, but we will concentrate on four, describing them from the child's perspective. First, if the child's sense of who counts as her family is taken seriously, she need not fear that she has lost the goods of family life, never to regain them. Even a young child can understand that although the family is going through an important change, it is not ending; that her relationships to both parents will endure even though the structure that once housed them did not, and that her family has now expanded to flow into two households instead of one. She can understand that "family" and "household" are not the same.

Second, by giving children a voice in structuring their new living arrangements, family members affirm children's moral agency at a time when children are in special need of such affirmation. All families contain a multiplicity of moral authorities, but at the time of divorce this multiplicity is particularly visible, and can be quite frightening to a child who once thought her parents presented a united moral front. If family members take the child's own agency seriously, and thereby encourage the child to trust her own best judgments about what is right and good, she will find parental disagreements less threatening to her own sense of self.

Third, by giving the child two households to be connected to, the child gets the good of living in two different worlds. When one world becomes tiresome or stale, the other world holds out, perhaps, the freshness of a different style of personal interaction, a different ambience, an alternative worldview, a change of scene. It can be comforting, when there is a quarrel or dispute in one of the child's worlds, to retreat at least mentally to the other world, where this particular altercation does not exist. And participation in two worlds can expand a child's mental horizons by teaching her that differences can be taken in one's stride—that they are interesting and ordinary, and needn't be feared as deviant.

Fourth, by endorsing the idea that families come in many shapes and flow across households, family members can teach children to accept fluidity in their own future family lives. The divorce rate nationally now hovers at just under 50 percent, and there is no reason to suppose that it will decrease when it has been rising steadily since the Civil War. Postdivorce families confer a lasting benefit on children by preparing them for the possibility that their own marriages or other committed relationships may not endure forever, and modeling for them the loving, creative, and moral responses that are available should this possibility come to pass. Moreover, as the family structure in postdivorce families is rendered particularly visible by the divorce that preceded it, it cannot be taken for granted, and so offers children the lesson that there is nothing particularly inevitable or natural about their intimate relationsips: they then have the opportunity of learning to *attend* to them, to cultivate them. That too is a benefit. And finally, if children become accustomed to the idea that how we structure our families is not merely a matter of private preference but also a matter for public discussion and concern, there is a chance that the next generation of Americans will arrive at a better understanding than we as a society currently share of the many satisfying possibilities there can be for good family life.

Divorce is painful, and as we three know very well, when children are involved it can take years for the wounds to heal. We do, however, believe that things can go better or worse as the family shifts its shape, and that the process of reconfiguring interfamilial relationships can illuminate important and interesting features of families that the sentimental ideal ignores or conceals. The thoughts we offer here are intended primarily to unseat certain beliefs about families and to challenge others, leaving the real work of theorizing divorce for another time. However, we would also like to suggest that the time for such work to begin is now, and that many of us have a stake in how well it is done.

Acknowledgments

We owe thanks to Linda Nicholson for her helpful criticisms and encouragement. This paper was presented at the Eastern Division meetings of the American Philosophical Association, New York, 1995.

Notes

1. See, among other accounts, Steven Mintz and Susan Kellogg, *Domestic Revolutions: A Social History of American Family Life* (New York: Free Press, 1988).

2. Eleanor E. Maccoby and Robert H. Mnookin, *Dividing the Child: Social and Legal Dilemmas of Custody* (Cambridge: Harvard University Press, 1992).

3. Bertrand Russell, *Marriage and Morals* (New York: Bantam, 1968), ch. 13.

4. Jeffrey Blustein, *Parents and Children: The Ethics of the Family* (New York: Oxford University Press, 1982), pp. 238, 245.

5. James C. Black and Donald J. Cantor, *Child Custody* (New York: Columbia University Press, 1989), p. 82.

6. Sara Ruddick, *Maternal Thinking: Toward a Politics of Peace* (1989; Boston: Beacon Press, 1995), p. 17.

7. The locus classicus of the family systems approach to identity formation is Salvador Minuchin, *Families and Family Therapy* (Cambridge: Harvard University Press, 1974).

8. See James Lindemann Nelson and Hilde Lindemann Nelson, "Other 'Isms' Aren't Enough: Feminism, Social Policy, and Long-Acting Contraception," in *The Ethics of Long-Term Contraception*, ed. Ellen Moskowitz and Bruce Jennings (Washington, D.C.: Georgetown University Press, forthcoming), excerpted as "Feminism, Social Policy, and Long-Acting Contraception," special supplement, *Hastings Center Report* 25, No. 1 (1995), pp. S30–S32.

9. Harry Frankfurt, "Freedom of the Will and the Concept of a Person," *Journal of Philosophy* 68 (1971), pp. 5–20; Peter Strawson, "Freedom and Resentment," in *Free Will*, ed. Gary Watson (New York: Oxford University Press, 1982).

10. Paul Benson, "Feminist Second Thoughts about Free Agency," *Hypatia* 5, No. 3 (Fall 1990), 47–64.

11. This story is adapted from E. Annie Proulx, *The Shipping News* (New York: Macmillan, 1994).

Part III

Intimate Knowings

8
Privacy, Self-Knowledge, and Pluralistic Communes: An Invitation to the Epistemology of the Family

John Hardwig

What follows is a lightly edited version of an essay I wrote more than twenty years ago, in the heyday of the communal living movement. Despite its antiquity, I still like it—it still has the ring of truth to my ear. In the meantime, however, feminist epistemology has developed and has given us much better tools than any I had available twenty years ago for understanding why it is true.

—Austin, Texas, August 1974

Advocates of communal living often urge that life in a commune provides the framework for a deeper knowledge of other people. I believe this is clearly true, and because it is true, communal living is also instrumental in promoting self-knowledge. The dialogue that is part of the life of a commune enables one to incorporate the insights of the other members into his understanding of himself and his world.

My experience with living in an urban, middle-class, pluralistic commune has taught me that: (1) life in a pluralistic commune is more conducive to dialogue than the available alternatives (living by oneself, living with a roommate, a couple, the nuclear family, and the monistic commune), and (2) pluralistic communes enable dialogue to be more penetrating with respect to issues concerning one's personal life than it could be under conditions found in other lifestyles. In this paper, I have not developed these points in the usual fashion by constructing an abstract analysis to support them. The autobiographical, anecdotal style aims to be evocative and suggestive; it is intended as an indication, not a demonstration.

The loss of privacy involved in communal living is obvious, and often mentioned. However, I believe that communes are so productive of self-knowledge precisely because of this loss of privacy. To understand why this is so, we must first understand something about what kind of privacy is lost and why.

The loss of privacy is not a loss of solitude brought about by the constant presence of others. (In our commune, you can go into your room and shut the door; no one will disturb you, object, feel affronted, or feel personally excluded.) Rather, the loss of privacy is due simply to the fact that you are known by people who care for you. If you retreat into solitude for long periods of time, people who care about you will notice this and wonder about it. If you are not on good terms with your spouse, lover, or friend, good friends cannot fail to be aware of this fact. If your children are aggravating you or if you are too preoccupied for days or weeks to really be with them, people who like both you and your children will be concerned. If elements of your lifestyle or your ways of relating to others are harming yourself or others, this will be observed and noted. Other members of the commune may ask what's bothering you or whether you want to talk about it. Privacy is lost, then, mainly because so much of what you are and do is a matter of public knowledge and concern within the commune. If there is a loss of autonomy due to a feeling that you owe others an explanation, it is largely a result of their awareness and concern.

The impetus toward self-examination, dialogue, and shared deliberation grows out of this knowledge and concern. The superior quality of dialogue in a commune also results from the fact that you are known. If someone is to make you aware of aspects of your self or your practice that you are not aware of, they must be allowed to see what you do, not just listen to what you say. If someone is to challenge assumptions that are so long-standing and seem so unquestionable that you never bother to mention them (not even to yourself), they must somehow have access to your "private life." "Don't you see that you're treating Bill like an *adult*? A five-year-old couldn't possibly understand what you're expecting him to understand." No, I hadn't noticed that. "You and Marilyn just don't fight with each other because you're both so quick to dismiss your feelings—even strong feelings—as irrational and hence to relegate them to the realm of your own problems." No, I'd assumed that other explanations better accounted for our relative lack of fights. "You are an honesty freak! You refuse to lie out of loyalty to your wife or friends, or to protect the feelings of others and their needs for privacy or secrecy." It had been an awfully long time since I'd seriously considered any other way of operating.

I found that when I kept my personal life private, it was relatively easy to defend myself against these charges, even if someone had been perceptive, impolite, and bold enough to make them. In a commune, too much is known to escape so easily.

The fact that others need to have the information that enables them to

pursue me beyond my initial (often defensive) reply is crucial to the epistemology of self-knowledge and self-evaluation. The first fruits of self-
knowledge are often bitter and one naturally resists upsetting and
potentially disruptive insights into oneself. Consequently, each of us has
good reason to be suspicious of his own assessments of himself.

In other words, self-judgment is necessarily interested judgment, for no
one can be indifferent to evaluations of himself and his practice. An interested judgment is not inevitably erroneous, mistaken, or biased. But an interested judgment is always epistemically suspect, not only because a
person who is the judge in his own case may knowingly tip the scales of
justice, but also because he may unknowingly do so. For these reasons and
because I have learned so much about the blindnesses, biases, and epistemic weaknesses of my own internal self-examination, I have become
skeptical of any methodology for deliberation that relies solely or ultimately on one's own judgment.

To some extent, of course, dialogue with one's partner in the context of
living as a couple can strengthen and sharpen self-examination in ways
similar to the dialogue of a commune. However, my own experience is that
my wife's ability to help me in these ways is limited in comparison to that
of the commune.

There are two other sources of limitations. First, it is relatively easy to
dismiss one person's observations about you, especially if accepting his
comments would force changes in established and comfortable patterns of
action and interaction. And most especially if you think he is disqualified
as a judge because he has an interest in the change that would be entailed.
(As a member of another commune so eloquently put it: "If one chick tells
you you're doing something, you think she's crazy. But if three chicks tell
you you're doing it, you've got to start listening.")

Second, stable relationships tend, I believe, to be stable because they
begin with or quickly evolve an ideological as well as a psychological compatibility. A couple will share a large number of common assumptions
about themselves, each other, and their relationship. Consequently, a stable
couple will tend to share a way of seeing . . . and also a way of not seeing.

The point in all this is not, of course, that others should be included in
one's self-examination and self-evaluation because they are ideal observers
or speak with the voice of Pure Reason. The point is that there is no Pure
Reason or ideal observer to which anyone can appeal in deliberation. Others can, however, observe your statements and your action without this observation having been filtered through your own conception of who you
are and what you are doing. To the extent that others do not share your
perspective, they can observe you in a way that is in principle impossible
for you to observe yourself. Because it is impossible for anyone to have an
external perspective on himself and an internal perspective on someone
else, the person who is familiar with you is in a position to perform a service for you that no one could possibly perform for himself.

Now, I do not wish to stretch the point about the role of communes in dialogue and self-knowledge further than is warranted. I believe that dialogue is essential to self-knowledge, not that communes are necessary for dialogue or for self-knowledge.[1] If a person has friends of widely divergent viewpoints, if he can learn to be open and honest enough with them and if he also spends enough time with them so they can become thoroughly familiar with his practice and not just his own account of his practice, perhaps conversation with friends could serve the same function that living in a commune has served for me.

My claim, then, is twofold: (1) In a commune, one must try to avoid dialogue and be willing to pay a price for doing so in order to prevent it. To the extent that one lives by oneself or with those who share one's views, one must continually pursue dialogue for it to occur. (2) If others are to be optimally qualified to serve as touchstones for deliberation and self-examination, they must have access to information about one's life. For an informed other is more capable of provoking and pursuing dialogue that penetrates, that is telling and to the point. Communes create informed others.

Perhaps the experience of others would differ significantly from my own on all these points. Perhaps my view that dialogue is essential to self-knowledge is a classic case of cosmologizing my embarrassments. Others might find that, being more reflective and self-conscious than I, they would have little or nothing to learn about themselves from living with others. Perhaps their relationships do not rest on hidden, though questionable agreements or on the results of domestic battles so definitively won so long ago that neither party ever thinks about them any more. Perhaps they are already aware of the assumptions on which their theory and practice of child-raising rest and of the points of divergence between the two. Maybe others are already aware of their priorities as evidenced by the way they spend their time and could explain satisfactorily (not just satisfactorily to themselves) why they have ordered their priorities in this way.

And yet, there is no way anyone could know that he has already anticipated all that he might have learned from others by allowing them to become familiar with his daily life, from observing their practices at close range, and from a confrontation by both of the evaluations of each. For there is no way to ascertain that one has nothing to learn from others except by sustained dialogue with them. For this reason, if for no other, any first-person, one-person method of self-examination and self-evaluation is epistemically suspect.

There is, then, a generally unnoticed tension between privacy and self-knowledge: a thoroughgoing commitment to self-knowledge requires a sacrifice of privacy, while preservation of privacy diminishes self-knowledge. For many people, an increase in self-knowledge would not suffice to justify the sacrifices of privacy (and perhaps also of autonomy) that are inherent in communal living.

However, I have come to see that the desire for privacy often hides and "justifies" a much less noble desire for a kind of fundamental irresponsibility. If the skeletons remain closeted and the dirty linen is never publicly aired, I can conduct my personal life free from the scrutiny of others. If others do not know what I am doing in my "private life," they will be unable to question, challenge, or accuse me. And if everyone is thereby disqualified from judgment due to my preservation of my privacy, I can conduct the reexamination of my values and conduct in front of a very sympathetic and friendly, all too understanding and forgiving, though somewhat ignorant judge—myself.

Postscript

The Morning After —
Some Sober Philosophical Reflections on an Impassioned Statement

In one sense, the decades since I wrote this essay have reduced it to something of mere academic interest: so far as I can tell, there is no longer widespread interest in communal living. I myself no longer live in a commune—I no longer know enough people who are interested in communal living. I have dusted off this early essay, then, partly as a requiem to the commune. I think it was/is a worthy institution that is likely never to get the serious reflection due it. But I have more than antiquarian interests. I believe there are implications here both for epistemology and for philosophical reflection on the family.

"The epistemology of the family" may seem more than a little odd, both from the side of epistemology and from that of the family. In terms of the latter, it may seem perverse to train an epistemological spotlight on the family. The family did not evolve as an institution for promoting self-knowledge . . . or any other kind of knowledge. It developed as a response to concerns about progeny, property, security, companionship, and perhaps even love. These may well be more important values than self-knowledge, values not to be sacrificed for mere self-knowledge. Similarly, self-knowledge is usually not the primary motivation for communal living.

From the side of epistemology, philosophers are only beginning to realize that institutions have anything at all to do with knowing. In traditional epistemology, knowers have been portrayed as fundamentally *a*institutional: independent, totally self-reliant, and self-sufficient. Indeed, this independence from the judgment and opinions of others has often been taken as one of the hallmarks of knowers, as opposed to mere believers. Knowers become knowers by transcending all institutions.[2] But even those philosophers who clearly recognize the importance of institutions for knowing—for instance, feminist epistemologists, social epistemologists—have been largely silent about families in epistemology.

Yet the family is important for epistemology. Let me briefly suggest three ways in which this is so.

1. Feminist epistemology has been one of the contemporary movements that have combined to teach us that knowers are always positioned or situated. The "God trick" is out; there is no disembodied view from nowhere. The question of positioning and of the relationships among knowers (and with the known) thus becomes critical for any "strong objectivity." But we must recognize that situated knowers are more than gendered, raced, and classed—they are also familied. Most were raised in some sort of family and even those who were not have experience that is decisively shaped by the *absence* of family. Moreover, unless knowers live entirely in their work, they still have relationships, friends, lovers, partners, marriages, and many live in families.

2. Epistemology is not, of course, only a theory about science. It is also an account of self-knowledge, including self-examination, self-evaluation, and self-transformation. Consequently, the theory of positioned rationality must be brought to bear on how we understand self-knowledge. No one can be completely transparent to herself, so we will need an account of how others can be best positioned to contribute to someone's self-knowledge. Nuclear families are one way of positioning others, communes another.

3. Self-knowledge (or lack thereof) influences knowledge of other things. As a result, one cannot successfully specialize in knowing particle physics, cancers, the economics of developing nations, or moral theory and leave self-knowledge aside, or put it off until later in life. Ultimately, each of us has only one instrument of observation and reflection—our self. The more someone knows about the strengths and weaknesses, capabilities and distortions of her own epistemic instrument, the better can she use it to arrive at reliable conclusions. For this reason, institutions that promote self-knowledge enhance the reliability of a society's knowers; institutions that impede self-knowledge leave us all epistemically more vulnerable.

Each of these observations requires much more detailed consideration. In fact, I believe that each points to a research program within epistemology. But the present volume is dedicated to reflection on the family, so we must return to the primary theme of this paper—epistemological evaluation of the family.

Patricia Hill Collins's powerful notion of an "outsider within" can be adapted to thinking about the epistemology of families.[3] The creation of intimacy involves the creation of a private, yet shared space by gradually allowing someone inside. But preservation of the privacy of an intimate relationship or a nuclear family keeps all others *outside*—ignorant, uninformed, marginalized, unable to knowledgeably or effectively comment.

Because we are all positioned and no one is completely transparent to herself, we all need touchstones with whom to work out epistemically sensitive and reliable portraits of ourselves. Since no one speaks with the voice of Pure Reason and a view from nowhere, there is no one ideal touchstone. The best we can do is to tie our reflections—not only about ourselves, but especially about ourselves—to potential insights gathered from those occupying a variety of positions.[4]

Thus our self-portraits should be constructed through interaction and discussion with many others, all inevitably imperfectly positioned. If I recognize that everyone—myself included—is imperfectly positioned to know me, I should not decide to rely on the observations of only one or two. I would almost always be better served if more than one other person were positioned to comment knowledgeably on me and my life, and if I were to work out my view of myself through a complex process of checking various reports against each other in order to try to figure out how important and accurate are the comments of each. This already argues against the preservation of privacy and points to an epistemic advantage of communes over couples and nuclear families.[5]

In terms of cognitive features, at least some others need to be intellectually distant—far enough outside so that they do not share all the forms of life or ways of seeing that are to be the subject of investigation. Otherwise, our self-examination will be too circumscribed by the very paradigms, assumptions, and commitments that are to be reexamined—by the ideological similarity I spoke of as characterizing stable relationships. But others also need to be close enough to have considerable information about our practice. They have to be far enough inside to be positioned to watch how we live, not just listen to what we say about how we live. (Listening to what we say could suffice only if we already had perfect self-knowledge and were also completely open.) If others are not close enough to have a rich basis of firsthand observation, they will usually not be well positioned to be able to recognize our distortions, self-deceptions, lies, and the discrepancies between our practice and our accounts of it.

There is also an inside and outside in terms of emotional closeness to—and one hopes also care for—the observed other. Traditional scientific methodology strives to create detached others, others who care about but not *for* the "object of investigation." The detached observer is an emotional outsider, if you will. The sheer possibility and also the strengths and weaknesses of the stance of an emotional outsider have been the subject of intense discussion within feminist epistemology, science studies, and the methodological reflections of cultural anthropologists.

Completely detached observation seems impossible, certainly for a subject matter everyone is emotionally involved with, such as relationships and families. Moreover, almost all of us strive to shield ourselves and our loved ones from the scrutiny of uncaring, detached observers.[6] But especially when we're talking about knowing other people, there may also be too much emotional closeness or involvement to see well—either too much positive emotional connectedness (love, caring, commitment) or too much negative emotional connection (anger, resentment, outrage, hostility, even fear).

The inside/outside of traditional epistemology and that of emotional involvement are intertwined in all sorts of interesting ways. But the present point is that our self-reflection and self-examination will tend to be epistemically better if they are conducted in dialogue with at least some others who are close but not too close, who have enough distance in both the cognitive and the emotional sense without being strangers or uninvolved observers.

In these terms, the epistemic problem of the nuclear family (and the couple) is twofold: (1) those who are "inside" enough in terms of information are too ideologically similar and also too emotionally close; (2) those emotionally detached enough and ideologically different enough are too unaware of important information. The nuclear family (and private relationships) tend to restrict observation and evaluation to those who are *very* close or *very* distant and removed. The nuclear family tends to force everyone to the epistemological extremes of these two polarities of cognitive inside/outside and emotional inside/outside.

But we have just seen that our self-reflection needs to be shared with those who occupy some sort of intermediate position—close, but not too close. By contrast, pluralistic communes strive to create and maintain precisely such intermediate positions. They create "outsiders within." If an outsider within plays an important epistemic role, she does so for a couple or a family, not just for an academic discipline or a university.

I will close now by putting some of the same points in the language of private and public. As a companion to Collins's notion of an "outsider within," I propose that of a "private public." As they have evolved in our culture, home and family are private spaces. Moreover, one common use of our increasing disposable income is to buy additional privacy, both privacy within the family (each family member often now has her own room) and privacy of the family unit, as neighbors are kept at greater and greater distance.

Of course, if you preserve your private space, others will not normally know what is going on in it. They know primarily what you choose to tell them and, often, not much more. This means that others will have to rely largely on your own interpretation of events in your family. (Surely, it is not only because I am male that I know so little about what goes on in other people's marriages and families!)

Communes strive to make the private public. They are created by inviting other people into the private space which couples and nuclear families normally consider exclusively their own. Pluralistic communes are attempts to create and sustain a special kind of space in which you can risk being known and evaluated due to the context of support and care that characterize this space—but not so much support and care that the knowledge and evaluation are myopic, prejudged, biased by ideological uniformity, and so on.

But the public which a commune creates is a *"private public."* It is not a public that any and everyone can inhabit—you must be trusted and approved to be invited in. You must also invest a lot of yourself to belong—in fact, you must agree to share a major portion of your life with these people in order to belong to this public. So a private public is created.[7] Accordingly, much that is common knowledge within the commune will not be shared with outsiders. Indeed, some of it *cannot* be shared with outsiders. (Those who were invited to our communal meals often remarked that they just couldn't follow a lot of the banter among us, just as a guest at a family reunion often can't understand or fully appreciate what is being said.)

Like marriages and families, pluralistic communes can fail, and they can fail epistemically. Although I believe communes normally have epistemic strengths that traditional nuclear families lack, communal living is no royal road to self-knowledge. There *is* no royal road to self-knowledge, no institution that can guarantee greater self-knowledge. Some of the ways communes can fail epistemically can be understood as the collapse of the private public. Serious personal conversation may end and living together may become mechanical and superficial. The commune then degenerates into a boarding house or a rooming house in which people live for reasons of cost, convenience, companionship, or comradery. (All perfectly valid reasons.)

Theoretically, the private public can collapse (or fail to materialize) through either a deficiency or an excess of closeness (cognitive and/or emotional). The Ogilvys theorize that communes have a "natural [epistemic] half-life," after which familiarity leads to diminishing returns from dialogue.[8] However, I suspect the private public in communes most often collapses due to excessive emotional distance. The mutual respect, acceptance, support, or trust requisite to sustain a private public evaporates, and people are returned to their private realms of solitude, relationships, or families, even if some form of group living continues.

Communal living is clearly neither a necessary nor a sufficient condition for self-knowledge. Still, to the extent that it is always epistemically important for others to be positioned to see how I live and respond to what I do, not just to listen to what I say, the epistemic strengths of living together remain. To the extent that we are all positioned or situated knowers, living with several people will have epistemic advantages over living with only one other adult.

Feminism has surely taught us that the personal is political. The feminist movement has tried and—on a general, impersonal level, at least—partly succeeded in casting light on the private sphere of couples and families. But we still need an epistemology of the family. Moreover, each of us also needs epistemic light cast on us individually, on our personal lifestyles and on our private lives. That's why we need a private public. Finally, if anyone is interested in circling back to where we began, that's why a pluralistic commune is epistemically better than a couple or a nuclear family.

Acknowledgments

I wish to thank Jim Bennett, Kathy Bohstedt, George Brenkert, Nanne Johnson, Hugh LaFollette, Hilde Nelson, John Nolt, and especially Mary English for helpful comments on earlier versions of this paper. Several of these friends lived in a commune with me. But it should come as no surprise to anyone that these friends do not all agree with everything I say about communes . . . or even about the commune some of us lived in.

Notes

1. For an argument that dialogue is necessary for the kind of self-knowledge ingredient in moral rationality, see another ancient paper of mine: John Hardwig, "The Achievement of Moral Rationality," *Philosophy & Rhetoric* 6 (1973), pp. 171–185.

2. My own contribution to the attack on this paradigm of the knower is found in two papers: John Hardwig, "Epistemic Dependence," *The Journal of Philosophy* 82 (July, 1985), pp. 335–349; John Hardwig, "The Role of Trust in Knowledge," *The Journal of Philosophy* 88 (December, 1991), pp. 693–708.

3. Patricia Hill Collins, "Learning from the Outsider Within: The Sociological Significance of Black Feminist Thought," *Social Problems* 33, No. 6 (1986), pp. S14–S32.

4. There is no ideal position which others *must* occupy to contribute to self-knowledge. This alone implies that fellow members of pluralistic communes are not the only ones positioned to contribute to self-knowledge. Indeed, it implies that there are valuable things to be learned about yourself from a variety of positions—from friends, from strangers, from family members, from therapists, from fellow employees, and so on. (To some extent, one can also vary one's own position—insights into oneself can also be gained from various jobs and other activities, from travel, from reading . . . and also from extended periods of solitude, especially unoccupied solitude.) But those who live in communes can also read, have a lover, talk to strangers, go rock climbing, participate in various groups. Indeed, people living in many communes also have marriages or other long-term relationships and families within the commune.

5. Is it also necessary to say that I would not argue that living in a pluralistic commune with closed, unobservant dullards would be epistemically superior to a nuclear family composed of bright, articulate, perceptive, self-conscious, and forthright people? Like many philosophical points, the idea that pluralistic communes are epistemically superior to the alternatives (living by oneself, in couples, the nuclear family) is true only standardly, normally, usually, or *ceteris paribus*. But this is not to minimize the importance of this point—in social philosophy, most of the critical and evaluative points we can make are true only standardly, normally, for the most part, or *ceteris paribus*.

6.   Our commune, located in a town with a large research university, became a magnet for sociology graduate students in need of thesis or dissertation topics. They were detached—they wanted to study us, but not to become involved or to help us in any way. We felt uncomfortable subjecting ourselves and our lives to constant, detached observation. Besides, it threatened to overwhelm us—it looked like we would be the subject of many sociological investigations. After some fumbling, we hit upon a way to deal with this problem. We told these potential observers that they could study us, but in return we would like to study them, too. For we were interested in them and had a number of questions about their lives—how their marriages or relationships worked, how tasks were divided, how they made decisions or who made them, who the leader in *their* relationships was, how he/she was selected, etc. Having been told of our conditions, the would-be observers left and never returned. Presumably, most of them decided to study people who are further outside the academy than they (and some of us) were.

7.   It is worth noting that dialogue within the private public of a commune is not an epistemic substitute for a genuine public or community discussion. There are too many different people and too many different viewpoints for any commune to encompass them all. Moreover, no one would choose to share her life with all the different kinds of people there are. Most of us need the familiarity, comfort, and support of a private public to discuss our personal lives in any depth. But it is also important to talk with people who are genuinely outside your circle of friends and the people you live with.

8.   Jay and Heather Ogilvy, "Communes and the Reconstruction of Reality," in Sallie TeSelle, ed., *The Family, Communes and Utopian Societies* (New York: Harper & Row, 1971), pp. 83–99.

9

Addiction and Knowledge: Epistemic Disease and the Hegemonic Family

Judith Bradford and Crispin Sartwell

If one goes to a bookstore at, say, the local mall, and asks for books on "the family," one will be guided to a smorgasbord of dysfunction: self-help literature for raising difficult children, for living with an alcoholic or drug addict, for dealing with the loss of sexual desire or romance in marriage. This literature both acknowledges the existence of a powerful norm of the family in the culture of those at whom it is aimed, and acknowledges (indeed requires, for marketing purposes) the frequency with which actual families diverge from the norm. Self-help literature addresses a variety of family "failures," a taxonomy of dysfunctions arranged around a central norm of balanced, healthy functionality. The basic self-help strategy of much of the material on codependency, marital romance, and so forth is a program for the return of the failed or failing family to the central ideal of "health" or "functionality."

In this paper, our contention will be that the "disease" addressed in some versions of self-help practice is primarily *epistemic*, and can be understood fruitfully as a set of situated responses to the strong deployment of the hegemonic ideal of family. Ironically, this ideal is treated as unproblematic and desirable by much self-help literature. In the actual development of small-scale social arrangements, the strength of the deployment of a certain ideal of family as the standard by which families are recognizable constrains the production of seeing and the contents of knowing; it defines and regulates a structure of epistemic communities, as well (and relatedly) as communities of race, class, and sexual orientation. From this analysis of epistemic dysfunction, we will seek to draw some fairly general conclusions for the notion of epistemic community as developed in feminist epistemologies.

I

Like "gender," the notion of "family" has been criticized by several contemporary feminisms as a descriptive and normative term. Two very general strains of critique have emerged from different standpoints. Both general trends—the critique of the "traditional" nuclear family "from the inside" and "from the outside"—identify the same ideal of family as the dominant model. The ideal has this content: the family is white, nuclear, and coresident, and in it, heterosexual, biological parents raise their children. This content of the notion of "family" is what Naomi Zack attacks as "what is assumed to be the dominant family form (and) taken to be the only 'morally good' form of the family" (Zack, p. 45) in our cultural imagination. It is also the apparently calm eye of the hurricane of dysfunctional families that appear in self-help literature.

The emphases of the critiques of the normative family, however, vary. In some feminist analyses of the family central to the emergence of some strains of second-wave and radical feminisms, the point is that traditional, gendered, family arrangements contribute to the perpetuation of gendered subjectivity and sexist power relations (Chodorow). These accounts credit the existence of the (white) nuclear family as normative but damaging; they say, in effect, that "the family" is a mechanism of the reproduction of sexism insofar as actual family arrangements match the contents of the dominant definition.

Various black and lesbian feminisms, on the other hand, have tended to stress the inapplicability of that white nuclear model to the forms of "family" practiced and valued in social, historical, and political spaces other than the relatively privileged world from which such second-wave analyses proceeded. In the process of pointing out, among other things, the racism of white middle-class feminism's equation of their forms of family with *the* family, some black feminist accounts have pointed out that other configurations of social, economic, erotic, and affective bonds count as families in their communities and traditions. In addition, much black feminist work (Collins, hooks 1993) has examined the effects on black families of the nuclear family ideal and its deployment in institutional and cultural contexts (see also Fraser). Such analyses highlight the specificity of the nuclear coresident family to the white Western patriarchal tradition, and trace the class and race effects of its insertion as the standard by which "family" is defined. Thus the norm of "family" in common circulation, the notion inscribed in our institutions, is under attack both when it *does* describe actual lived family relations and when it does *not*.

In the wake of such critiques from both "inside" and "outside," the hegemonic ideal of family looks as though it should have little remaining power; it seems that no one should, or could, hang on to that definition as descriptive or prescriptive. Yet, despite critical attack from theorists and from political movements, this ideal of family is still strong. The hegemony of this model is expressed, first, in its semantic status as the meaning of "family" per se; in legal and social contexts similarity to the dominant ideal of family is the functional index of the ability of anything that claims to be a family to be recognized as such. Other arrangements (such as non-coresident families, or families in which grandparents assume the primary responsibility for child care) are "disintegrated" or "pathological." The now-habitual reference to one-parent households, for example, as "broken" tends to reinscribe the ideal of the "whole" two-parent family, even after critiques of that notion.

Thus one interesting feature of the family norm is that its force has little to do with how many actual families "like that" one actually knows; everything purporting to be a family, especially in contexts of the attempt to claim legal and social benefits (or to fend off social and legal attack), situates itself as close to that ideal as possible.

II

So though the hegemony of the norm has been thrown into question along the lines of race, gender, and sexuality, it remains not only a myth of normality, but a standard by which alternatives can be articulated. In some of the self-help literature aimed at the production of functioning families, this picture of the family is reinscribed as the healthy and unproblematic state with which the reader is supposed to be reconciled. The taxonomy of dysfunction is a grid constructed according to distance and direction from the norm. Extended black families that do not fit the requirement of co-residence of biological parents are "broken"; white, bourgeois families that do not fit the requirements are, in some cases, "sick."

It is above all families who appear to live in proximity to the ideal of the normal family who are addressed by the self-help literature, especially its more commercially successful forms. We think it is a fair generalization to say that most such literature presumes an audience that is middle-class, heterosexual, and perhaps white. The problems addressed by this literature are not, for example, the "family problems" that occur in conditions of poverty, homophobia, or systematic racism. Rather, a set of characteristic psychological and existential difficulties faced by "normal" people, the putatively "unraced" and "unclassed" problems of family failure, are articulated. What problems do these "normal" folks have, according to this literature?

Starting with formation of Alcoholics Anonymous, and subsequently Al-Anon Family Groups, a particular story of family dysfunction has been told. This model is conveniently described by the term "fortress family." In Alcoholics Anonymous, the "Big Book" and basic text of the twelve-step movement, the "alcoholic" is more or less presumed throughout to be a middle-aged, middle-class, family man. In the model of the dysfunctional family set forth in AA and Al-Anon literature, the problems of a family revolve around the existence of an addict within the family system. Since alcoholism is both socially stigmatizing and professionally endangering, the addiction of one member (especially, in this particular model, the primary wage earner) causes the family to create a system of concealment that denies the addiction while working to compensate for its effects. This system of secrecy, typically, has the effect of "enabling" addiction: nurturing it through simultaneous lack of acknowledgment and practical mitigation of its consequences. The role of the "wife" is conceived as the preserver of appearances; she attempts to plug the leakage of information about the family into social space. She becomes obsessed with the preservation of appearances according to the dominant family norm, including the appearance of her husband as head of the household. The manufacture of the appearance of "normal" gender relations is one facet of what grows into a deadly contradiction: normal, unstigmatized appearances must be maintained, while the work of maintaining them must itself remain invisible. This process may begin with small concealments (calling the office to make an excuse, for example), but it expands into an entire deportment toward the world, and, finally, to herself.

The system of concealment, that is, extends into "denial"—the concealment of one's own efforts at concealment from oneself as well as from everyone else. At this point, the fortress family has become an epistemic regime, an all-encompassing relation to the world in which any eruption of the (unmanaged) truth of addiction and dysfunction is dangerous. The primary control over acknowledgment of addiction (or, on other applications of the notion of the fortress family, family secrets such as incest and abuse) becomes a mania for epistemic (and not only epistemic) control of the family and, above all, the appearances produced by family members. The system of secrecy and control attempts to encompass the appearances presented by family members both to each other and to "outsiders"; even when no nonfamily members are present, mention of the family secret by word or deed is forbidden. Thus the fortress family is the private family grown *pathologically* private, isolating itself in the attempt not to let its deviance from the successful family norm become a social reality. As long as addiction, for example, is kept from wider social acknowledgment, the failure of recognition shores up the ability of the family to hide it from themselves. Social norms of politeness and privacy interact with the fortress family system to produce a regime of nondeviance that erases the signs of the family secret and perpetuates the appearance of functionality. In turn, the ability of fortress family members to hide a secret from themselves shores up their ability successfully to hide it from others; no conscious dissimulation is needed, so none can be detected.

The self-help literature and the programs of recovery that tie into that literature are deeply concerned with the epistemic issues involved in the diagnosis and amelioration of these fortress family systems. The processes of "recovery" that identify one's own inability accurately to name what one sees (since one's seeing and naming abilities have been formed in systems of intense fear, even as that very fear and the conditions that cause it have been denied) provides alternate vocabularies in which to describe one's experience. Recovery processes on the twelve-step model work by allowing suspicion of the entering addict's, or codependent's, epistemic abilities. An addict or codependent's own technologies of representation are distorting and dangerous, and this is central to his or her illness. Hence, such programs must provide an alternative representative repertoire. "Admitted we were powerless over alcohol and that our lives had become unmanageable"—the first of Alcoholics Anonymous's twelve steps—allows the addict to name himself as an addict and declares an inability to see rightly without participation in the epistemic community of recovery. This community is an ongoing forum in which one's perceptions are admitted, validated, checked, and reinterpreted by people in various stages of the same recovery process.

Quite generally, addictive behavior comes close to being identified, in some ways, with the system of obsessive manipulation and concealment that tries to fit the actualities of one's life into a more acceptable, less painful or threatening mold. In the emphasis on the necessity of shared, ongoing, safe communicative space for personal transformation and healing, twelve-step practice resembles the consciousness-raising practices of, for example, the early women's movement. In other respects, however, such as the strict depoliticization of recovery practice (the insistence that recovery lies outside collective social transformation, which is enshrined specifically in AA's twelve traditions), the recovery movement can seem opposed, even antithetical, to politically based movements for personal and social change. For these reasons, the story of addiction as told in twelve-step groups is open to suspicion; it medicalizes the condition of addiction and codependency to an extent that underplays the possible social and political roots of these problems. Kay Leigh Hagan, among others, criticizes codependency treatment and self-help programs for their failure to place codependency into a wider political context of sexist oppression.

Transforming the conditions of the oppressed, including the epistemic disabilities of compulsive and unconscious self-deception, involves collective social action along with communicative exchange and the invention and circulation of new terms to make oppression visible. The invention of such new discursive collectivities in which to understand female or black selves is a necessary part of progressive movement for social change to end sexism and racism.

One important difference between the problems and processes of recovery and those ameliorating the condition of the oppressed, however, is the availability of various kinds of leverage against the norms of the oppressive culture. Considered in relation to the hegemonic family ideal as set forth above, for example, the normative whiteness and heterosexuality of the family ideal provide avenues of leverage against it. When one notices, say, that the standard of family is a white standard and that one is black (or that the standard is heterosexual and one is a lesbian) then one gains also the thought that perhaps the norm by which one has been steering is not the right one, that it is inimical to you and your kind. Thus when aspects such as class, race, or sexuality enter into the considerations of one's relation to the dominant family norm, part of the leverage one gains against it will be articulated in terms of political analysis and social action.

In the case of white, middle-class, heterosexual families, such structural possibilities of leverage are less prominent. What insight is gained, for example, when a white, middle-class, straight person realizes that the normal appearances they are trying to produce are white, middle-class, and straight? In the case of recovery rhetorics and practices, the vocabulary of illness and health serves the function of distancing one's (sick) family (which may, in most of its visible features, resemble the dominant family image) from a "healthy" family. This may explain, in part, the demographics of the market for self-help literature of the "recovery" genre.

In her essay, "Codependency and the Myth of Recovery," Kay Leigh Hagan examines the popular codependency literature in order to draw a strong parallel between codependency, as defined there, and "internalized oppression" (Hagan 1993, chap. 3). Hagan uses the definitions and descriptions of codependency provided in books such as Melody Beattie's bestselling *Codependent No More*, along with statistics that imply that codependency so defined is a quite general condition of women in contemporary American culture, to suggest that "codependency" is not a psychological "disease" but a set of traits present in women as a response to widespread sexist oppression. This line of comparison is plausible and insightful. Yet the generalized condition of "codependency" as described in work such as Beattie's may be less plausibly assigned to the category of "disease" than the more deadly forms of epistemic disability found in severe cases of alcoholism and coaddiction. Hagan's critique is plausible insofar as she is correct that social ills are being misunderstood as personal psychological problems. Yet there is still some cogency in the assignment of alcoholism, and the epistemic derangements to which alcoholics and their children are subject, to a medical category (depending, of course, on your theory of what counts as a disease). Beattie's "disease" of codependency makes you miserable, but alcoholism is a condition that can make you dead. Even epistemic diseases can be fatal.

III

Much recent feminist epistemology and other critiques of subject-centered conceptions of knowledge, such as those advanced by versions of pragmatism and hermeneutics, have attempted to reconceive the project of knowledge in historical and social terms. Lynn Hankinson Nelson, for example, suggests in her paper "Epistemological Communities" that the primary epistemic agents are not individuals (as they are conceived to be in the mainstream, Western, epistemological discourse stretching back at least to Descartes) but rather communities.

> My claim is that the knowing we do as individuals is derivative, that your knowing or mine depends on our knowing, for some "we." More to the point, I will argue that you or I *can* only know what *we know* (or could know), for some "we." . . . The "we" as I understand things, is a group or community that constructs and shares standards of evidence—a group, in short, that is an "epistemological community." (Alcoff and Potter, p. 124)

If Hagan is right, then Cartesian individualism might itself be understood as epistemic disease, and furthermore as a disease that has much in common with addictive family systems, especially the isolation of the knower from wider discursive communities. Yet the material we have just surveyed suggests a conclusion that Nelson does not draw, but which there is no reason for her to reject: namely, that all epistemological communities in her sense are not created equal. Nelson appears to identify an epistemic community simply in terms of shared standards of evidence. This identification may stem in part from her primary purpose of characterizing the *scientific* community (which is not, historically speaking, a particularly oppressed group!) as an agent of knowledge dependent on its embeddedness in wider contexts of communal knowing. But some communities that have very well-defined shared standards of evidence endanger the lives or sanities of the persons embedded in them. So, to make any sense out of the diagnosis of the fortress family as in some way productive of epistemic disabilities, we need to find either some criteria to sort out better from worse epistemic communities (productive of better or worse forms of epistemic abilities) or a definition of epistemic community by which we might describe how the fortress family fails to be a community at all.

The fortress family is to some extent a closed epistemic community; it isolates itself from the standards of evidence current in the communities that surround it, and institutes a regime of evidential constraint that compromises the access of the family and of its members to certain facts that would or could be obvious in a wider social context. Along one axis, this demonstrates the danger inherent in very small, insulated epistemic systems (a danger, too, to the Cartesian isolated knower), and thus pinpoints one of the epistemic dangers inherent in the dominant norm of the nuclear, private family itself. To say, in the present context, that something is a "family matter" is to say precisely that it is private; the nuclear family is conceived of as being largely self-contained epistemically, though the members of such families are certainly participants in larger social contexts in their capacity as, say, executives, or consumers, or students. The model of the family residence is a "detached" suburban house, in which the family can be both enclosed and sheltered from wider physical and social embeddedness.

The "family space" that accompanies the model of the nuclear family is both a social and physical space. Polite neighbors avert their eyes from family matters, and house walls hide them. When a family secret turns privacy to pathology, the insulating layer of politeness and physical separation aids in the production of normal appearances. Thus certain forms of social and economic privilege are enabling conditions of the fortress family. Privilege preserves the nuclear family from both visibility and questionability. No one asks: "What the hell is wrong with your mother?"

This is not to deny that the "normal" family could function as a successful epistemic community, or that it often does. But the recovery movement thematizes certain epistemic derangements which are always present as possibilities in small, closed systems, especially authoritarian systems, such as often occur in relations of parents to very small children. Nor is it only small epistemic communities that enforce and display such derangements; indeed, in large-scale social arrangements characterized by oppression, epistemic agents are systematically undermined as knowers and as self-knowers precisely as a strategy of oppression.

Such observations suggest that a "social" or "standpoint" epistemology, such as that developed in the works of Sandra Harding, Nancy Hartsock, and Donna Haraway, needs to be supplemented by an account that allows some sort of distinction between epistemic communities that are nurturing to their members as knowers and epistemic communities that are inimical to life or health. One obvious way in which such a distinction could be framed is by recourse to truths that are conceived to be nonepistemic: a functional epistemic community, by this standard, is simply one in which the truth can be made public within the community, and the dysfunction of the fortress family could be accounted for simply as its repression of the facts. This would present no difficulties, for example, for Hartsock or Harding, who regard their accounts of social epistemology as a defense of "objective" or nonepistemic truth.

But such an account would face many difficulties, some of them especially vexed within a feminist epistemological framework. For it may well be asserted that individual knowers can have access to the truth only through the social. On such accounts, it is hard to see how epistemic communities could be judged by whether or not they deliver truth to their members or allow their members to speak the truth; in that case, truth is conceived as being presocial, or something "out there" to which various communities have access or fail to have access. Further, it should be remembered that, though lying to oneself and others can bring one to the point of illness or death, so can telling the truth to oneself and others. Fortress families are configured precisely so as to "shut out" such dangerous truths, and often their social cohesion as coresident families is shattered once the truth is spoken. And even if we were prepared to judge epistemic communities by their relation to truths, we might still ask how communities that are open to truth are possible; we might still ask for at least a rough characterization of a successful or healthy epistemic community.

Here is our attempt to identify the criteria for such a community. (1) Though we may wish, with Nelson, to shift the locus of epistemic agency from individuals to communities, we need to emphasize that, as knowers, individuals and communities are in a reciprocal relation. Any community that makes it impossible or superhumanly difficult to speak certain experiences may be epistemically dangerous to its members. (2) Epistemic arrangements are often most successful when they are fairly small-scale (when it is possible, for example, to know the other members), but when they are diverse and shifting. The fact that people can enter and leave yields the continual possibility of corrigibility. (3) Successful epistemic communities may depend both on some commonality of experience and on the allowance of diversity. Large-scale, hegemonic, social arrangements are problematic precisely in their foreclosure of ways of knowing and ways of speaking knowledges that diverge from the hegemonic prescription. Both such hegemonies and the insular world of the fortress family force knowledges and ways of knowing into concealment; they operate by seeking to eradicate knowledges that they regard as illegitimate, problematic, incomprehensible, or threatening. (4) Power can have various equivocal relations to knowledge; it can, for example, constrain one to produce lies, and if this production is thorough enough, it can constrain one to deceive even oneself. Communities that are nonhierarchical and nonoppressive are more likely to produce knowers whose knowledge is adequate to living. (5) Social processes of knowing involve relationships among individuals that allow them to learn from each other. In such processes authority is important; deciding whose accounts are trustworthy and whose ways of seeing are most worthy of consideration is part of learning how to "go on" epistemically. Forms of authority recognition that are, to some extent, driven by personal trust and earned in personal interaction have different existential effects from oppressive authority relations. Oppressive authority relations involve accreditation in which those over whom authority is exercised have few choices about whom to accredit or why to accredit them. Abstract and untrusted authorities, experts, police, authoritarian parents, can tell a person what they "ought" to believe, even force them to act as if they believed, but not teach them how to have good epistemic abilities.

Some elements of the picture of the family that recovery literature and practice take as normative are desirable features of a more inclusive and accurate picture of family life. Loving relations, mutual support, trust, openness, and loyalty are characteristics of both the picture of the "ideal family" and the notion of the functioning epistemic community that emerges from examination of recovery practice. The manipulation, deceit, and epistemic illness that arises in families that try too hard to conform to the "ideal picture" are productive of various human miseries, in people separated from the fulfillment of the "ideal family" by systematic oppression, as well as in those most able to fulfill it by virtue of their privileged social locations. Our primary criticism, then, is not directed at the ideal itself, but at its semantic and normative hegemony; the notion of family should be pluralized or multiplied, and its normative weight should be lessened. It is precisely the normative force of the ideal, and not its specific content, that involves families in a police state of appearance production. The point is not to get rid of the picture, but to identify the various social configurations that could embody its positive aspects.

IV

The rough guidelines of successful epistemic communities explored above bear some similarity to the normative guidelines set out, for example, in Helen Longino's "Subjects, Power, and Knowledge: Description and Prescription in Feminist Philosophies of Science." The point of our account, however, is a little different; it is meant to mark different problems about closed, authoritarian, or rigid epistemic systems. The point of much recent feminist epistemology has been to show that the wrong kinds of constraint on scientific practice, for example, tend to inhibit the production of truth by those communities. Longino recommends openness to critique as one criterion by which epistemic communities, and the knowledge they produce, can be "graded" for objectivity. Whether different subjects are able to raise their voices to problematize a research program or model is seen as central to the achievement of better science. Nelson's work, as well, is primarily concerned with the analysis of communal knowing in order properly to understand how the scientific community operates in truth-seeking and how it is embedded in larger knowing communities.

Our account, like Longino's and Nelson's, is meant to highlight the situatedness of knowers and communities. But in addition, it is meant to demonstrate that knowledge production and its constraints are by no means a problem only for the philosophy of science. All of us, scientists or not, are engaged in practices of knowledge production and belief formation crucial to our possibilities of happiness, not to mention our continued existence. Our bodies are situated in communities, as is our doxastic agency. Being a good knower, embedded in a community that allows critique and exploration to proceed without undue threat to our bodies or livelihoods, is an urgently practical matter.

In this way we attempt a rapprochement between feminist epistemologies such as Nelson's and the histories of women's lives and knowing abilities described in, for example, *Women's Ways of Knowing*. Individual knowers and communities in which individuals know have geneses and histories that shape our possibilities of speaking. Families are our first, and often most important, communal contexts. It is in our families that we receive our first trainings in how to know and act, and frequently we most urgently need to know *about* our families in order to understand ourselves. The possession of good epistemic abilities is an exigency of everyday existence, intimately bound up with (or perhaps indistinguishable from) what we do and how we live. If this emphasis, as well as the foregoing analysis, is correct, then the amelioration of the conditions that produce the various epistemic vices we sketch out is vitally important. Naturalized epistemologies claim that actual knowing practices are what epistemology needs to study; we extend the claim, with a twist, to suggest that normative epistemology should stay close to analysis of actual epistemic problems of real people.

The analysis of the effects of the normative family ideal, its semantic position and social force, becomes politically and epistemologically significant as soon as we admit that knowers are persons, fully embedded in social relations, and vulnerable as *embodied* persons are vulnerable: to hurt, to need, and to habit. Each individual knower—even if the individual's epistemic agency is conceived as derivative from that of a community—had a childhood, a family, and an upbringing; each individual knower is subject to fears and hurts, and has undergone an epistemic initiation variously "pressed" by threats to their bodies and necessary social relations. It is in our families that we "get going" as knowers, well or badly; in our families, as well as in wider contexts, we were encouraged or discouraged to develop our voices. Knowers begin their epistemic lives in situations of profound dependency on others, and that dependency can, in families, be given the shape of help or harm to our later voices.

Clearly, our implication is that epistemic and social ills go hand in hand, as our epistemic and social positions inflect one another. This conclusion is also reached by other feminist epistemologists, and it should not be surprising that epistemology in which "having a voice" is central leads us to social, psychological, and familial aspects of the politics of voices and voicelessness. Every voice emerges as the babbling of children, and is encouraged or discouraged in complex ways. Knowing, like speech, like charity, begins at home.

Bibliography

Alcoff, Linda and Potter, Elizabeth eds., *Feminist Epistemologies* (New York: Routledge, 1994).

Beattie, Melody, *Codependent No More: How to Stop Controlling Others and Start Caring for Yourself* (New York: Harper and Row, 1987).

Belenky, Mary Field, Clinchy, Blythe, Goldberger, Nancy, and Tarule, Jill, *Women's Ways of Knowing* (New York: Basic Books, 1986).

Chodorow, Nancy, *The Reproduction of Mothering* (Berkeley: University of California Press, 1978).

Collins, Patricia, *Black Feminist Thought: Knowledge, Consciousness, and the Politics of Empowerment* (New York: Routledge, 1991).

Fraser, Nancy, *Unruly Practices* (Minneapolis: University of Minnesota Press, 1989).

Hagan, Kay Leigh, *Fugitive Information: Essays From a Feminist Hothead* (New York: Pandora Press, 1993).

Haraway, Donna, *Simians, Cyborgs, and Women: The Reinvention of Nature* (New York: Routledge, 1991).

Harding, Sandra, *Whose Science? Whose Knowledge?* (Ithaca: Cornell University Press, 1991).

Harding, Sandra, and Hintikka, Merrill, eds., *Discovering Reality: Feminist Perspectives on Epistemology, Metaphysics, and the Philosophy of Science* (Dordrecht: Reidel, 1983).

Hartsock, Nancy, "The Feminist Standpoint: Developing the Ground for a Specifically Historical Materialism," in *Discovering Reality*, ed. Harding and Hintikka.

hooks, bell, *Feminist Theory From Margin to Center* (Boston: South End, 1984).

———*Sisters of the Yam: Black Women and Self-Recovery* (Boston: South End, 1993).

Longino, Helen, "Subjects, Power, and Knowledge: Description and Prescription in Feminist Philosophies of Science," in Alcoff and Potter, eds. *Feminist Epistemologies*.

Zack, Naomi, *Race and Mixed Race* (Philadelphia: Temple University Press, 1993).

Part IV

Who's In, Who's Out?

10

Family's Outlaws: Rethinking the Connections between Feminism, Lesbianism, and the Family

Cheshire Calhoun

How should we understand lesbians' relation to the family, marriage, and mothering? Part of what makes this a difficult question to answer from a feminist standpoint is that feminism has undertheorized lesbian and gay oppression as an axis of oppression distinct from gender oppression.[1] As a result, lesbians' *difference* from heterosexual women is often not visible—even, oddly enough, within explicitly lesbian-feminist thought. In Parts I, II, and III of this essay, I critically review feminist analyses—particularly lesbian-feminist ones—of lesbians' relation to the family, marriage, and mothering. In Part IV, I develop a historical account of the construction of lesbians (and gays) as outlaws to the family.

My aim is to suggest that lesbians' distinctive relation to the family, marriage, and mothering is better captured by attending to the social construction of lesbians as familial outlaws than by attending exclusively to the gender structure of family, marriage, and mothering.

I. Feminism and the Family

Feminist depictions and analyses of the family, marriage, and mothering have been driven by a deep awareness that the family centered around marriage, procreation, and child-rearing has historically been and continues to be a primary site of women's subordination to and dependence on men, and by an awareness that the gender ideology that rationalizes women's subordinate status is heavily shaped by assumptions about women's natural place within the family as domestic caretakers, as reproductive beings, and as naturally fit for mothering. It has been the task and success of feminism to document the dangers posed to women by family, marriage, and mothering in both their lived and ideological forms.

The ideology of the loving family often masks gender injustice within the family, including battery, rape, and child abuse. Women continue to shoulder primary responsibility for both child-rearing and domestic labor; and they continue to choose occupations compatible with child care, occupations which are often less well paid, more replaceable, and less likely to offer benefits and career-track mobility. The expectation that women within families are first and foremost wives and mothers continues to offer employers a rationale for paying women less. Women's lower wages in the public workforce in turn make it appear economically rational within marriages for women to invest in developing their husband's career assets. No-fault divorce laws, which operate on the assumption that men and women exiting marriage have equally developed career assets (or that those career assets could be developed with the aid of short-term alimony) and that fail to treat the husband's career assets as community property, result in women exiting marriage at a significant economic disadvantage.[2] Women's custody of children after divorce, their lower earning potential, the unavailability of low-cost child care, the absence of adequate social support for single mothers, and, often, fathers' failure to pay full child support combine to reduce divorced women's economic position even further, resulting in the feminization of poverty. The ideology of the normal family as the self-sufficient, two-earner, nuclear family is then mobilized to blame single mothers for their poverty, to justify supervisory and psychological intervention into those families, and to rationalize reducing social support for them.

This picture, although generally taken as a picture of women's relation to the family, marriage, and mothering, is not, in fact, a picture of *women's* relation to the family, but is more narrowly a picture of *heterosexual* women's relation to the family, marriage, and mothering. It is a picture whose contours are shaped by an eye on the lookout for the ways that marriage, family, and mothering subordinate heterosexual women to men in the private household, in the public economy, and in the welfare state. Thus it fails to grasp lesbians' relation to the family.[3]

It has instead been the task of lesbian feminism from the 1970s through the 1990s to develop an analysis of lesbians' distinctive relation to the family. However, although lesbian feminism has developed feminist arguments for rejecting lesbian motherhood, lesbian marriages, and lesbian families, it too has failed to make lesbian difference from heterosexual women central to its analyses. It is to the promise and, I will argue, the failure of lesbian feminism to grasp lesbians' distinctive relation to the family that I now turn.

II. Lesbian Feminism, the Family, Mothering, and Marriage

In understanding what lesbians' relation to the family, motherhood, and marriage is and ought to be, lesbian feminists took as their point of departure feminist critiques of heterosexual women's experience of family, motherhood, and marriage. Lesbian feminists were particularly alive to the fact that lesbians are uniquely positioned to evade the ills of the heterosexual, male-dominated family. In particular, they are uniquely positioned to violate the conventional gender expectation that they, as women, would be dependent on men in their personal relations, would fulfill the maternal imperative, would service a husband and children, and would accept confinement to the private sphere of domesticity. Because of their unique position, lesbians could hope to be in the vanguard of the feminist rebellion against the patriarchal family, marriage, and institution of motherhood.

Family. In the 1970s and '80s, lesbian feminists used feminist critiques of heterosexual women's subordination to men within the family as a platform for valorizing lesbian existence. Lesbian feminists like Monique Wittig and Charlotte Bunch, for instance, argued that the nuclear family based on heterosexual marriage enables men to appropriate for themselves women's productive and reproductive labor.[4] Because lesbians do not enter into this heterosexual nuclear family, they can be read as refusing to allow their labor to be appropriated by men.

Lesbian feminists similarly made use of feminist critiques of heterosexual women's confinement to the private sphere of family and exclusion from the public sphere of politics and labor to argue for a new vision of lesbians' personal life. In that vision, passionate friendships, centered around a common life of work, could and should replace the depoliticized, isolated life within the nuclear family. Janice Raymond, for instance, argued for the feminist value of historical all-women's communities, such as the pre-enclosure nunneries and the nineteenth-century Chinese marriage resisters' houses where women combined intimate friendships, community, and work.[5]

Lesbian-feminist interpretation of lesbians' relation to the family as nonparticipation in *heterosexual*, male-dominated, private families is then translated into nonparticipation in *any* form of family, including lesbian families. In a 1994 essay, for instance, Ruthann Robson argues against recent liberal legal efforts to redefine the family to include lesbian and gay families that are functionally equivalent to heterosexual ones.[6] She argues that, in advocating legal recognition of lesbian families, "we have forgotten the lesbian generated critiques of family as oppressive and often deadly."[7] In particular we have forgotten the critiques of the family as an institution of the patriarchal state, of marriage as slavery,[8] and of wives as property within marriage.[9] In her view, the category "family" should be abolished.

Motherhood. Feminist critiques of heterosexual women's experience also supplied the point of departure for lesbian-feminist critiques of lesbian motherhood. Lesbian motherhood, on this view, represents a concession to a key element of women's subordination—compulsory motherhood. By refusing to have children, or by giving up custody of their children at divorce, lesbians can refuse to participate in compulsory motherhood. They can thus refuse to accept the myth "that only family and children provide [women] with a purpose and place, bestow upon us honor, respect, love, and comfort."[10] Purpose and place is better found in political activities in a more public community of women. Lesbian feminists thus challenge lesbians contemplating motherhood to reflect more critically on their reasons for doing so and on the political consequences of participating in the present lesbian baby boom.

Not only does resistance to motherhood signal a rejection of conventional understandings of womanhood and women's fulfillment, it also frees lesbians to devote their lives to public political work for lesbians and heterosexual women. Thus lesbian resistance to motherhood is seen as instrumental to effective political action. Nancy Polikoff, for instance, claims that "[t]o the exent that motherhood drains the available pool of lesbians engaging in ongoing political work, its long-term significance is overwhelming."[11]

Lesbian motherhood also facilitates the closeting of lesbian existence. Even when lesbian mothers are careful not to pass as heterosexual, their very motherhood works against their being publicly perceived as deviants to the category "woman." And in her study of lesbian mothers, Ellen Lewin argues that motherhood enables lesbians to claim a less stigmatized place in the gender system; in particular, it enables them to claim for themselves the conventional womanly attributes of being altruistic, nurturant, and responsible—attributes which lesbians typically are stereotyped as lacking.[12]

Marriage. Like lesbian motherhood, lesbian (and gay) marriage seems antithetical to the lesbian-feminist goal of radically challenging conventional gender, sexual, and familial arrangements. Historically, the institution of marriage has been oppressively gender-structured. And, as Polikoff points out in a recent essay, the historical and cross-cultural record of same-sex marriages does not support the claim that same-sex marriages will revolutionize the gender structure of marriage. On the contrary, same-sex marriages that have been legitimized in other cultures—for instance, African woman-marriage, Native American marriages between a berdache and a same-sex partner, and nineteenth-century Chinese marriages between women—have all been highly gender-structured. Thus there is no reason to believe that "'gender dissent' is inherent in marriage between two men or two women."[13]

Moreover, the attempt to secure legal recognition for lesbian and gay marriages is highly likely to work against efforts to critique the institution of marriage. In particular, by attempting to have specifically *marital* relationships recognized, advocates of marriage rights help to reinforce the assumption that long-term, monogamous relationships are more valuable than any other kind of relationship. As a result, the marriage rights campaign, if successful, will end up privileging those lesbian and gay relationships that most closely approximate the heterosexual norm over more deviant relationships that require a radical rethinking of the nature of families.[14]

Finally, arguments for lesbian and gay marriage rights on the grounds that lesbians and gays lack privileges that heterosexual couples enjoy—such as access to a spouse's health insurance benefits—are insufficiently radical.[15] Distributing basic benefits like health insurance through the middle-class family neglects the interests of poor and some working-class families as well as single individuals in having access to basic social benefits. If access to such benefits is the issue, then universal health insurance, not marriage, is what we should be advocating.

III. Lesbian Disappearance

The difficulty with the lesbian-feminist viewpoint is that it is one from which lesbian difference from heterosexual women persistently disappears from view.

First, the value of the family and marriage for *lesbians* is judged largely by evaluating the *heterosexual* nuclear family's effects on *heterosexual* women. Lesbians are to resist family and marriage because the family centered around the heterosexual married couple has been gender structured in a way that made marriage a form of slavery where heterosexual women could be treated as property and their labor appropriated by men. But to make this a principal reason for lesbians' not forming families and marriages of their own is to lose sight of the difference between lesbians and heterosexual women. Lesbian families and marriages are not reasonably construed as sites where women can be treated as property and where their productive and reproductive labor can be appropriated by men. It thus does not follow from the fact that heterosexual marriage and family has been oppressive for heterosexual women and a primary structure of patriarchy that *any* form of marriage or family, including lesbian ones, is oppressive for women and a primary structure of patriarchy.

The alternative argument—that creating lesbian families and marriages will not remedy the gender structure in heterosexual marriages and families—drops lesbians from view in a different way. Here, heterosexual women's interests are substituted for those of lesbians as the touchstone for determining what normative conclusions about the family, marriage, and mothering lesbians should come to. Lesbians are to resist forming marriages and families of their own because heterosexual women's struggle against the institution of marriage and family will not be promoted and may in fact be hindered by lesbian endorsement of the value of marriage and family. This line of reasoning ignores the possibility that lesbians may have interests of their own in forming families and marriages, interests that may conflict with heterosexual women's political aims.

Second, resistance to the forms of gender oppression and gender ideology to which lesbians, *as women*, are subject is presented as a distinctively lesbian task (that is, as a distinctively lesbian version of feminist resistance), when in fact these are broadly feminist tasks whose burden should be equally shared by heterosexual women and lesbians. Both lesbians and heterosexual women have reason to resist the construction of mothering as an unpaid, socially unsupported task. Both have reason to reject women's confinement to the domestic sphere and reason to value participation in politically oriented communities of women. Both have reason to resist their gender socialization into the myth of feminine fulfillment through mothering and to assert their deviance from the category "woman." Both can have justice interests in objecting to a social and legal system that privileges long-term, monogamous relationships over all other forms of relationship and that does not provide universal access to basic benefits like health insurance. All of these are broadly feminist concerns. As a result, the lesbian-feminist perspective does not articulate any distinctively *lesbian* political tasks in relation to the family, marriage, and mothering. Instead, lesbians are submerged in the larger category "feminist."

Finally, the political relation between heterosexuals and nonheterosexuals and the ideologies of sexuality that support the oppression of lesbians and gays simply do not inform the lesbian-feminist analysis of lesbians' relation to the family, marriage, and mothering. What governs the lesbian-feminist perspective is above all the political relations between men and women, and to a lesser extent class relations and the political relations between those in normative long-term, monogamous relations (whether heterosexual or nonheterosexual) and all other human relations. As a result, the radicalness of lesbian and gay family, marriage, and parenting is measured on a scale that looks only at their power (or impotence) to transform gender relations, the privileging of long-term, monogamous relations, and class privilege. Not surprisingly, lesbian and gay families, marriages, and parenting fail to measure up. But this ignores the historical construction of lesbians and gays as outlaws to the natural family, as constitutionally incapable of more than merely sexual relationships, and as dangerous to children.

Within gender ideology, for instance, lesbians have not been and are not constructed as beings whose natural place is within the family as domestic caretakers, as reproductive beings, and as naturally fit mothers. On the contrary, the gender ideology that rationalizes the oppression of both lesbians and gays consists in part precisely in the assumption that both are aliens to the natural family, nonprocreative, incapable of enduring intimate ties, dangerous to children, and ruled by sexual instincts to the exclusion of parenting ones. Moreover, unlike heterosexual women, it is not their subordination *within* the family that marks their oppression but rather their denial of access *to* a legitimated and socially instituted sphere of family, marriage, and parenting.

Lesbians and gays are, for instance, denied the legal privileges and protections that heterosexuals enjoy with respect to their marital and familial relations. Among the array of rights related to marriage that heterosexuals enjoy but gays and lesbians do not are the rights to legal marriage, to live with one's spouse in neighborhoods zoned "single-family only," and to secure U.S. residency through marriage to a U.S. citizen; the rights to Social Security survivor's benefits, to inherit a spouse's estate in the absence of a will, and to file a wrongful death suit; the rights to give proxy consent, to refuse to testify against one's spouse, and to file joint income taxes.

Lesbians and gays similarly lack access to the privileges and protections that heterosexuals enjoy with respect to biological, adoptive, and foster children. Sexual orientation continues to be an overriding reason for denying custody to lesbian and gay parents who exit a heterosexual marriage. Gays and lesbians fare equally poorly with respect to adoption and foster parenting. New Hampshire prohibits gay and lesbian adoption and foster parenting, while others states, like Massachusetts, have policies making a child's placement with lesbian or gay parents unlikely. Even when adoption is successful, joint adoption generally is not—nor is adoption of a partner's biological child.

What comes into view in this picture of the legal inequities that lesbians and gays confront is the fact that the family, marriage, and parenting are a primary site of heterosexual privilege. The family centered around marriage, procreation, and child-rearing has historically been and continues to be constructed and institutionalized as the natural domain of heterosexuals only, and thus as a domain from which lesbians and gays are outlawed. This distinctively lesbian and gay relation to family, marriage, and parenting is what fails to make its appearance within feminist analyses and critiques of the family. But so long as the political position of lesbians and gays in relation to heterosexual control of family, marriage, and parenting remains out of view, distinctively lesbian (and gay) interests in family, marriage, and parenting and distinctively lesbian (and gay) political goals in relation to the family cannot make their appearance. It is to the construction of lesbians and gays as outlaws to the family that I now turn.

IV. Familial Outlaws

A constitutive feature of lesbian and gay oppression since at least the late nineteenth century has been the reservation of the private sphere for heterosexuals only. Because lesbians and gays are ideologically constructed as beings incapable of genuine romance, marriage, or families of their own, and because those assumptions are institutionalized in the law and social practice, lesbians and gays are displaced from this private sphere.

In what follows, I want to suggest that the historical construction of gays and lesbians as familial outlaws is integrally connected to the history of social anxiety about the failure and potential collapse of the heterosexual nuclear family. In particular, I want to suggest that in periods where there was heightened anxiety about the stability of the heterosexual nuclear family because of changes in gender, sexual, and family composition norms within the family, this anxiety was resolved by targeting a group of persons who could be ideologically constructed as outsiders to the family, identifying the behaviors that most deeply threatened the family with those outsiders, and stigmatizing that group. In each of the periods of anxiety about the family that I intend to consider, lesbians and gays had achieved fairly high social visibility, making them natural candidates for the group to be constructed as outsiders to the family. The construction of gays and lesbians as highly stigmatized outsiders to the family and as displaying the most virulent forms of family-disrupting behavior allayed anxieties about the potential failure of the heterosexual nuclear family in three ways. First, it externalized the threat to the family. As a result, anxiety about the possibility that the family was disintegrating from *within* could be displaced onto the spectre of the hostile outsider to the family. Second, stigma threatening comparisons between misbehaving members of the heterosexual family and the dangerous behavior of gays and lesbians could be used to compel heterosexual family members' compliance with gender, sexual, and family composition norms. Third, by locating the genuinely deviant, abnormal, perverse behavior outside the family, members of heterosexual families were enabled to adjust to new, liberalized norms for acceptable gender roles and sexual behavior within families[16] as well as new, liberalized norms for acceptable family composition. They could, in essence, reassure themselves with the thought: "At least we aren't like them!"

The coincidence of anxiety about the failure of the heterosexual nuclear family and the ideological construction of gays and lesbians as familial outlaws is particularly striking in three periods: the 1880s to 1920s, the 1930s to 1950s, and the 1980s to 1990s. Although a variety of factors threatened the family in each of these periods, I want to suggest that the three periods differ with respect to the familial norms that were most seriously challenged. In the 1880s to 1920s it was especially norms governing (women's) gender behavior, in the 1930s to 1950s, it was most critically norms governing (male) sexuality, and in the 1980s and 1990s it has been, above all, norms governing acceptable family composition that have been most centrally challenged.

1880s to 1920s. The 1880s to 1920s witnessed significant challenges to the gender structure of marriage. By the mid-1800s, the first wave of the feminist movement was underway, pressing for changes in women's gender roles within the family. First-wave feminists pushed for legal reforms that would recognize women as separate individuals within marriage by, for example, securing women property rights within marriage, and that would give women access to divorce. (Between 1860 and 1920 the divorce rate increased over 600 percent.[17]) They also pushed for increased access to higher education and employment as well as for contraception, abortion, and (through the temperance movement) control of male sexuality, all of which would enable women to limit family size and free women from a life devoted exclusively to childbearing and child-rearing.

First-wave feminists' explicit critique of women's gender role within the family produced an anxiety about the family that focused on its gender structure. Because turn-of-the-century gender ideology tied gender tightly to biology, the violation of gender norms was interpreted as having significant biological repercussions. From the mid-1800s on, physicians argued that "unnatural" women—that is, "over"educated women, women who worked at gender-atypical occupations, and women who practiced birth control or had abortions—were likely to suffer a variety of physically based mental ailments including weakness, nervousness, hysteria, loss of memory, insanity, and nymphomania.[18] Worse yet, their gender-inappropriate behavior might result in sterility or inability to produce physically and mentally healthy offspring. In particular, they risked producing children who were themselves inappropriately gendered—effeminate sons and masculine daughters. Not only could departure from women's traditional gender role as wife and mother have dire physical and mental consequences for both herself and her offspring, she herself might be suspected of being at a deep level not really a woman. Indeed, she might be suspected of being one of the third sex.

Beginning roughly in 1869 with the publication of Carl von Westphal's essay on the congenital invert, medical theorists began developing a new gender category variously labelled the sexual invert, the intermediate sex, the third sex, the urning, the man-woman. The image of the sexual invert crystallized anxiety about women's, and to a lesser extent, men's gender-crossing and symbolized the dangers of deviance from conventional gender norms. Although the invert is the historical precursor to the contemporary categories "lesbian" and "homosexual," the turn-of-the-century sexual invert was not constructed primarily *sexually*. What distinguished the invert was her or his *gender* inversion. The sexually inverted woman, for example, was distinguished from noninverted women by her masculine traits: short hair, independent and aggressive manner, athleticism, male attire, drinking, cigarette and sometimes cigar smoking, masculine sense of honor, dislike of needlework and domestic activities, and preference for science and masculine sports. The sexually inverted woman's attraction to conventionally gendered women and to effeminate men was simply a natural result of her generally masculine genderization. In her sexual relations, whether with women or with a husband, she would wear the pants.

Medical theorists postulated that, at a biological level, sexually inverted women were not real women. Some imagined that inverts were really hermaphrodites. Others, like Havelock Ellis, imagined that they possessed an excess of male "germs."[19] Others, like Krafft-Ebing, imagined that the invert was a throwback to an earlier evolutionary stage of bisexuality (that is, bi-*genderization*) and that in spite of her female brain and body, the psychosexual center in her brain was masculine.[20]

Because the mark of the sexual invert was her lack of conformity with women's conventional gender role, the line between the nonconforming sexual invert and the nonconforming feminist was often blurred. Feminist views and feminist-inspired deviance from gender norms might be both symptom and cause of sexual inversion. Like sexual inverts, feminists threatened to disrespect appropriate gender relations between women and men in marriage. One author of a 1900 *New York Medical Journal* essay, for instance, "warned that feminists and sexual perverts alike, both of whom he classed as 'degenerates,' married only men whom they could rule, govern and cause to follow [them] in voice and action."[21]

In short, the sexually inverted woman, sometimes indistinguishable from the feminist, symbolized the dangers of departing from women's conventional gender role. The idea that this new medical category of sexual inversion was created in direct response to first-wave feminists' challenge to gender norms is not new. Both Lillian Faderman and George Chauncey, Jr., for instance, have argued that given both the influence of feminist ideas and the burgeoning of economic opportunities for women, there was a cultural fear that women would replace marriages to men with Boston marriages or romantic friendships.[22] One response to that fear was greater attention to the ideal of companionate marriage, and thus to making marriage more attractive to women.[23] A second response, however, was a cultural backlash—or as Chauncey describes it, a heterosexual counter-revolution—against Boston marriages, romantic friendships, schoolgirl "raves," and same-sex institutions. The pathologizing of both gender deviance and same-sex relationships brought what were formerly taken to be innocent and normal intimacies between women under suspicion of harboring degeneracy and abnormality.

The pathologizing of relations between women was not confined to medical literature. As Lisa Duggan has documented, newspapers sensationalized violent intimate relationships between women, such as the case of Alice Mitchell, a sexual invert, who intended to elope with and marry Freda Ward and to cross-dress as a man, adopting the name Alvin. When their plan was discovered and the engagement forcibly terminated, Alice Mitchell murdered Freda so that no one else could have her. Duggan argues that Alice's clear intent to forge a new way of life outside the heterosexual, gender-structured family marked her as dangerous. In sensationalizing cases like Alice's,

> [t]he late-nineteenth century newspaper narratives of lesbian love featured violence as a boundary marker; murders or suicides served to abort the forward progress of the tale, signaling that such erotic love between women was not only tragic but ultimately hopeless. . . . The stories were thus structured to emphasize, ultimately, that no real love story was possible.[24]

Not only was no real love story possible, no real family relation was possible either. And this is the point I want to underscore. Controlling challenges to the conventional gender structure within heterosexual marriages was accomplished by constructing the fully gender-deviant woman as someone who was not only pathological and doomed to tragedy, but who was constitutionally unfit for family life. Her masculinity unfitted her for the marital role of wife, unfitted her for the task of producing properly gendered children, and unfitted her for any stable, intimate relationships. The cultural construction of the lesbian was thus, from the outset, the construction of a kind of being who was, centrally, an outsider to marriage, family, and motherhood.

The image of the doomed, mannish lesbian could be used to compel heterosexual women's compliance with gender norms. In addition, by equating the worst forms of gender deviance with lesbians, heterosexual families were helped to adjust to new gender norms for women (which, by comparison to lesbians, seemed normal). Finally, attributing the worst forms of gender deviance to a third sex externalized the threat to the heterosexual family, suggesting that the heterosexual family was not in fact being challenged from within by *real* women.

1930s to 1950s. The Depression of the 1930s and World War II in the 1940s created a new set of threats to the stability of the heterosexual family.[25] During the Depression, many men lost their traditional gender position in the family as breadwinners as a result of both massive unemployment and a drop in marriage rates. The sense of a cultural crisis in masculinity was reflected in numerous sociological studies of "The Unemployed Man and His Family."[26] Men's traditional position in the family and family stability itself was additionally undermined during World War II, which brought a rise in the frequency of prolonged separations, divorce, and desertion.[27]

One response was the attempt to reposition men as primary income earners in their families by discouraging or prohibiting married women from working. A second response, however, appears to have been a shift in the cultural construction of masculinity from being gender-based to being sexuality-based. In his historical study of New York gay culture during the first third of the twentieth century, for instance, George Chauncey argues that sexual categories for men underwent a significant transformation during the '30s and '40s. The gender-behavior-based contrast between "fairies," that is, effeminate men and "men" (who might be "queer," "trade," that is, heterosexual men who accepted advances from homosexual men, or strictly heterosexual) gave way to the contemporary binarism between homosexual and heterosexual. Real manhood ceased to be secured by simply avoiding feminine behaviors, and instead came to rest on exclusive heterosexuality.[28] The depiction of gay men, during the sex crime panics of 1937 to 1940 and 1949 to 1955, as violent child molesters further solidified the boundary between real, heterosexual men and homosexuals, while depiction of the heterosexual sexual psychopath as hypermasculine underscored the centrality of (hetero)sexuality to manhood.[29]

Compounding the shifts in gender arrangements within the family brought on by the Depression and World War II were shifts in cultural understandings of women's and children's sexuality. The idea of female sexual satisfaction, the use of birth control, and sexuality outside of marriage all gained increased acceptance. And the publicization of Freudian ideas underscored not only the sexuality of women, but the sexuality of children as well. The sexualization of women and children meant that both might fail to be merely innocent victims of male sexual aggression; they might instead play a role in inviting it.[30] These factors contributed to a changed understanding of sexuality and sexual norms both outside and inside the family. They also contributed to cultural anxiety about the power of sexuality to destabilize and undermine the family.

Those anxieties were crystallized during the sex crime panics in the twin figures of the heterosexual psychopathic rapist and the homosexual psychopath who seduced youth and molested children. Both figures symbolized sexuality run dangerously amok. The image of the dangerously sexual homosexual received added reinforcement during the McCarthy era's purge of "sex perverts" from governmental service on the grounds that they threatened not only the nation's children but its national security and the heterosexuality of its adult population as well.[31]

The images of the sexual psychopath and the homosexual child molester helped to redefine the sexual norm, setting the outer limits of acceptable sexual behavior: violent sex, sex with men, and sex with children.[32] By constructing new understandings of sexual abnormality, the images of the sexual psychopath and the homosexual child molester also helped Americans adjust to new sexual norms, such as the acceptability of nonprocreative sex, as well as to new understandings of both women and children as "normally" sexual beings. The location of the sexual danger posed to women and children outside the family also allayed anxiety that the family risked disruption by the potentially violent sexuality of its own members.

Again, the point I want to underscore is that resolving cultural anxiety about shifting gender and sexual patterns within the family was integrally connected with the social construction of gay men as familial outlaws. The very nature of homosexuality unfitted gay men for family. Constitutionally prone to uncontrolled and insatiable sexuality, gay men (and lesbians) could not be trusted to respect prohibitions on adult-child sexual interactions.[33] Nor, given the compulsive quality of their sexual desire, could gay men or lesbians be expected to maintain stable relationships with each other.

1980s to 1990s. The 1980s and 1990s have posed a different challenge to the family. Technological, social, and economic factors have combined to produce an explosion of new family and household forms that undermine the nuclear, biology-based family's claim to be *the* natural, normative social unit.

Increasingly sophisticated birth control methods and technologically assisted reproduction using in vitro fertilization, artificial insemination, contract pregnancy, fertility therapies, and the like undermine cultural understandings of the marital couple as a naturally reproductive unit, introduce nonrelated others into the reproductive process, and make it possible for women and men to have children without a heterosexual partner. The institutionalization of child care, as mothers work to support families, involves nonfamily members in the familial task of raising children. Soaring divorce rates have made single-parent households a common family pattern—so common that Father's Day cards now include ones addressed to mothers, and others announcing their recipient is "like a dad." The high incidence of divorce has also meant an increase in divorce-extended families that incorporate children, grandparents, and other kin from former marriages as well as former spouses who may retain shared custody or visitation rights.[34] As a result of remarriage, semen donation, and contract pregnancy, the rule of one-mother, one-father per child (both of whom are expected to be biological parents) that has dominated legal reasoning about custody and visitation rights has ceased to be adequate to the reality of many families. Multiple women and/or multiple men become involved in children's lives through their biological, gestation, or parenting contributions.[35] The extended kinship networks of the Black urban poor, including "fictive kin," which enable extensive pooling of resources, have become increasingly common in the working class as the shift from goods to service production and the decline of industrial and unionized occupations has made working class persons' economic position increasingly fragile.[36] And the impoverishment of single-parent households has increasingly involved welfare agencies in family survival.

In short, as Judith Stacey observes,

> No longer is there a single culturally dominant family pattern to which the majority of Americans conform and most of the rest aspire. Instead, Americans today have crafted a multiplicity of family and household arrangements that we inhabit uneasily and reconstitute frequently in response to changing personal and occupational circumstances.[37]

We now live, in her view, in the age of the postmodern family. It is an age where one marriage and its biological relations have ceased to determine family composition. Choice increasingly appears to be the principle determining family composition: choice to single-parent, choice of fictive kin, choice to combine nuclear families (in extended kin networks, in remarriage, or in divorce-extended families), choice of semen donors or contract birthgivers, choice to dissolve marital bonds, choice of who will function as a parent in children's lives (in spite of the law's failure to acknowledge the parental status of many functional parents). That is, what Kath Weston describes as a distinctively gay and lesbian concept of "chosen families," contrasted to heterosexuals' biological families, in fact characterizes the reality of many heterosexual families who fail in various ways to construct a nuclear family around a procreative married couple.[38]

As family forms multiply, the traditional, heterosexual and procreative, nuclear family delimited by bonds of present marriage and blood relation and capable of sustaining itself rather than pooling resources across households has ceased to be the "natural" family form.[39] Not only has the pluralization of family forms undermined the credibility of the claim that the traditional family is the most natural family form, it has also highlighted the failure of the traditional family to satisfy individual needs better than other personal relationships or alternative family forms.[40]

Cultural anxiety about the future of the family crystallized in the 1980s and 1990s in at least two major images: those of the unwed welfare mother and of the lesbian or gay whose mere public visibility threatens to undermine family values and destroy the family. The depiction of lesbians and gays as beings whose "lifestyle" contradicts family values was preceded in the 1970s by the gay liberation movement, and with it, a rise in lesbian custody suits and in litigation contesting the denial of marriage licenses to gays.[41] Both the sheer visibility of gays and lesbians as well as their specific bid for acknowledgment of gay and lesbian marriages and families made gays and lesbians natural targets for the expression of cultural anxieties about the family.

In the late 1980s, for instance, Britain passed Clause 28 of the Local Government Act that, in addition to prohibiting the promotion of homosexuality, also forbade local authorities from promoting "the teaching in any maintained school of the acceptability of homosexuality as a pretended family relationship."[42] The pretended nature of gays' and lesbians' family relationships has, in the United States, been repeatedly underscored in court rulings affirming that marriage requires one man and one woman. The pretend nature of lesbian motherhood has also been underscored in custody rulings that have assumed that being parented by a lesbian is not in a child's best interests—because the child may be molested, or may fail to be socialized into her or his appropriate gender or into heterosexuality, or may be harmed by the stigma of having a lesbian parent.[43]

Not only are gays and lesbians constructed as beings whose "marriages" and "families" fail to be the genuine article, they are also constructed as beings who, simply by being publicly visible or mentionable, assault family values. As a result, antidiscrimination measures are equated with hostility to the family, even though ending workplace discrimination or punishing hate crimes would appear to have little to do with advocating one family form rather than another. So, for instance, the author of a 1995 law journal article argues that gays and lesbians should not be protected against discrimination because gay sexuality is "deeply hostile to the self-understanding of those members of the community who are willing to commit themselves to real marriage."[44] He makes it clear that any policy protecting a "gay lifestyle" threatens the stability of the family, and for that reason should be rejected:

A political community which judges that the stability and protective and educative generosity of family life is of fundamental importance to that community's present and future can rightly judge that it has a compelling interest in denying that homosexual conduct—a "gay lifestyle"— is a valid, humanly acceptable choice and form of life, and in doing whatever it *properly* can, as a community with uniquely wide but still subsidiary functions, to discourage such conduct.[45]

So threatening to the family are gays and lesbians taken to be that even protecting them against hate crimes may be interpreted as dangerously close to attacking the family. Thus the Hate Crimes Act passed by Congress in 1990 (which covers sexual orientation) includes the affirmation that "federal policy should encourage the well-being, financial security, and health of the American family," almost immediately followed with the warning that "[n]othing in this Act shall be construed, nor shall any funds appropriated to carry out the purpose of the Act be used, to promote or encourage homosexuality."[46]

As in previous periods, constructing lesbians and gays as dangerous outlaws to the family serves several functions. First, it externalizes the threat to the heterosexual, procreative, nuclear family, diverting attention from heterosexuals' own choices to create multiple, new family arrangements that undermine the hegemony of the traditional family. Second, depicting gay and lesbian relationships as "pretended" families, by comparison to which even the most deviant heterosexual families can appear normal, helps heterosexual families adjust to changing norms for family composition. Finally, the equation of heterosexuality with family values and homosexuality and lesbianism with hostility to the family serves to compel loyalty to the sexual norm prescribing heterosexuality. It also renders suspect some of the alternative family arrangements that heterosexuals might be inclined to choose, such as supportive, familylike relationships between women involved in single parenting.

V. Not for Heterosexuals Only

I have argued for the existence of a historical pattern in which anxiety about the stability of the family goes hand in hand with the ideological depiction of gays and lesbians as unfit for marriage, parenting, and family. The construction of lesbians and gays as natural outlaws to the family and the masking of heterosexuals' own family-disrupting behavior results in the reservation of the private sphere for heterosexuals only.[47]

It is because being an outlaw to the family has been so central to the social construction of lesbianism that I think lesbians' relation to the family is better captured by attention to their outlaw status than to the gender structure of marriage and motherhood (as is characteristic of lesbian feminism). Indeed, on the historical backdrop of the various images of family outlaws—the mannish lesbian, the homosexual child molester, and their pretended family relationships—lesbian-feminist resistance to lesbian and gay marriages, lesbian motherhood, and the formation of lesbian and gay families looks suspiciously like a concession to the view of lesbians and gays as family outlaws. Because being denied access to a legitimate and protected private sphere has been and continues to be central to lesbian and gay oppression, the most important scale on which to measure lesbian and gay political strategies is one that assesses their power (or impotence) to resist conceding the private sphere to heterosexuals only. On such a scale, the push for marriage rights, parental rights, and recognition as legitimate families measures up.

For similar reasons, it seems to me a mistake to make advocacy of "queer families" *the* political goal for lesbians and gays. By "queer families" I mean ones not centered around marriage or children, but composed instead of chosen, adult, supportive relationships (which would include lesbian-feminist politicized communities of women).

Equating gay families with queer, nonmarital, and nonparenting families concedes too much to the ideology of gays and lesbians as family outlaws, unfit for genuine marriage and dangerous to children. In addition, describing families that depart substantially from traditional family forms as distinctively gay conceals the queerness of many heterosexual families. I have tried to show that, historically, gays and lesbians have become family outlaws not because *their* relationships and families were distinctively queer, but because *heterosexuals'* relationships and families queered the gender, sexual, and family composition norms. The depiction of gays and lesbians as deviant with respect to family norms was a product of anxiety about that deviancy within heterosexual families. Thus claiming that gay and lesbian families are (or should be) distinctively queer and distinctively deviant helps conceal the deviancy in heterosexual families, and thereby helps to sustain the illusion that heterosexuals are specially entitled to access to a protected private sphere because they, unlike their gay and lesbian counterparts, are supporters of the family.

All this is not to say that there is no merit in lesbian feminists' concern that normalizing lesbian motherhood will reinforce the equation of "woman" with "mother." Overcoming the idea that lesbian motherhood is a contradiction in terms may very well result in lesbians' being expected to fulfill the maternal imperative just as heterosexual women are. But this is just to say that the oppression of lesbians and gays is structurally different from gender oppression. Thus, strategies designed to resist *lesbian* oppression (such as pushing for the legal right to coadopt) are not guaranteed to counter *gender* oppression (which might better be achieved by resisting motherhood altogether). In gaining access to a legitimate and protected private sphere of mothering, marriage, and family, lesbians will need to take care that it does not prove to be as constraining as the private sphere has been for heterosexual women.

Nor have I meant to claim that there is no merit in both lesbian feminists' and queer theorists' concern that normalizing lesbian and gay marriage will reinforce the distinction between good, assimilationist gays and bad gay and heterosexual others whose relationships violate familial norms (the permanently single, the polygamous, the sexually nonmonogamous, the member of a commune, and so on). Overcoming the idea that lesbian and gay marriages are merely pretended family relationships may very well result in married lesbians and gays being looked upon more favorably than those who remain outside accepted familial forms. But this is just to say that countering lesbians' and gays' family outlaw status is not the same thing as struggling to have a broad array of social relationships recognized as (equally) valuable ones. It is, however, important not to exaggerate the level of conformity involved in having familial status. I have argued that families often fail to conform to gender, sexual, and family composition norms. This has not prevented heterosexuals from claiming that, their deviancy notwithstanding, they still have real marriages and real families, and are themselves naturally suited for marriage, family, and parenting. Thus, lesbians and gays who resist their construction as family outlaws are not bidding for access to one, highly conventional family form (such as the nuclear, two-parent, self-sufficient, procreative family). They are instead bidding for access to the same privilege that heterosexuals now enjoy, namely the privilege of claiming that *in spite of their multiple deviations* from norms governing the family, their families are nevertheless *real* ones and they are themselves naturally suited for marriage, family, parenting *however* these may be defined and redefined.

Notes

1. I have argued for this claim in both "Separating Lesbian Theory from Feminist Theory," *Ethics* 104 (1994), pp. 558–581, and in "The Gender Closet: Lesbian Disappearance Under the Sign 'Women'," *Feminist Studies* 21 (Spring 1995), pp. 7–34.

2. For discussions of women's vulnerability in marriage and after divorce, see Susan Moller Okin, *Justice, Gender and the Family* (New York: Basic Books, 1989), and Lenore J. Weitzman, *The Divorce Revolution: The Unexpected Social and Economic Consequences for Women and Children in America* (New York: Free Press, 1985).

3. This is not to say that lesbians are entirely left out of the picture. Although drawn from a heterosexual viewpoint, this picture of the family, marriage, and mothering as a primary site of women's subordination and dependence is one that lesbians do nevertheless fit into in many ways. Lesbians, too, can find themselves in heterosexual marriages, undergoing divorce, becoming single parents, disadvantaged in a sex-segregated workforce that pays women less, without adequate child care or child support, vulnerable to welfare bureaucracies, and so on.

4. Monique Wittig, *The Straight Mind and Other Essays* (Boston: Beacon Press, 1992); Charlotte Bunch, "Lesbians in Revolt," in *Passionate Politics, Essays 1968–1986* (New York: St. Martin's Press, 1987).

5. Janice G. Raymond, *A Passion for Friends* (Boston: Beacon Press, 1986).
6. Ruthann Robson, "Resisting the Family: Repositioning Lesbians in Legal Theory," *Signs* 19 (1994), pp. 975–996.
7. Ibid., p. 977.
8. Ibid. p. 976
9. Ibid., p. 986–987.
10. Irena Klepfisz, "Women Without Children/Women Without Families/Women Alone," in *Politics of the Heart: A Lesbian Parenting Anthology*, ed. Sandra Pollack and Jeanne Vaughn (New York: Firebrand Books, 1987), p. 57.
11. Nancy D. Polikoff, "Lesbians Choosing Children: The Personal Is Political," in Pollack and Vaughn, *Politics of the Heart*, p. 51.
12. Ellen Lewin, *Lesbian Mothers: Accounts of Gender in American Culture* (Ithaca, N.Y.: Cornell University Press, 1993), p. 16.
13. Nancy D. Polikoff, "We Will Get What We Ask For: Why Legalizing Gay and Lesbian Marriage Will Not 'Dismantle the Legal Structure of Gender in Every Marriage'," *Virginia Law Review* 79 (1993), 1535–1550, p. 1538.
14. Robson's objection to functionalist approaches to the family in legal thinking is precisely that functionalist approaches are inherently conservative and "guarantee exclusion of the very relationships that might transform the functions," such as sexual relationships among three lesbians (Robson, "Resisting the Family," p. 989).
15. Paula Ettelbrick, "Since When Is Marriage a Path to Liberation?" in *Lesbians, Gay Men, and the Law*, ed. William B. Rubenstein (New York: The New Press, 1993); and Polikoff, "We Will Get What We Ask For."
16. Estelle B. Freedman develops this thesis in "'Uncontrolled Desires': The Response to the Sexual Psychopath 1920–1960," in *Passion and Power: Sexuality in History*, ed. Kathy Peiss and Christina Simmons with Robert A. Padgug (Philadelphia: Temple University Press, 1989).
17. Eli Zaretsky, "The Place of the Family in the Origins of the Welfare State," in *Rethinking the Family: Some Feminist Questions*, ed. Barrie Thorne with Marilyn Yalom (New York: Longman, 1982), p. 199.
18. Carroll Smith-Rosenberg and Charles Rosenberg, "The Female Animal: Medical and Biological Views of Woman and Her Role in Nineteenth-Century America," in *Concepts of Health and Disease: Interdisciplinary Perspectives*, ed. Arthur L. Caplan, H. Tristram Engelhardt, Jr., James J. McCartney (Reading, Mass.: Addison-Wesley Publishing Co., 1981).
19. Havelock Ellis, *Studies in the Psychology of Sex*, Vol II: *Sexual Inversion* (Philadelphia: F.A. Davis Co., 1928).
20. Richard von Krafft-Ebing, *Psychopathia Sexualis: A Medico-Forensic Study* (New York: Pioneer Publications, Inc., 1947).
21. Quoted in George Chauncey, Jr., "From Sexual Inversion to Homosexuality: The Changing Medical Conceptualization of Female 'Deviance,'" in *Passion and Power*, p. 92.
22. Chauncey, Jr. "From Sexual Inversion to Homosexuality"; Lillian Faderman, *Surpassing the Love of Men: Romantic Friendship and Love between Women from the Renaissance to the Present* (New York: William Morrow, 1981); Lillian Faderman, "Nineteenth-Century Boston Marriage as a Possible Lesson for Today," in *Boston Marriages: Romantic but Asexual Relationships*

Among Contemporary Lesbians, ed. Esther D. Rothblum and Kathleen A. Brehony (Amherst: University of Massachusetts Press, 1993).

23. Chauncey, Jr., "From Sexual Inversion to Homosexuality."

24. Lisa Duggan, "The Trials of Alice Mitchell: Sensationalism, Sexology, and the Lesbian Subject in Turn-of-the-Century America." *Signs* 18(1993), 791–814, p. 808.

25. See Estelle B. Freedman, "'Uncontrolled Desires'"; John D'Emilio, "The Homosexual Menace: The Politics of Sexuality in Cold War America," in *Passion and Power*; and George Chauncey, Jr., *Gay New York: Gender, Urban Culture, and the Making of the Gay Male World, 1890–1940* (New York: Basic Books, 1994).

26. Chauncey, Jr., *Gay New York*, pp. 353–354.

27. D'Emilio, "The Homosexual Menace," p. 233.

28. Chauncey, Jr., *Gay New York*. One of his central aims in this work is to argue that the hetero-homosexual binarism is of significantly more recent invention than generally acknowledged.

29. This point is made by Freedman in "'Uncontrolled Desires'."

30. Freedman, "'Uncontrolled Desires'," p. 212.

31. John D'Emilio, in "The Homosexual Menace," points out that there was virtually no evidence supporting McCarthy-era allegations that lesbians and gays were vulnerable to blackmail and hence unsuitable for government employment. He suggests that the massive efforts to counter the "homosexual menace" can only be explained as a result of the Depression and World War II's disruption of family life, gender arrangements, and patterns of sexuality.

32. Freedman, "'Uncontrolled Desires'," and D'Emilio, "The Homosexual Menace."

33. Fear that the child will be sexually molested is one reason for denying *lesbians* custody of their children.

34. Judith Stacey cites one San Francisco study of divorced couples as revealing that one-third of them sustained kinship ties with former spouses and their relatives; *Brave New Families: Stories of Domestic Upheaval in Late Twentieth Century America* (New York: Basic Books, 1990), p. 254. "Divorce-extended" is her term.

35. For an exhaustive discussion of the inadequacies of the one-mother, one-father assumption to both heterosexual and gay/lesbian families see Nancy D. Polikoff, "This Child Does Have Two Mothers," *The Georgetown Law Journal* 78 (1990), 459–575.

36. Stacey, *Brave New Families*.

37. Ibid., p. 17.

38. Kath Weston, *Families We Choose: Lesbians, Gays, Kinship* (New York: Columbia University Press, 1991).

39. Indeed, it has become doubly denaturalized. First, in failing to be repetitively enacted by individuals creating families, the heterosexual, procreative, nuclear family has lost its appearance of being the natural family form. That is, just as gender is "naturalized" through repeated performances (Judith Butler, *Gender Trouble: Feminism and the Subversion of Identity* [New York: Routledge, 1990]), so too one might imagine that the family itself is naturalized through being repetitively enacted. Second, family composition extends well

beyond those "naturally" linked by blood and those whose marital coupling "naturally" issues in progeny.

40. Jeffrey Weeks, "Pretended Family Relationships," in *Against Nature: Essays on History, Sexuality, and Identity* (London: Rivers Oram Press, 1991), p. 143.

41. For 1970s marriage cases, see *Lesbians, Gay Men, and the Law*.

42. Quoted in Jeffrey Weeks, "Pretended Family Relationships," p. 137.

43. Although courts are moving to the assumption that the mother's lesbianism per se is not a bar to her fitness as a parent, this did not prevent the Virginia Supreme Court in the recent case of *Bottoms v. Bottoms* from ruling that, even so, *active* lesbianism on the part of the mother could be a bar to her fitness.

44. John M. Finnis, "Law, Morality, and 'Sexual Orientation'," *Notre Dame Journal of Law, Ethics, and Public Policy* 9 (1995), 11–39, p. 32.

45. Ibid., pp. 32–33.

46. U.S.C. #534, quoted in Robson, "Resisting the Family," p. 981 ftn. 16.

47. Justice White, in *Bowers v. Hardwick* argued that homosexual sodomy is not protected by the right to privacy because, in his view, the right to privacy protects the private sphere of family, marriage, and procreation and he opined that there was no connection between family, marriage, and procreation on the one hand, and homosexuality on the other.

11

Who Takes Care of the Maid's Children?
Exploring the Costs of Domestic Service

Mary Romero

When I was presenting my research on college campuses, students, faculty, and administrators who are the adult children of private household workers sought me out to share their accounts of domestic service. Having never been confronted with the attitudes of their mother's employers in a public setting, they were almost always surprised and shocked to hear their colleagues or professors speak from the standpoint of employers of private household workers. Their initial reaction was a response to employers' paternalizing claims that workers received various hidden benefits from the occupation, such as the opportunities to learn English and the use of modern appliances, or the claims that their cleaning lady was just like "one of the family." Their next response was a recollection of the physically hard work of domestic service, the low pay, and the impact the occupation had on their families. Their stories provide the answer to the question: Who takes care of the maid's children when she is taking care of the mistress's children?

In my book *Maid in the U.S.A.*, I identified elements of paid and unpaid labor and explored the work experiences of Chicana private household workers, particularly the structure of domestic work as manual, mental, and emotional labor. I argued that the work became genderized and racialized through everyday interactions between employer and employee. An analysis of the structure of the work pointed to ways in which women employers shift the burdens of sexism onto women employees. However, the cost of maintaining the privileges of a middle-class, patriarchal lifestyle is paid not only by private household workers. The women's families also pay a price. This essay explores the impact of domestic service on the workers' families.

I conducted seventeen interviews with persons affiliated with higher education whose mothers worked in domestic service.[1] All of the interviewees' mothers worked as day workers and four also had experience as live-in workers. Nine of the interviewees were women and eight were men. I interviewed six African Americans (four men and two women) and two Caribbean women. The others were Latino; six were Mexican American (five women and one man), and the others were either Salvadorean, Nicaraguan, or Costa Rican (all men). They ranged in age from their early twenties to mid–forties.

Exploring domestic service from the perspective of the workers' children provides insights into the hidden costs of maintaining the white, middle-class, patriarchal ideal of the American family; revealing the domino effects of domestic service on the workers' children. Before describing specific working conditions that affect private household workers' families, I will discuss arrangements workers made for their own child care and household labor.

Reproductive Labor in the Private Household Workers' Families

Like other mothers employed outside the home, private household workers are faced with the problem of child care. Unless older children or relatives are available, the worker has only two alternatives: leave them home alone, or take them to work. William Taylor, an African-American child in the 1950s in Cleveland explains:

> I remember going there [employer's house] and it was a fancy place. Kind of impressive and a lot of work. . . . I just tried to stay out of the way. I only went on days in which, you know, for some reason I couldn't go to school or was home alone.

Six of the interviewees who accompanied their mothers to work recall spending time with the employer and their family. Growing up in Pittsburgh in the '50s, Alex Conrad recalled that he and his brother spent time with his mother's employer participating in a children's television program:

> It was bizarre. This woman was an artist and had a kid's TV show. Saturday morning was her thing, she was one of the co-hosts, and just sort of took us in. We were in the studio audience for this show where she would sit and interview us. We did this kind of thing periodically. We must have done this three or four times. She would pick us up and take us places . . . bought us Christmas trees and it was sort of a fun relationship. I got to do some things that little black kids from the projects didn't get to do, because this white lady would come and take us places.

And then suddenly it just sort of stopped and I never had any idea of what became of it. My mother's interpretation of it years later was that when we started getting a little more—because my mother was quite frugal and little things, would try to build on things—that suddenly this woman wasn't as interested in us when we weren't as needy. So it was almost as if little successes drove her away.

The interpretation of the employer's action suggests that Alex and her brother no longer functioned to enhance and affirm the employer's self-perception as kind and generous. This explanation is consistent with perceptions reported by other domestics.[2]

There were times when bringing children to work became part of the job. One African-American male and one Latina remembered when their mothers' employers requested that they bring their children to work to play with their children or grandchildren. Edward Miller grew up in South Carolina in the '40s and he recalled an employer who expected him to play with his youngest child. He felt the request reduced him to a toy for the employer's son:

> As a child I met the children of a couple that my mother was working for and the little boy, Danny, who was about, I guess I must of been about eight years old, and Danny was about six and a little spoiled brat, and he—I was his pickaninny and he just wanted to play with me. So anytime he would act up or demand what he wanted, my mother would call me or my father to come and get me, "Danny wants to play with you," so I would come over and I would play with the kid. Danny was the little brat who saw me as a huge big black toy, you know, to play with.

Growing up in Los Angeles in the '70s, Rosa Garcia's mother received similar requests to bring her daughter to work:

> They had a granddaughter and so they asked me to spend the night. The granddaughter asked me to spend the night and I did. And my mom was gonna pick me up the next day cause she had apartments to do in that building and stuff. . . . What a nightmare that was. I really don't know why she [granddaughter] got so mad at me. She was really mad at me. And when her sister came over I could hear them talking about me. So it was just waiting for my mother to pick me up. It was a horrible experience. Really bad.

Two male and one female interviewee were separated from their mothers for a period of time. Edward Miller's mother left their home in the South during an economic crisis to take a job as a live-in domestic in New York. His father was unemployed, and higher-paying domestic jobs in

New York were attractive enough to separate the family for a time. Ricardo Olivas, a Latino growing up in San Francisco in the '50s, was also separated from his mother while she took a live-in position. Although she was a single mother and her relatives had not yet immigrated to the United States, she was able to find affordable care in a boys' school for her two sons:

> When she lived as a maid we had to go to boarding school because she couldn't keep us . . . but we would come and stay occasionally with her.

Like many Caribbean children of live-in workers, Sophia Cliff was separated from her mother until Ms. Cliff received a green card and was able to bring her children to New York City. In Sophia's case, the separation lasted four years.

> I didn't see her [mother] at all because she couldn't travel. We didn't get to see her until she came that year in '89. When she left I had just turned twelve and when she came back, I was sixteen, going on seventeen. . . . I wrote her a lot and she wrote me back sometimes. She send like a lot of barrels and packages and clothes and money and all that stuff because my grandmother doesn't work so she had to send us money and stuff to take care of us.

Live-in conditions had the most drastic impact on the family, usually separating mother and child for months and even years. Day work was less disruptive and provided working mothers with some opportunity to care and nurture their own children.

More than half of the interviewees were cared for by relatives or siblings, particularly African Americans from the South and second-generation Chicanos who were more likely to live near relatives:

> I remember staying with neighbors, with my grandmothers for awhile, with other neighbors and stuff before I started first grade because my mother was working as a domestic. (Edward Miller)

> My uncle and my aunt came from Mexico to live and they moved into one of the back apartments. So I think that was a big help too for her [mother] cause my aunt would take care of my brother. When he'd come home from school she'd give him something to eat and stuff. So that helped out. So it sort of worked out kind of within the family. (Rosa Garcia)

Older children frequently were responsible for caring for their younger brothers and sisters:

Basically I took care of the kids and stuff. So I was a very young mother myself. Because I was in second grade. I think Tomas [brother] must have been in kindergarten. He was still very young when she [mother] started working. And how it worked out was that we were in school most of the day and then we would get home like at three o'clock and she would get home like at five o'clock. So there was never long periods where she wasn't around. (Rosa Garcia)

If the children were old enough to go to school they frequently spent a few hours alone before their mothers returned from work. During this time, they were expected to contribute to housecleaning. Rosa Garcia described her work and how the allocation of tasks changed to include her father when her mother's work schedule extended into the evenings:

I was responsible for all the housework. Except my sister Josephina and I would—we would draw little papers of who gets what [the household chores to do]. So she did that. But I did the cooking because she couldn't cook and stuff. And I was like the supervisor. Whatever she cleaned I had to make sure it was right because my mother, given what she does, was a perfectionist about it. And my father would do some of the cooking too occasionally, like if my mother would serve parties at night [and wasn't home to cook].

For Edward Miller, an African American growing up poor during the '50s in the South, the labor not only included housecleaning but also chopping wood:

But that work had to be done and so you know you thought about it. I mean in class, when school was out at two o'clock, you went right home because you knew you had this work to be done. And of course if it wasn't done, if your parents came home, my mom came home at five, my dad at five-thirty, if this work wasn't done, you caught hell. I mean you got whippings. You actually got whippings so you knew the work that had to be done, the wood had to be chopped. The wood box had to be full.

Reproducing the gendered division of household labor was not limited to the separation between work in the house and outside the house, but extended to the allocation of workload and responsibility. Daughters were more likely to take over the majority of the housecleaning in their mothers' absence. The responsibility of domestic labor, child care, or cooking was never shifted to the male children; however, in several households, the oldest daughter was expected to take over the work and "be the mom." A similar account appears in Elaine Bell Kaplan's writings: "As the oldest daughter I acted as the substitute mother. At the age of 12, I was scolding and bossing my brothers and sisters."[3]

Unlike the employers' children, who were free to participate in after-school activities, most of the domestics' children had to return home and do housework or child care. Growing up in Arizona in the '50s, Antonia Zamora recalled the limitations housework had on her extracurricular activities:

> I tried it [to get involved with activities at school] one year in my eighth grade. And I got into what was our drill team, that's it. They were just starting up a drill team for girls and I tried it for a while but they [parents] kept saying you need to come home because this needs to be done and that has to be done and you can't stay after school to practice, blah, blah, blah. So I missed too many times so I finally dropped out. It wasn't worth it. And then I didn't get involved again with the school until I was in high school and I think I was in my sophomore year.

A recurring theme throughout the interviews was the relationship between the kind of parenting the children received and their mothers' paid housework and child care. Working conditions had an impact not only on the economic status of the employee's family, but also on social relationships within the family. Long workdays filled with strenuous labor resulted in household workers having fewer hours and less energy to mother their own children. Under these conditions, parenting becomes a privilege and is secondary to the basic need to provide financially for the child. Attending school meetings and activities, as well as spending "quality time" with the children, competes with the paid labor household workers do for employers and their families. The major factor was the time their mothers had to spend with them. As Edward Miller noted:

> I only experienced her [mother] from I guess 5:30 to 8:00 at night, for three hours of the day, because we had to go to bed at that time, at eight or eight-thirty at night and the little white kids got to benefit from her all day.

Time spent with their mothers decreased with the demands made by employers, and parenting became a privilege. The feeling that they were competing with the employer and her children for their mothers' time remained long after childhood:

> When I go home now and I bump into some of these kids who knew my mother when she was [working]—you know—it's still a first name basis. Oh yes, Darlene, I know your mother, oh she raised me and all that you know. I want to say yeah she raised me too you know. (Edward Miller)

An employers' labor was transferred to the domestic's home in a variety of ways. The most common extension of the work was phone calls requesting advice or information about the whereabouts of employer's belongings. Having the worker do the ironing in her own home not only extended the length of the working day but shifted the cost of equipment and electricity. Workers sometimes cared for employers' children in their homes, especially when the employers left town for the weekend. Requests to do cooking also blurred divisions between work and family. Sal Lujan remembers his mother cooking Mexican food for her employer's party in Texas:

> They've asked her to make Mexican food and they give her a lot of money. They paid like sixty bucks or something. They give her sixty bucks and she'd make tamales or something like that, and plus she tells them "you have to buy everything." So they buy everything and she gets to make the whole thing at home.

Although Sal viewed sixty dollars as a lot of money, he did not calculate the value of his mother's time or the expense for providing cooking utensils and equipment.

A few of the interviewees had firsthand experience doing paid housework. Some began working with their mothers as children and continued as adolescents during vacations and summers. Antonia Zamora described the tasks her mother assigned her and the precautions taken:

> I would go with her maybe during the summer. I would go with her maybe an afternoon or a full day. But I still had to stay in an area of the house where the valuables were not there. Like in the kitchen or in the family room or something like that. And yes, I would help clean up a little bit. Like dusting, those kinds of things. But that's basically all. I couldn't roam around the house. I remember that. I couldn't roam around the house. And I had to stay confined to certain areas.

Rosa Garcia recalled that working with her mother in Los Angeles was one way to earn extra money.

> But then I did it pretty consistently during Christmas vacations. And my sister and I, Josephina, the second oldest, would fight about whose turn it was to work with my mom because that's how we would make our Christmas money to buy people gifts.

Male children were more likely to be hired by the employers to mow the lawn and to do other yard work. William Taylor was employed to do yard work in Cleveland in the '50s.

I used to go and do yard work for people. I wasn't good at it so it didn't last for long. They used to say, "Well your son if he wants to work, he can come over on the weekend and cut the grass," and stuff like that. I did that three or four times. I didn't like it and I didn't want to do it. . . . I remember going to these big houses and the grass—the yards were too large and too much work. I didn't want to do it. I was about in the seventh and eighth grade I remember, doing it.

After leaving home, some found themselves occasionally working with their mothers in order to have more time for family activities. For instance, Luis Chavez described working with his mother while on leave from the Army in the early '80s.

I went with her to help her clean so we could get it done faster because I wanted to spend more time with her. So I didn't get paid or anything.

All of the interviewees voiced a dislike of domestic service. As Gloria Salas stated:

It was boring and it was, it really is a lonely job. And when I was younger in junior high I used to go a lot more than I did in high school. And my mom would tell me, "Oh, just dust." Because she never had me do anything harsh, never. Like the worst I did I think was maybe mop the kitchen floor and vacuum. But all she had me do was dusting. And I never liked it because it was hard work and sometimes the employers would be at home.

Luis Chavez felt the stigma of serving others, and attempted to protect his dignity:

I went into the house. I just detached myself from whose house it was. I didn't put a face to any of the people there. I just followed her instructions as to what she wanted done and did it. Get it out of the way and get out of the house.

Three of the interviewees recalled replacing their mothers' labor when necessary. For instance, Antonia Zamora filled in as a live-in when her mother was called home to nurse her grandfather. Her experiences are typical of situations reported by live-in workers:[4]

My grandfather got sick during the time when she [mother] was in Malibu [working]. And I graduated and I had to take her place for the next two weeks. It was very lonely [laughs] because all I did was take care of the kids. I didn't have to cook. I mostly took care of the kids. I cleaned up. It was lonely because I didn't have anybody to pal around with or anyone to really talk to. I talked with them once in a while. And there wasn't a daily conversation. You know mostly it was dealing with the children. And that's basically all there was.

Child care and cleaning were not the only kind of labor the children replaced. The two Latino interviewees who grew up in live-in situations in Los Angeles performed emotional labor for the employer. For example, Jim Trevino described the companionship he provided the employer in his mother's absence:

> I think to a large extent I filled a lot of the companion role. She had some boyfriends and sometimes she'd break up and she'd feel really bad. And she likes to go out and she had no one to go out with so I'd go out with her. To movies and stuff. She'd feel bad. She wanted to talk to somebody. She was in therapy from the time I was a teenager on. But sometimes she just wanted to talk to somebody else and she could talk to me a lot. And I'm sure she talked to my mother also when I was away to school [college] or something like that.

Through the paid and unpaid physical and emotional labor that household workers' children did for employers, they served in the reproduction of the middle-class family. The children were ascribed the same status as their mothers, and were treated as a source of cheap labor for housecleaning, yard work, baby-sitting, and companionship. The interaction not only reproduced the gendered relationships in the "American family," but also class and race relations.

Rituals and Everyday Practices in Domestic Service

Almost all of the interviewees expressed discomfort with the interaction their mothers had with the employers' children. They reported that their mothers spent an enormous amount of time with the employers' children and participated in activities they considered parenting, and thus crossed the bounds of paid child care. As Edward Miller concluded:

> She [mother] actually raised their kids. And she knew more about what was going on in their lives than they did.

William Taylor similarly perceived the employer's requests crossing the line into parenting.

> My mother took care of these kids. I think the girl and I were the same ages, and I used to go over once in a while. This woman [employer] just kind of turned over her house to my mother and she ran it. This woman kind of depended on her [mother] for all these little things in life that

we normally take care of. But she [mother] just kind of took over the house, took over the kid. She [employer] would say, "Look, could you take the kid out"—I don't remember the kid's name—"and get clothes, school clothes." So then my mother would get in the car and they'd go out and she'd buy her school clothes for the year. She [employer] would leave them money to buy school clothes for the year.

Conflicts between the worker and her children frequently resulted when the employer increased the amount of child care, sometimes requesting her do the child care in her own home. Luis Chavez recalled that the employer's children occasionally spent the night:

And now it's taken a strange twist. During football season the admiral [employer] flies in his children for a big football party and while they're at the football games, all of his children's children, the young kids, are at the house and my mother's there baby-sitting them. Still to this day.

Interviewees were concerned with the respect that employers' adolescent children showed when interacting with their mothers:

I heard stories of how older people, high school age interacted with her. The younger children were more like she was a baby-sitter and they basically had to do what she said. And I think she had more control over them because she took them out of their environment and put them in her house. But the high schoolers I think were a lot more rude to her. Thinking that she didn't have any power over them. (Luis Chavez)

As they got older their attitude became exceedingly patronizing. That is what I couldn't handle. That was the thing I couldn't handle. . . . And their attitude is just very patronizing. When they really owe her a lot for all she did and sacrificed for them. But I don't know, I guess I don't know how else I would expect them to act. Just a little more respectful, that's all. (Edward Miller)

Domestics' children were keenly aware that the behavior their mothers tolerated from the employers' children was not allowed in their own families:

When the Smiths [employers] weren't home Richard and Jane, Barbara, and Ted [children] would get stoned in their room and my mother would come upstairs and she knew that they were getting high. She smelled the house and she came and said, "Open the windows! Air out the room! And don't leave the house." It was like my mother knew she wasn't going to change them or change the habits or anything. My mother cleaned around their pot. They had a shoe box under the bed with their pot and paper and all the stuff. My mother took it out and cleaned around it and put it back. She never threw it away. Or she'd find it in Ted's pants and she'd go and put where it was suppose to go [in the shoe box under the bed]. . . . I couldn't understand why she just accepted their rules and stuff. (Teresa Guiterrez)

Recognizing the double standard in child-rearing pointed to their mothers' inability to act according to their own values. The experience served to socialize the children to the appropriate behavior within each class and the interpersonal class relationships.

For the most part, employers' children were merely characters in their mothers' stories, but some interviewees remembered meeting the employers' children. Frequently the encounters occurred when the employer drove their mother home or when they were with their fathers picking their mothers up from work. Edward Miller described awkward encounters with the white children his mother was paid to care for:

No we didn't speak. It was like . . . we wanted to . . . we just didn't know what to say or . . . if we did we would be crossing some invisible boundary that we weren't supposed to. So whether they were boys or girls my age, . . . we just kind of stared at each other and that was it you know. No expression. No smile, no ugly faces. Nothing. Just a kind of look like we were both aliens from another planet. And we could see each other but we couldn't understand each other.

The mothers' interaction with the employers' children served to teach her children class differences. Class distinctions were not limited to material possessions but included the privilege of having constant caring and nurturing, and the "deprivation" of not having someone else pick up after you. Recounting her mother's complaints about the employer's child, Linda Duran pointed to the different class expectations that middle-class parents hold and the extra work those expectations meant for her mother:

They're too submissive, you know, the kids run wild. One kid has a room full of stuffed animals. Evidently they're all over the dresser and the bed and the floor and this angers her [mother] because she's got to pick them up to dust underneath it and that sort of thing. "The kid's too damn old to be having all this stuff in there anyway" and "I don't understand why they have to have so many." "The kid is twelve and why do they have to have teddy bears." She decided that the kid's not growing up fast enough. So she does talk about it [the employers children], usually when it affects her work somehow.

Edward Miller told a disturbing story of seeing the employer's son clinging to his mother as she tried to leave work.

> I remember going with my father, I guess I must have been four years old, because I could actually physically stand up on the seat, back then they didn't have car seats and seat belts and all of that, so I would drive with him standing up on the seat, the front seat of this forty-seven Chevy we had, and we went over to the house where my mother worked, the white family that my mother worked for, and this little boy, this little white boy about my age was crying his eyes out because my mother was leaving and I remember feeling a twinge of jealousy and downright anger because I had been taught never to cry when my mother left, because that was something she had to do. So I had already been trained not to express that kind of emotion, "Get use to it! Your mother has to go to work." And here is this little white boy expressing all of this anguish and emotion because my mother was leaving him. My father had gone to pick my mother up from work and she was trying to excuse herself from the little brat and he was crying his eyes out. And I am sitting there watching this and I couldn't cry, I wasn't suppose to cry. So that was the first hint of caste and class differences, and culture and all that.

The children of private household workers may not understand the class and racial hierarchy, but they clearly learned their place in it, as well as their parents' place.

The most common type of interaction between domestics' children and employers was nightly telephone calls. Employers and their families called the workers to inquire about misplaced household items, to renegotiate verbal work contracts, to ask advice and to arrange additional hours. For instance, William Taylor knew the range of phone calls his mother received from employers:

> I remember a lot of the younger women that she would work for would call her for child care—help—"look my baby is this, what do I do?" And so I mean it was kind of like "you're the only person I know that can tell me these things." I remember those kinds of calls. There would be on occasion, as I say . . . someone would call and complain.

Mariah Thomas's mother received similar calls:

> The second couple [my mother worked for], when the woman [employer] got pregnant, she kept on calling my mother. "What should I do? What should I eat? da da da da" to the point where my mom just had to say, "Well it's kinda late, do you mind?" When she [employer] was pregnant she went into a panic. She was calling like eleven, twelve o'clock at night. But usually they [employers] called before eight.

Teresa Gutierrez recalled even the employer's children calling her mother:

> I remember when I was younger, Tommy the [employer's] only son, wore glasses and he used to lose his glasses all the time. He used to call my mother to find out if she knew where his glasses were. I am talking—like ten o'clock at night, after my mother had already gone home and four hours after she had left and Tommy is looking for his glasses. There are many times the [employer] misplaced something. They are completely dependent on my mother!

Intrusion on family life was not the only criticism the children had with the phone calls. They frequently heard employers treat their mothers as inferiors. The accounts provide first-hand knowledge of how linguistic deference dominates the occupation:

> They [employers] were very rude. They were just nasty over the phone. "Well where is she?" One woman in particular, I can't even remember what her name is but my mom would just say, "Oh, she's just crabby. She doesn't mean anything by it." We [siblings] couldn't stand her. I think in fact my little sister told one of these old ladies off one time. I was already gone. I had already moved out of the house. But I think she did that. It's like they owned her or something. It's strange. That they could call at any hour and be you know nasty and demand you know to know where she is. It was horrible. (Rosa Garcia)

In phone calls children learned that the employer referred to their mother by her first name while the employer was always "Mrs." A child growing up in Pittsburgh in the '50s, raised to refer to adults as Mr. and Mrs., Alex Conrad was shocked to hear the employer's son refer to his mother in a familiar manner:

> I can remember my reaction of calling my mother at one job she was on and a kid answered the phone and I asked for Mrs. Conrad. I heard this kid, who had to be my age, call my mother by her first name.[5]

Elizabeth Carter grew up in New York in the '50s and heard her mother treated as inferior:

> I don't remember them [employer] calling her Mrs. Carter at all. It was always Jessie and she was always the girl. I remember her saying she didn't like that when they called her the girl or my girl—that's the sense of attachment that they tried to make out of it.

Latino children learned that employers changed their mothers' names for their convenience. Some employers anglicized names:

> This is such a joke with my sister. We'd always say, "Is Molly home?"
> It's Amalia [mother's name]. But of course they can't pronounce it so
> they call her Molly. (Rosa Garcia)

Gloria Salas noted the common employer practice of referring to all Latina
domestic workers as Maria.

> Judith [employer] would call Mom Maria. My mom would always say,
> "My name is Laura, not Maria." And I remember one time I went to go
> help at Judith's place and she goes, "Maria, how's school?" And I im-
> mediately told her, "My name's Gloria, not Maria."

Phone calls revealed other aspects of the relationship, exposing manipulative aspects of the interpersonal dynamics in the employee-employer relationship. For instance, Alex Conrad was present when an employer called
his mother to request that she work on the holidays. The employer pressured
Alex's mother by implying she owed her a debt.

> This judge [employer] I mentioned, he was instrumental in our lives.
> My brother got a scholarship to college because he pulled strings. My
> brother's very bright, but it helped that he could pull some strings. But
> years later [the judge was dead], this woman [judge's wife] would call
> my mother and say, "Would you come out on Saturday and work." One
> time she called, it happened that we were home for the holidays, and I
> got angry and my brother got angry and said, "No. We don't want you
> to go." And this woman would invoke, "After all the judge did for
> you." Our response was, "Tell her that your son the college professor
> and your son the lawyer said that we want you home for the holidays
> and not going out cleaning her house." There was this real tension be-
> tween just the fact that we felt that early on, but we could play her elit-
> ist games now and argue back. My mother felt obligation and she felt
> bad for this woman.

The most widely practiced ritual in domestic service is giving discarded
items to employees. All but one interviewee had memories of their mothers bringing home old clothes, furniture, books or leftover food. Several interviewees, like Jim Trevino, noted the importance of the old clothes
during periods of economic crisis.

> I know that a lot of these people [employers] you know as time went by
> didn't want their clothes anymore. They would want to throw them
> away. And sometimes she'd [mother] ask for them. After a while they
> were just given to her. And I wore some of those clothes. Especially
> when Alice [live-in employer] wasn't paying my mom. And my mom

was doing day work. I think that was part of her way to supplement the cost of things that I needed. (Jim Trevino)

In the following quote, Edward Miller captures the reality of needing the clothes, while recognizing the symbolism of old clothes from employers who paid low wages and no benefits:

> I had to wear that garbage [laugh]. That happened quite a bit, hand-me-downs, old clothes, secondhand presents. You could tell that they were things—ashtrays and stuff—that they probably got from their rich relatives and couldn't use them, so they rewrapped them and gave them to my mom. My mom would bring that stuff home. We did pick through those clothes to see what we could use because we damn sure needed them but it wasn't anything that we were proud of, even back then we had pride—we knew where it was coming from—Salvation Army stuff like that, it wasn't no buffalo exchange where it was kind of neat, you know, like after the sixties—to wear these Annie Hall stuff, and to have the kind of worn clothes to identify with the downtrodden. We were not romanticizing being poor. Not at all. No. That stuff was secondhand. We knew it was secondhand. It was worn. It had the smell of someone else's sweat in it no matter how many times you washed it. It was a statement about your class. It was a statement about your economic level and it was a statement about who was keeping you there and so we weren't at all happy about it at all.

Hidden Costs of Reproducing Families

The experiences of the domestics' children raise several issues affecting families in middle-class as well as working-poor households with mothers employed outside their homes. The time children and mothers share together during the week may average as little as two or three hours a day; and during the week, as well as the weekend, some of this time is filled with mothers doing cooking, laundry, cleaning, shopping, and other family chores. In both classes, a child may be expected to help her or his mothers in her "double day"; and the work is frequently accomplished without the assistance of paternal labor. Affordable child care is a problem for all employed mothers, particularly for women working full-time, or overtime, or having long commutes. Arranging family schedules around an eight- to ten-hour workday and a four- to five-hour schoolday, with doctor appointments and school activities is a challenge for working mothers in manufacturing, service, and professional occupations. Middle-class working mothers may even take their children to work with them or arrange for them to be hired for the summer. However, domestic labor and child care are shaped by the economic status of the family, resulting in significant differences that reproduce the different class positions of working-poor and middle-class families.

While not all middle-class families hire private household workers, their purchasing power alters the fundamental nature of the employed mothers' "double day," as well as the quality of work that her children do. For example, laundry is drastically different when a family owns a washer and dryer, has dress shirts washed and ironed and dress clothes dry cleaned at the cleaners. The task is qualitatively altered if the employed mother has to take clothes to the laundromat or washes clothes by hand. Asking children to help with the laundry may also not involve the same experience. Removing the clothes from the dryer and folding them while watching TV or doing homework at home is different from waiting in a crowded laundromat for the next available dryer. The different options available for preparing meals similarly illustrate how family purchasing power shapes the work. Unlike employed mothers among the working poor, middle-class employed mothers have a wide variety of options that range from cooking a meal from scratch, to using prepackaged food, buying take-out, or eating at a restaurant.

Child care options are also significantly different. The quantity and quality of licensed and unlicensed day care facilities and home care arrangements are largely determined by the parent's income. More centrally and often overlooked, middle-class neighborhoods are specifically constructed with recreational facilities that are safe and available; poor neighborhoods are not. In middle-class neighborhoods, there are parks and bike paths, school yards are safe and supervised after hours, and it is easier for neighbors to "keep an eye on" the children. Middle-class parents have the disposable income to purchase a wide range of educational and social activities, such as lessons (tennis, swimming, piano, dancing), clubs, and associations. Low-income families do not have the money to afford these educational and social activities. Leaving older children in charge of their younger siblings for a few hours in the afternoon is an option used by many working mothers regardless of class; however, the decision to do so in a high crime area is more likely to be made because the family has no other options. For the working poor these are not cost-benefit decisions but rather zero-sum games.

Although an increasing number of middle-class families are hiring private household workers to clean their house two to four times a month, many middle-class families choose not to spend their disposable income in this way. Families not purchasing cleaning services must distribute the household labor, and this includes the children. Based on resources and the value system of the family, children may even "earn" an allowance for their contribution. The inclusion of children in the division of household labor is sometimes used as a lesson to teach responsibility. However, middle-class families are not likely to assign cooking, cleaning, or child care duties *at the expense of* school or other educational and sport activities. Nor are their work demands likely to jeopardize middle-class notions of childhood. When families depend on the reproductive labor of children, issues surrounding the division of labor are not optional and may indeed take priority over extracurricular activities.

The options of having children help with housework, and the related issue of "taking the children to work," are central in my analysis. They reveal cleavages and critical symbolic differences between working mothers in white-collar positions or the professions who ask their daughters to pitch in and help do the vacuuming, dusting, and scrubbing the kitchen floors, and working mothers who clean and scrub houses for a living. Daughters of domestics see their mothers' labor and perceive domestic work as a real possibility in their own life. Simultaneously, they are deeply aware of the shame and stigma attached to the occupation. For these working mothers, "taking their daughters to work" carries very different messages from working mothers employed as secretaries, much less college faculty, lawyers, or managers. For the latter, colleagues welcome the children and encourage them to follow in their mother's footsteps. Daughters of the middle class are unlikely to observe their mothers on their hands and knees scrubbing someone else's floor, much less being patronized or treated as inferior. In these ways "taking our daughters to work" has multiple and contradictory meanings; it assists in the reproduction of class relations. It is an empowering event for some, and a ritual of degradation for others. Children's memories of their mothers' employment forces us to look more closely at the impact that parental working conditions have in shaping, limiting, and creating options for doing the everyday work of maintaining the family.

Acknowledgments

An earlier version of this paper was presented at the Pacific Sociological Association Meeting in San Diego, April 15–17, 1994. I want to thank Eric Margolis and Shelly Kowalski for their editorial comments.

Notes

1. While the sample is not necessarily representative of the children of private household workers, interviews with adults who have experienced social mobility capture the "view from inside" as well as a "view from both sides." For a more detailed description of the experiences of a child "living in" with her mother, see Romero, "Cuentos From a Maid's Daughter: Stories of Socialization and Cultural Resistance," *Latino Studies Journal* 4, No. 3 (1993), 11–22. "Life as the Maid's Daughter: An Exploration of the Everyday Boundaries of Race, Class and Gender," in *Feminisms in the Academy*, ed. Domna C. Stanton and Abigail J. Steward (Ann Arbor: University of Michigan Press, 1995), pp. 157–179.

2. See Shellee Colen, "With Respect and Feelings: Voices of West Indian Domestic Workers in New York City," in *All American Women: Lines That Divide and Ties That Bind*, ed. Johnetta B. Cole (New York: Free Press, 1986), pp. 46–70; Judith Rollins, *Between Women* (Philadelphia: Temple University

Press, 1985); Mary Romero, *Maid in the U.S.A.* (New York, Routledge, 1992); Julia Wrigley, *Other People's Children* (New York: Basic Books, 1995); Bonnie Thornton Dill, *Across the Boundaries of Race and Class: An Exploration of Work and Family among Black Female Domestic Servants* (New York: Garland Publishing, 1994); Evelyn Nakano Glenn, *Issei, Nisei, War Bride* (Philadelphia:Temple University Press, 1986).

3. Jacklyn Cock also comments on the mother-daughter relationship among domestics and the pressure placed on the female children to assume the responsibility. She notes that this frequently forced the eldest female child to "relinquish the opportunity of going to school and stay home." *Maids and Madams: A Study in the Politics of Exploitation* (Johannesburg: Raven Press, 1980).

4. See Grace Chang, "Undocumented Latinas: The New 'Employable Mothers'," in *Mothering: Ideology, Experience, and Agency*, ed. Evelyn Nakano Glenn, Grace Chang, and Linda Rennie Forcey (New York: Routledge, 1994), pp. 259–286; Colen, "With Respect and Feelings"; Romero, *Maid in the U.S.A.*; Wrigley, *Other People's Children*.

5. In her study of domestics and employers in the South, Susan Tucker interviewed several daughters. Martha Calvert, the daughter of a domestic worker, recounted a story similar to Alex Conrad's. "I couldn't understand why some woman that called my mamma—and I could tell by her voice, she got to be younger than my mother—called Mama by her first name. I got a spanking in the first grade for that—because I corrected a white lady that called my mama Joanne. I told her, 'You sound the age of one of my sisters, so I think my mother's name is Mrs. Perdue to you.'" *Telling Memories among Southern Women: Domestic Workers and Their Employers in the Segregated South* (Baton Rouge: Louisiana State University Press, 1988), p. 39.

Bibliography

Chang, Grace, "Undocumented Latinas: The New 'Employable Mothers,'" in *Mothering: Ideology, Experience, and Agency*, ed. Evelyn Nakano Glenn, Grace Chang, and Linda Rennie Forcey (New York: Routledge, 1994), pp. 259–286.

Cock, Jacklyn, *Maids and Madams: A Study in the Politics of Exploitation* (Johannesburg: Raven Press, 1980).

Colen, Shellee, "With Respect and Feelings: Voices of West Indian Domestic Workers in New York City," in *All American Women: Lines That Divide and Ties That Bind*, ed. Johnnetta B. Cole (New York: Free Press, 1986), pp. 46–70.

Coley, Soroya Moore, "'And Still I Rise': An Exploratory Study of Contemporary Black Private Household Workers," Ph.D. diss., Bryn Mawr College, 1981.

Dill, Bonnie Thornton, *Across the Boundaries of Race and Class: An Exploration of Work and Family among Black Female Domestic Servants* (New York: Garland Publishing, 1994).

Glenn, Evelyn Nakano, *Issei, Nisei, War Bride: Three Generations of Japanese American Women in Domestic Service* (Philadelphia: Temple University Press, 1986).

Kaplan, Elaine Bell, "'I Don't Do No Windows': Competition Between the Domestic Worker and the Housewife," in *Competition: A Feminist Taboo?*

ed. Valerie Miner and Helen E. Longino (New York: Feminist Press, 1987), pp. 92–105.

Rollins, Judith, *Between Women: Domestics and Their Employers* (Philadelphia: Temple University Press, 1985).

Romero, Mary, *Maid in the U.S.A.* (New York: Routledge, 1992).

———, "Cuentos From a Maid's Daughter: Stories of Socialization and Cultural Resistance," *Latino Studies Journal* (1993) 4(3), pp. 11–22.

———, "Life as the Maid's Daughter: An Exploration of the Everyday Boundaries of Race, Class and Gender," in *Feminisms in the Academy*, ed. Domna C. Stanton and Abigail J. Steward (Ann Arbor: University of Michigan Press, 1995), pp. 157–179.

Sennett, Richard and Jonathan Cobb, *The Hidden Injuries of Class* (New York: Vintage Books, 1973).

Tucker, Susan. *Telling Memories among Southern Women: Domestic Workers and Their Employers in the Segregated South* (Baton Rouge: Louisiana State University Press, 1988).

Wrigley, Julia, *Other People's Children* (New York: Basic Books, 1995).

Part V

Families and Medicine

12

Child Abuse and Neglect:
Cross-Cultural Considerations

Françoise Baylis and Jocelyn Downie

In many countries the world over, the view that it is acceptable for parents to indenture, trade, sell, beat, starve or abandon their children has changed and changed quite dramatically over the last several decades. Consistent with the United Nations' *Convention on the Rights of the Child*, many jurisdictions have taken:

> legislative, administrative, social and educational measures to pro-
> tect . . . |children| from all forms of physical or mental violence, injury
> or abuse, neglect or negligent treatment, maltreatment or exploitation,
> including sexual abuse.[1]

These measures typically prohibit practices that were once common but are now considered abusive or neglectful; they also establish minimum standards for parenting to help ensure that children are protected from harm.

Responsibility for ensuring that children have the opportunity to grow and develop in safe and healthy environments rests first with the parents, and second with the state. Parents, alone or in concert with others (such as family members, teachers, spiritual advisers, and health care providers), are expected to promote their children's well-being. Failure to do so invites state intervention—the state may not only suspend or permanently trans-fer the parents' custodial rights, but may also prosecute the parents, de-pending upon the nature and severity of the child abuse or neglect.

The state, however, is often loath to exercise its *parens patriae* authority and "act as a parent" in cases of suspected child abuse or neglect. In a liberal pluralistic society, state intervention is problematic when behaviors considered abusive or neglectful from the perspective of the dominant group fall within nondominant ethnic, cultural, or religious boundaries of acceptability.

This essay focuses narrowly on cross-cultural conflict that arises in a North American context between non-Western cultural communities and the dominant Western cultural community. It takes seriously the view of Edmund Pellegrino[2] and others that there is a *prima facie* obligation to respect diverse cultural beliefs and values.

The classic definition of culture is that offered by the social anthropologist Sir Edward Tylor: "that complex whole which includes knowledge, belief, art, morals, law, custom and any other capabilities and habits acquired by man [sic] as a member of society."[3] A contemporary reformulation of this definition defines culture as that "complex range of beliefs, values, and attitudes shared and perpetuated by members of a social group."[4] Both definitions imply that culture is learned (not inherited), and shared (not individual property).

In addition, culture is not static. This feature is captured by Clifford Geertz in his definition of culture as:

> an historically transmitted pattern of meanings embodied in symbols, a system of inherited conceptions expressed in symbolic forms by means of which men [sic] communicate, perpetuate, and develop their knowledge about and attitudes toward life.[5]

It is now also widely understood that groups, including cultural groups, are not territorially based, spatially bounded, historically unself-conscious, or homogeneous.[6]

A commitment to respecting cultural diversity raises the following questions: What does respect for a people's evolving culture entail? Does respect simply require an understanding of the culture, or does it require that the culture be acknowledged as legitimate, or perhaps even as "intrinsically valuable"? Considered from another perspective, what should be the limits of tolerance and deference to various cultural beliefs or values? Focusing more specifically on the issue of child abuse and neglect, what is an appropriate response to practices that, from the perspective of the dominant cultural community, constitute child maltreatment, but from the perspective of a nondominant cultural community constitute appropriate child treatment? For example, should the response include legally compelling the nondominant cultural community to abolish practices deemed "fundamental" to that community?

This essay focuses narrowly on one aspect of these questions; namely, how to respect the beliefs and values of nondominant cultural communities without thereby contributing to the oppression of vulnerable members of these same communities. Consider the following scenarios:

1. A newborn is bounced and jiggled while riding in a truck over bumpy roads.

2. A 12-year-old girl is kept away from school to care for her two younger male siblings.

3. Parents, aunts, uncles, and neighboring friends repetitively ask a small child, "Why don't you kill your baby brother?" "Why don't you die so I can have your nice new shirt?" ... "Your daddy's no good, shall I stone him to death—like this?"[7]

4. A four-month-old baby is restless, crying, and agitated. The mother responds by burning spots on her baby's stomach.

5. The parents of a three-year-old deaf boy refuse to consent to a cochlear implant for their son.

6. The parents of a young girl seek out a physician to excise their daughter's genitals.

7. The parents of a child who is dying of liver failure refuse to consent to a liver transplant for their child.

Which, if any, of these scenarios constitute(s) child abuse or neglect?

Consider these same scenarios with their respective cultural elements added.

1. A newborn is bounced and jiggled while riding in a truck over bumpy roads. The family lives in a small rural community where the roads are not paved. The child is strapped in a car seat and the parents are not particularly concerned about the "bumpy ride." Women from the neighboring Hawaiian community believe that the *haole* (non-Hawaiian) couple's behavior violates standards of proper child care. They believe the bouncing and jiggling causes *ōpū huli*, a "turned stomach," the symptoms of which resemble colic.[8]

2. A 12-year-old girl is kept away from school to care for her two younger male siblings. Her mother, a Nigerian immigrant, believes that the girl's proper place is in the home and that the responsibility of caring for her younger siblings without adult supervision is important in preparing her for her future role as mother. The mother's coworkers, who are not themselves Nigerian, are angry that this young girl is being denied a formal education.

3. Parents, aunts, uncles, and neighboring friends repetitively ask a small child, "Why don't you kill your baby brother?"

"Why don't you die so I can have your nice new shirt?"...
"Your daddy's no good, shall I stone him to death—like
this?" The Inuit adults initiate these small dramas to "cause
thought" (isumaqsayuq). This sort of questioning is an essential part of the Inuit educational process and is "highly
uniform across Inuit time and space—from West Alaska to
East Greenland, among groups that have not been in contact
for generations or centuries."[9] A nurse recently stationed to
Northern Canada is very concerned about the harmful psychological consequences of such "verbal abuse."

4. A four-month-old baby is restless, crying, and agitated. The
    mother responds by burning spots on her baby's stomach.
    Following a traditional Laotian healing technique aimed at
    the Mien folk illness of Gusia mun toe, she has burned a
    special reed dipped in pork fat and used it to raise blisters
    on her baby's abdomen. A physician who later examines the
    child is concerned about the burns that resulted from the
    mother's use of this traditional healing technique.[10]

5. The parents of a 3-year-old deaf boy refuse a cochlear im-
    plant for their son. The parents, who are members of the
    deaf community, equate "the cochlear implant with 'child
    abuse', 'Nazi experimentation', and 'genocide'."[11] They in-
    sist that deafness is not a disability. In their view, deaf peo-
    ple are members of a distinct cultural community. The
    family's caseworker believes this technology will help the
    boy overcome his disability.

6. The parents of a young girl seek out a physician to excise
    their daughter's genitals. This is an accepted practice in
    Ethiopia, their country of origin. It is routinely practiced to
    prevent sexual activity and provide proof of virginity at the
    time of wedlock. Excision of the genitalia of female children
    is not tolerated in North America, which is where the fam-
    ily now resides.

7. The parents of a child who is dying of liver failure refuse to
    consent to a liver transplant for the child. Organ transplan-
    tation is contrary to the parents' First Nations cultural be-
    liefs and values concerning the role of the Creator and the
    Fundamental Order. The physician who recommends the
    transplant believes that the parents' decision to refuse
    surgery constitutes medical neglect.[12]

Which, if any, of these scenarios constitute(s) child abuse or neglect?
    One extreme position is that none of these cases involves child abuse or
neglect. In this view, determinations of child abuse and neglect are cultur-

ally relative—there are no absolute right or wrong child care practices, but rather child care practices that are "right" for this cultural community and "wrong" for this cultural community given certain widely accepted endogenously derived standards for parenting. The position at the other extreme is that many (perhaps all) of the practices described above are examples of abuse or neglect. In this view, there are universal parenting standards. The problem with the first viewpoint is that complete deference to nondominant cultural communities' understandings of child maltreatment risks abdicating moral responsibility to care for the vulnerable. The problem with the second viewpoint is that it may not be appropriately respectful of nondominant cultural views about the proper treatment of children.

The usual approach to navigating between these extremes of cultural relativism and cultural imperialism involves attempts to specify objective criteria on the basis of which specific parental choices or behaviors might authoritatively be labelled abusive or neglectful. To date, this approach has proven unsuccessful. While there is significant agreement on the *definition* of child abuse and neglect (claims to the contrary notwithstanding), there is no agreement as to which practices are captured by this definition. Child abuse and neglect are terms that name inexcusable harm that has been visited upon children by specific acts of commission or omission—on this there is agreement. Agreement is lacking, however, regarding the criteria upon which specific acts of commission or omission might be deemed inexcusable or harmful. For some, the relevant criterion is the parents' intentions; others focus on the potential and/or actual physical, psychological and emotional consequences; still others are concerned about the nature of the act itself.[13] Abuse involves active mistreatment that results in serious harm. But "harm" according to whom, and "serious" according to whom? Neglect involves a failure to perform an expected or required action. But "expected or required" by whom? The key question is: Who decides, and on what authority, that a specific behavior is abusive or neglectful? There is no easy answer to this question.

A Feminist Reconceptualization

Within and between sovereign states a number of cultural communities usually coexist, some of which are overlapping, and one of which (a numerical majority or a powerful elite) typically exercises power and authority over the others. When parents who claim membership in a nondominant cultural community offer a culturally based justification of child care practices deemed abusive or neglectful by members of the dominant community, the cultural claim must be carefully and critically examined.

In this essay we develop an alternative feminist approach to the problem of cross-cultural conflict in cases of suspected child abuse and neglect, which is grounded in the following beliefs: (1) women and others are oppressed on the basis of one or more morally irrelevant characteristic(s) (gender, as well as race, ethnicity, religion, class, disability, and sexual orientation); and (2) this oppression must be exposed and eliminated. "Oppression" is here defined as an unwarranted reduction in options, or freedom to choose among options, available to members of a group that is defined by one or more morally irrelevant characteristic(s). An "unwarranted reduction" is a reduction that is not the result of nature, free choice, or practices aimed at *redistributive* justice.

The proposed methodology recommends a careful assessment of all culturally based claims offered by parents who are suspected of child abuse or neglect. The objective is to identify those claims which are unavailable, unsustainable, unsubstantiated, inaccurate, or morally indefensible. When parents explain a controversial parenting choice or behavior with reference to the beliefs or values of a nondominant cultural community, the following questions must be asked: Are the parents capable and well-intentioned? If not, a cultural defense is not available to them. Is there a nondominant cultural community to which the parents belong? If not, their cultural claim cannot be sustained. Can the parents provide a full description of the cultural claim? If not, the claim must be substantiated by others. Is the cultural claim advanced by the parents accurate? If not, an accurate account of the cultural beliefs and values must be sought from others. If none of the above conditions obtains, the parents' "cultural" defense of their controversial child care practice can be dismissed without being imperialistic.

On the other hand, if all of the above conditions obtain, a difficult moral question must be confronted; namely, whether the culturally informed practice, accurately understood, should be respected. In this essay we maintain that if the practice is oppressive of an internal marginalized group, the answer to this question must be a resounding no.

To some, the proposed methodology will appear unnecessarily complicated, since the last question seems to be determinative. In our view, however, a narrow focus on the last question misses several opportunities to resolve conflict between dominant and nondominant communities in a manner that does not involve one cultural community dominating the other.

1. Are the Parents Capable and Well-Intentioned?

A few parents are sadistic and they should not be allowed to stand behind a protective shield of culture. For example, a parent who slashes his adolescent son's face with the intention of asserting his authority cannot excuse the injury as ritual scarring.

Other parents are incapable of caring properly for their children due to: (1) an underlying physical or mental disorder; (2) limited financial or social resources; or (3) a general lack of parenting skills that may stem from emotional, physical, or intellectual impairment. They, too, cannot excuse their behavior on cultural grounds. For example, a vegan parent whose child is dehydrated and demonstrates failure to thrive cannot excuse her child's malnourishment on cultural grounds since this is not a necessary consequence of veganism, but rather is the result of the parent's limited knowledge about proper nutrition.

More frequently, however, parents are both capable and well-intentioned. When capable and well-intentioned parents appear to be making independent, culturally informed decisions about what is in their child's best interests, and these decisions are dissonant with the dominant cultural community's understanding of proper child care, further inquiry is necessary.

2. Is There a Nondominant Cultural Community to Which the Parents Belong?

In most instances of suspected child abuse or neglect in which a cultural defense is offered, questions about the existence of a nondominant cultural community will be uncontroversial. In a few cases, however, this issue will be problematic. For example, culture is a concept sometimes used to serve personal, political, or ideological goals. In pursuit of such goals, some will choose to justify their beliefs or actions on cultural grounds, just as others will attempt to strip themselves and/or others of a cultural defense or explanation.

Consider the current controversy about whether deafness is a disability or a common characteristic of members of a minority cultural community within the dominant hearing majority. There are many deaf people who insist that they are members of a unique cultural community with its own values, visual language, social organization, and history. But are the deaf a cultural community? Or, given that culture is learned, are some deaf people members of the deaf cultural community, while others are members of the dominant cultural community? It has been suggested that "a primary prerequisite for being a member of the Deaf Culture is knowing American Sign Language."[14] Is this claim accurate? This issue is of some importance in addressing scenario number 5, in which a young boy's parents refuse a cochlear implant for their son. According to the parents, their consent to the implant would deny their boy his culture and contribute to genocide. According to the dominant cultural community, deafness is a disability, and refusal of the implantation could be considered medical neglect. When addressing this thorny issue, a great deal depends upon whether the deaf are a cultural community, and whether deafness is both a necessary and sufficient condition for membership within this community.

In cases of suspected child abuse or neglect where a cultural defense is offered but there is no nondominant cultural community that informs the cultural claim, then barring other relevant considerations, the dominant community's beliefs and values should prevail. In such cases, cultural imperialism is not at issue; there are not two cultural communities, one of which is imposing its views on the other.

Similarly, if it is unclear whether there is a nondominant cultural community to which the parents belong, then on a balancing of the competing harms and benefits, the parents should be treated as though they were members of the dominant cultural community. The rationale for this conclusion is as follows. If the views of the dominant community are followed and at some later date the existence of the nondominant cultural community to which the parents claimed membership is established, then the harm of cultural insensitivity will have been realized. If there is no such determination, however, then the harm of child abuse or neglect will have been averted. In the face of uncertainty, it is better to risk being culturally insensitive than to risk failing to prevent avoidable harm to a child.

However, if the parents are clearly members of a nondominant cultural community, then an effort must be made to understand the cultural claim they offer in defense of their choices or behaviors.

3. Can the Parents Provide a Full Description of the Cultural Claim?

In some cases of suspected child abuse and neglect, the dominant cultural community will have no knowledge or understanding of the beliefs and values that inform the choices and behaviors of parents of nondominant cultural communities. In other cases, relevant cultural beliefs and values may be *familiar* to members of the dominant community, but may not be *well understood*—consider, for example, the refusal of medically indicated blood transfusions by Jehovah's Witness parents.

Whenever a nondominant cultural community's child care practices conflict with the dominant cultural community's understanding of proper child care, it is imperative that the parents provide a full description of the cultural basis for the controversial practice. This should include a description of the nature and history of the practice, and perhaps also some explanation of the context for the practice. Some information about the relative importance of the practice would also be helpful—specifically, whether the practice is vital to the cultural community or is merely peripheral to it. Perhaps of equal or greater importance is information about whether the practice is contested from within and if so, on what basis.

In some cases parents will not be able to provide a full description. Not all parents will be knowledgeable about the various required elements for a full description as outlined above. In other cases, there will be reason to question the accuracy/validity of the parents' description (for instance, conflicting information is presented, or the mother is silent and defers to the male parent or other male authority figure). In such cases, there is legitimate reason to approach others to understand better the content of the parents' cultural claim, to resolve apparent inaccuracies or contradictions, and to address any lingering concerns.

4. Is the Cultural Claim Advanced by the Parents Accurate?

Cultural claims made by parents in defense of specific parenting choices and behaviors may be inaccurate. For this reason, it is necessary to ascertain whether: (1) the nondominant cultural community to which the parents claim membership actually holds the beliefs ascribed to it by the parents; and (2) whether the parents' interpretation of these beliefs is accurate. To this end, cultural interpreters for the nondominant cultural community, who can explain or make known the expectations of the community, must be identified. Second, as necessary, any conflict between cultural interpreters must be resolved.

(a) Who speaks for the nondominant cultural community? There are two sorts of problems that can arise in attempting to identify who speaks on behalf of a nondominant cultural community—one pragmatic and the other substantive.

The pragmatic problem is that of finding cultural interpreters for the nondominant cultural community. In some cases, no such individuals or groups can be found. For example, consider a case in which a child is in need of emergency lifesaving medical treatment. The parents, recent immigrants to North America, are from a small tribe in a remote part of Africa. They claim that their cultural community opposes the use of any form of Western medicine. It is not possible in the time available to contact the tribal elders (or anyone who has studied the tribe) and ask them about the cultural community's position on the proposed treatment. Also, apart from the parents, there is no one in the immediate vicinity who can speak to the cultural community's beliefs and values. In this situation, there is no one to substantiate the parents' claim that the practice deemed neglectful by the dominant community is culturally mandated. The parents' claim is insufficient. Vulnerable children should not be abandoned in the face of unsubstantiated cultural claims.

The substantive problem is that of determining who, amongst those willing to serve as cultural interpreters for the nondominant cultural community, should be heard. Traditionally, when assessing the legitimacy of cultural interpreters, there has been a bias in favor of those who derive their legitimacy from sources familiar to the dominant cultural community (for example, powerful mainstream political or religious sources of authority). Restricting legitimacy in this way, however, reflects an unacceptable bias. In our view, it is important to recognize culturally specific sources of authority (that is, authority based on endogenously derived norms). For example, in some cultural communities authority is inherited, in others it is inspired, and in still other communities it is delegated by a select subgroup.

As well, there should be a commitment to privilege the views of those who speak for members of internal marginalized groups who have traditionally been deprived of power and voice. Arguably this is essential to ensure that in recognizing the claims of the nondominant cultural community, the dominant community does not thereby contribute to the oppression of vulnerable members of the nondominant community.

(b) Do the cultural interpreters agree on the cultural legitimacy of the practice?
If there is clearly only one cultural interpreter for the nondominant community, then this question does not arise. However, for cases in which there is more than one interpreter, it must be addressed.

Consider, for example, scenario number 7, in which the parents refuse a liver transplant for their child. An attempt to carefully and critically assess the cultural claim offered by the parents in defense of their decision might involve discussion with one or more cultural interpreter(s)—some might insist that the parents' viewpoint is consistent with First Nations beliefs and values; others might say that, although historically sanctioned, the refusal is now considered unacceptable.

One possible strategy for dealing with such conflict would be to compare each cultural interpreter's position on the controversial parental choice or behavior with the parent's position on other cultural practices. Only those interpretations that were internally coherent would be deemed credible. This approach, however, is problematic for at least two reasons.

First, as noted previously, cultural communities are not static. As they evolve, there will be internal inconsistencies between positions on various practices. It follows that coherence is not a necessary feature of culture and so cannot be a necessary feature of any credible cultural interpretation. Geertz is most eloquent on this point:

> coherence cannot be the major test of validity for a cultural description. Cultural systems must have a minimal degree of coherence, else we would not call them systems; and, by observation, they normally have a great deal more. But there is nothing so coherent as a paranoid's delusion or a swindler's story. The force of . . . interpretations cannot rest, as they are now so often made to do, on the tightness with which they hold together.[15]

Internal coherence is not a necessary condition of an accurate cultural interpretation. Views that appear inconsistent should not be discounted solely on this basis.

Second, those who disagree with the beliefs and values of persons more powerful than themselves may not always have their own views consistently developed. Furthermore, those who recognize a problem with, and openly contest, one traditional practice, may not recognize or have the courage to question other problematic practices and so their views may appear inconsistent. For example, early feminists identified sexism but were largely insensitive to problems of racism, ableism, heterosexism, and other forms of discrimination in their own lives and views. They may have appeared less consistent than those who simply asserted dominance and superiority over all "others."[16] These concerns apply strongly to cultural interpreters for nondominant cultural communities, and even more strongly to cultural interpreters for internal marginalized groups within either dominant or nondominant cultural communities.

(c) What is involved in assessing the accuracy of any cultural claim? In addition to establishing whether a practice is deemed to be legitimate by the cultural community, one must also ask whether the parents are proposing to conduct the practice as the cultural community believes it should be conducted.

Consider scenario number 4, in which a Laotian mother burns spots on her daughter's stomach to treat symptoms that resemble colic. There is indeed a traditional Laotian healing technique for *Gusia mun toe*, and the Laotian cultural community does believe that it is legitimate for the mother to treat her baby's restlessness, crying, and agitation with it. However, the mother in this scenario is performing the technique incorrectly. She is burning the baby, while the technique, correctly practiced, does not result in serious burns. Therefore, the mother's cultural claim in defense of her actions is inaccurate.

Consider also scenario number 6, in which parents seek out a physician to excise their daughter's genitals. Some cultural communities that approve of ritual female genital operations only require that the clitoris be nicked; others require removal of the prepuce of the clitoris (Sunna). A third common type of ritual female genital operation involves excision of the clitoris and the labia minora (clitoridectomy); and in its most severe form, the practice involves the excision of the clitoris, the labia majora and minora and sewing up of the vulva (infibulation or Pharaonic circumcision).[17] If the parents are from a cultural community that prescribes ritual Sunna genital operations and yet they want a ritual Pharaonic genital operation, then the parents' cultural claim in defense of their request for the ritual Pharaonic form is inaccurate.

This stage of the analysis requires asking both whether the practice proposed by the parents is seen as legitimate by the cultural community *and* whether the parents are proposing to conduct the practice as the cultural community believes it should be conducted.

d) What should be done? If it is not possible to identify relevant interpreters or to resolve conflict between them, then, on a balancing of the competing harms and benefits, one should proceed as if there were no countervailing cultural claim. The rationale for this conclusion is the same as the rationale for the conclusion regarding action in the face of uncertainty about whether there is a nondominant cultural community—namely, that it is better to err on the side of protecting children.

On the other hand, if it is possible to identify cultural interpreters and to resolve any conflict between them, then the cultural claim advanced by the parents can be compared with the claims advanced by the interpreters.

If these claims are inconsistent, then the parents' claim must be viewed as idiosyncratic, and treated like all other idiosyncratic claims. If the nondominant cultural community does not endorse the parents' position, then again, cultural imperialism is not at issue; there is no conflict between the claims of dominant and nondominant cultural communities.[18]

One final possibility is that the parents' claim is deemed inaccurate, but the nondominant cultural community does endorse a position that is contrary to that of the dominant cultural community. In such a situation, the analysis must proceed on the basis of the revised claim.

5. Is the Cultural Claim, Accurately Understood, One That Should Be Respected?
When it is clear that the parents are capable and well-intentioned, that they are members of a nondominant cultural community, that an accurate cultural claim explains the controversial child care practice, and that that claim conflicts with the views of the dominant cultural community, the question that remains is whether the cultural claim should be respected. A careful assessment of the anticipated consequences of the controversial practice is needed to answer this question. This assessment requires: (1) that the nature of possible conflicting views about consequences be recognized; and (2) that attention be given to more than just the consequences for the discrete child considered separate and detached from any cultural community.

First, it is important to distinguish between disagreement about whether the controversial practice will lead to particular consequences, and disagreement about whether the particular consequences that everyone agrees will likely result from the controversial practice constitute harm. It is important to recognize this distinction because it is often thought that overriding a nondominant cultural community on the second is culturally imperialistic, whereas doing so on the first is not. In our view, this perspective is mistaken. Overriding a nondominant cultural community on the basis of either of these disagreements may be culturally imperialistic; because of recent work in feminist epistemology and philosophy of science we view cross-cultural "factual" disagreements in the same spirit as cross-cultural "value" disagreements.[19]

Reference to the scenarios can help to illustrate this point. First, consider disagreement about whether the controversial practice will lead to particular consequences. In scenario number 1, members of the local community believe that jiggling a newborn will cause *ōpū huli*, while the parents, who are members of the dominant cultural community, do not. In scenario number 3, the parents believe that *isumaqsayuq* will not cause psychological harm, whereas the dominant cultural community believes it will. In scenario number 4, the mother believes that burning spots on her baby's stomach will cure the baby's restlessness, crying, and agitation; the dominant cultural community does not. In all of these examples, conflict is over what consequences will follow particular actions/omissions.

Second, consider disagreement about whether the particular consequences that everyone agrees will result from a controversial practice constitute harm. In scenario number 2, the mother does not believe that entrusting her daughter with the responsibility of caring for her younger siblings is harmful to her; the dominant cultural community does. In scenario number 6 the parents do not believe that excising their daughter's genitals is harmful to her; the dominant cultural community does.

The second important feature of any careful assessment of the consequences of controversial child care practices is the difference in the consequences for the discrete child, the embedded child, and any internal marginalized group of which the child is a member. The discrete child is a child in the abstract—that is, a child stripped of temporal, cultural, familial, geographical, and other characteristics. The embedded child is the particular child in his or her context—that is, a child in a particular time, place, cultural community, and family. An internal marginalized group is a marginalized group within a dominant or nondominant cultural community.

Typically, in an assessment of child abuse, only the consequences for the child are considered and they are considered for the discrete child rather than the embedded child. That is, the consequences for the internal marginalized group are ignored and the particular child in the case at hand is abstracted from his or her context. Because actual children exist only as embedded beings, it is essential to consider the embedded child rather than the discrete child. Because we are opposed to the oppression of women and other vulnerable groups, we also believe that it is essential to consider the consequences for internal marginalized groups.

Consider the practice of clitoridectomy and infibulation, the two most severe forms of ritual female genital operations. If the concern is only with the consequences for the discrete child, then arguably the harms of this practice outweigh the benefits, given the serious consequences experienced by the discrete child, including:

> severe pain, shock, infection, difficulty urinating and menstruating, malformation and scarring of genitalia, physical and psychological trauma with sexual intercourse, bleeding, increased vulnerability to the AIDS virus, difficulty in childbirth, increased risk of sterility and infant mortality.[20]

However, it may be the case that the benefits of ritual female genital operations outweigh the harms when the consequences for the embedded child are considered. Those who prescribe the practice can argue that the medical harms noted above are outweighed by endogenously defined physical, psychological, aesthetic, social, and economic benefits (although each of the claims can be independently critiqued).[21] But if the consequences for women as an internal marginalized group are considered, the harm-benefit ratio shifts again. In its broadest context, ritual female genital operations seriously harm women:

> A group of people can suffer real damage, real distortion, if the people or society around them mirror back to them a confining or demeaning or contemptible picture of themselves. . . . Their own self-depreciation, on this view, becomes one of the most potent instruments of their own oppression.[22]

If a child care practice endorsed by a nondominant cultural community contributes to the continued oppression of an internal marginalized group, the practice must be condemned.

The methodology proposed here clearly will not resolve all potential cross-cultural conflicts, with respect to child abuse and neglect. It will, however, facilitate an analysis of such conflicts, as some cultural claims can be set aside on nonimperialistic grounds because they are either unavailable, unsustainable, unsubstantiated, or inaccurate. In addition, other cultural claims can be dismissed on the grounds that they contribute to the oppression of internal marginalized groups within both the dominant and nondominant cultural communities. This approach, we believe, successfully navigates between the extremes of a standardless cultural relativism and a hegemonic cultural imperialism.

Acknowledgments

Research for this paper was supported in part by a grant from the Social Sciences and Humanities Research Council of Canada for a Strategic Research Network on Feminist Health Care Ethics (SSHRC #806-93-0016). As well, one of us (FB) had research support from the University of Tennessee Professional Development Award Program. Sincere thanks are also owed to Susan Sherwin, Brad Abernethy, and Margaret Lock for helpful comments on an earlier version of this essay.

Notes

1. United Nations, *Convention on the Rights of the Child*, as adopted by the General Assembly of the United Nations on November 20, 1989. Article 19.
2. Edmund Pellegrino, "Intersections of Western Biomedical Ethics and World Culture," in Pellegrino E., Mazarella P., Corsi P., eds., *Transcultural Dimensions in Medical Ethics* (Frederick, Md.: University Publishing Group Inc., 1992), p. 15.
3. Edward Tylor, *Primitive Culture*, Vol. 1 (1871; New York: Harper & Row, 1958), p. 1.
4. Robert Orr, Patricia Marshall, and Jamie Orborn, "Cross-Cultural Considerations in Clinical Ethics Consultations," *Archives of Family Medicine* 4 (1995), p. 159.
5. Clifford Geertz, *The Interpretation of Cultures: Selected Essays* (New York: Basic Books Inc., 1973), p. 89.
6. Arjun Apparudai, "Global Ethnoscapes: Notes and Queries for a Transitional Anthropology," In Richard G. Fox, ed., *Recapturing Anthropology: Working in the Present* (Santa Fe: School of American Research Press, 1991), p. 192.

7. Jean Briggs, "Mazes of Meaning: The Exploration of Individuality in Culture and of Culture through Individual Constructs," in *Psychoanalytic Study of Society*, Vol. 16 (New York: International University Press, 1991), p. 115.

8. Jill Korbin, "*Hana' ino*: Child Maltreatment in a Hawaiian-American Community," *Pacific Studies* 13.3 (1990), p. 19.

9. Jean Briggs, "Mazes of Meaning," pp. 116–117.

10. "Culture, Healing, and Professional Obligations," *Hastings Center Report* 23, 4 (July/August, 1993), p. 15.

11. Amy E. Brusky, "Making Decisions for Deaf Children Regarding Cochlear Implants: The Legal Ramifications of Recognizing Deafness as a Culture rather than a Disability," *Wisconsin Law Review* 235 (1995), pp. 241–242.

12. *Saskatchewan (Minister of Social Services) v. F.P. and L.P.* (April 20, 1990) Arnot Prov. J. (Sask. Prov. Ct.).

13. Natalie Abrams, "Problems in Defining Child Abuse and Neglect," in Onora O'Neill and William Ruddick, eds., *Having Children: Philosophical and Legal Reflections on Parenthood* (New York: Oxford University Press, 1979), p. 156.

14. Amy E. Brusky, "Making Decisions for Deaf Children," p. 240, n. 22.

15. Clifford Geertz, *The Interpretation of Cultures: Selected Essays* (New York: Basic Books Inc., 1973), pp. 17–18.

16. We thank Susan Sherwin for her insights on this point.

17. Stephen A. James, "Reconciling International Human Rights and Cultural Relativism: The Case of Female Circumcision," *Bioethics* 8.1 (1994), pp. 6–7.

18. For the purposes of this essay we assume that the interpreters for the dominant cultural community are the people charged to act as agents for that community with regard to child abuse and neglect (e.g., child welfare agents and the courts).

19. Sandra Harding. *The Science Question in Feminism* (Ithaca, N.Y.: Cornell University Press, 1986).

20. Stephen A. James, "Reconciling International Human Rights," pp. 8–9.

21. For an internal cultural critique of some of these claims, see Stephen A. James, "Reconciling International Human Rights," pp. 8–12.

22. Charles Taylor. *Multiculturalism and "The Politics of Recognition"* (Princeton: Princeton University Press, 1992), pp. 25–26.

13

Gays, Lesbians, and the Use of Alternate Reproductive Technologies

Sidney Callahan

Gays, lesbians, and the use of alternate reproductive technologies is a controversial topic. Should gay and lesbian couples be defined as families? Is it ethical to form a family through collaborative reproduction using third parties? Perhaps so much heat is generated in these controversies because there had been so little consensus in American society on the ethics of responsible parenthood *before* new reproductive technologies and new social movements came upon the scene. In the last thirty years there has been a rapid development of alternate reproductive medical technologies while at the same time the pace of social change has quickened; many women do paid work, families have been stressed by divorce and economic recessions, feminism has evolved, and a gay and lesbian movement has become more assertive. Today more moral reflection and dialogue is needed on the complicated interlocking questions of feminism, families, and reproductive ethics.

Defining the Family

Arguments over how to define the family have been fierce both in and out of feminism. Much of the recent debate in American society has been focused on whether a definition should be employed which would include gay and lesbian couples. Many practical and legal issues, such as insurance benefits, patient decisions, rental and lease requirements, inheritance laws, adoptive policies, custody disputes, and so on, are affected by who is going to be considered a family. Moral approbation and normative status are also implied when one's domestic lifestyle is considered to merit the label of family. Obviously different cultures and subcultures define the boundaries of family differently, manifesting a variety of kinship arrangements classified as the stem family, the conjoint family, the extended family, the symmetrical or asymmetrical family, and other variants.[1] Today in America, because of divorce and remarriages, we also have blended and reconstituted families, made up of stepparents, half-siblings, and other relationships that do not yet have kinship labels.

Another complication arises from the fact that all families are always developing through time and the reproductive life cycle. Particular families are in the process of being established, expanding, dividing through fission, and declining through death.[2] A picture drawn of a particular family in early formation may look very different from later versions in an established household, or later still, when fission has taken place and the original family members die. The "family of origin" is defined as the family into which one is born and the "family of procreation" has been the term for the family that a person forms in adulthood. But suppose there is no procreation of children? Is a couple living alone still a family? Should a family be synonymous with a household? Many households contain those with whom deep relationships beyond formal ties exist and these persons have been called "fictive kin." And what of the challenge of defining a family within a commune that practices experimental group living arrangements?

I think that it is sensible to see that a universal human institution like the family exists as a "group fact" or gestalt or holistic system with emergent properties and social existence beyond the aggregated individuals or their individualistic self-perceptions.[3] The family is partly a group involving subjective mutual consent, but it also takes on a life of its own which other observers can discern and define as a socially real entity. Prototypically, a family biologically reproduces itself as it socially continues to exist over intergenerational life spans. A family is a patterned, bounded system progressing through time with some permanent communal and behavioral commitments to a concrete specific kinship group formed by both biological reproduction and permanent personal commitments.

A permanent intergenerational focus on mating, biological reproduction, and nurturing offspring, while caring for old parents, distinguishes the family from other intentional institutions and groups. The family everywhere has been the mediating institution that produces and socializes new members of a community and takes care of the vulnerable, ill, impaired, and dying family members. Obviously too, the larger public communities in a society will also be affected by the families' abilities to engender emotional bonds of empathy and trust, the foundation of the mutual moral obligations of kinship and civic virtue.

Families reproduce and conserve the culture, but as a mediating institution, families affect the larger society as well. Families adapt to new social and economic conditions and can produce innovations by challenging the status quo and exerting pressure on existing institutions. As feminists are beginning to recognize, families *can* support their members in patterns of living that display "just care" and gender equality.[4] Within a good family it is possible for everyone to contribute according to their means while receiving according to their needs. Families are capable of displaying altruism and creating benevolent and loving bonds; they do not always manifest abuses of power. All of the social science literature attests that strong familial bonds contribute to individual economic welfare, health, psychological well-being, moral socialization, altruistic behavior, and general happiness.

Indeed, it is the potential of families for good experiences that makes the failure and abuse of power in families such devastating betrayals. Even nonviolent emotional abuses of competition, favoritism, ridicule, neglect, infidelity, and egotistic selfishness create suffering. Since families are the setting of the most interpersonal intimacy humans experience, emotional maturity and morally responsible character formation become paramount requirements for the well-being and happiness of family members. While many families may deny and blind themselves to any pathologies in their midst, it would be just as false for feminists to deny the positive experiences of families. If I know that my husband, daughter, and sons, along with my sister, parents, and other kin, have meant the world to me and given me as much joy as any other relationship or project in my life, I can hardly dismiss these experiences as "false consciousness" induced by patriarchal pronatal socialization.

In considering the powerful role of families in society, it is also short-sighted for feminists to slight the strength of those familial genetic connections we have metaphorically named "blood ties." Yes, permanent committed kinship bonds and moral obligations are a social invention and constructed by an articulate primate with a big brain.[5] The very idea of kinship requires an understanding of abstract relationships existing in a nonobservable, nonimmediate past which continues into a not-yet future. But these constructed bonds and promises rest on a biological foundation of bonds which are shared with other primates who nurture their young for long periods.

Human beings are animals, and it is not to the advantage of any practical thinker bent on reform to discount biological predispositions and capacities which (like the brain itself) have been inherited over millions of years of evolutionary processes and selection. Human beings can change themselves and their communities because, with their big brains and emotional capacities, they are "the self-interpreting animals"; but as a unique species they will be predisposed to favor certain self-interpretations over others. "Anthropological constants" exist which give enough evidence to rehabilitate the idea of a species-specific human nature with a measure of psychic unity.[6] Our wonderful brains, language, emotions, altruism, bodily capacities for activity and reproduction are part of the gifts of biological inheritance—along with, unfortunately, tendencies toward fear, anxiety, aggression, selfishness, and self-deception.

Intergenerational Obligations

Feminists who wish to stress how embodied and socially embedded human beings are, and who wish to change society, must not make the mistake of discounting new biological evidence. In the past feminists have often over-reacted against biological inquiries and findings because of the existence of ideologically biased determinist theories which employ distorted evidence to try to prove women's inferiority. These outmoded forms of scientism have been used to justify *socially* constructed oppression as natural, biological, and immutable. But astute thinkers can work to discriminate false claims from reliable scientific findings and avoid handicapping their emancipatory critiques of society by closing off sources of knowledge.

Today, the influence of genes and genetic inheritance has been recognized in medicine and psychology. Sociobiologists have also made a strong case for the importance of selected genetic programming in shaping reproductive patterns. But there is less recognition of the potent psychosocial role of genetic ties and blood relationships in families. Why do people, including gays and lesbians, desire children of their own? Is this only an example of a socially coerced desire? It seems inadequate to reduce the desires for one's own biological children to the need to sustain patriarchal dominance or to shore up capitalistic views of children as private property.[7] Nor is desire for children limited to a selfish need for social insurance in old age.

Mother, father, sister, brother, daughter, son, grandparents—human beings cherish their familial blood kin for many reasons that have nothing to do with patriarchy, property rights, or the unthinking following of tradition. The biological links in a family create powerful bonds because they are particular, specific, unique, and most important, irreversible connections. While one can divorce a spouse, the genetic tie between parent and child or between siblings can never be undone.

Moreover, genetic ties can be extended over time and space; they exist despite physical distance or the absence of daily encounters. Brothers, sisters, aunts, uncles, and cousins remain one's relatives no matter how far away they live. Grandparents, grandchildren, and more distant progenitors can be uniquely part of one's family. Even the dead and unborn generations can exert influence on the present.

Since biological relatives are irreversibly our own particular kin, we are stuck with them. But then they are stuck with us as well. You don't earn or achieve your status as a family member, you're born into the fold and your family is obligated to care for you, and you for them. Morally obligating ties of blood kinship produce responsibilities that no one contracts for or enters into with informed consent. Family obligations exert their claims prior to other freely chosen allegiances or promises. In the same way, as ecofeminists recognize, we are born into earth's ecosystem without informed consent, yet inherit a moral responsibility to take care of our environment for future generations.

When, in turn, we biologically engender a child with a partner, the two parents are equally invested and so considered equally responsible for the child. The embodied union of the heritage of two individuals in a new human being produces an irreversible connection between the two persons. Love for the other can engender a powerful desire to have a child together and produce a new creative one out of two. At the same time, two different family lineages are united and new extended bonds of biological kinship are created. Each child has two sets of kin to act as backups, and additional resources for nurturing and helpful launching into the community.

And yes, it is also true that the social capital provided by biological children extends through adulthood and into old age. This is not so much a matter of financial aid or care as it is that after one's spouse, friends, colleagues, and comrades have died or become frail, one's descendants remain on the scene as a direct connection to the human community—specific people to love and care about. In most cultures and civilizations, including our own, the care is reciprocal; elderly kin are cared for by their offspring out of either gratitude or duty.

In fact our immersion in biological kinship in families prepares us for old age and strengthens the obligations that we owe to older generations. In the mirror I see my face turning into my father's face, with the same wrinkles and deep shadows, while my body slowly begins to resemble my mother's in her advanced old age. Having loved these physical bodies I can better come to terms with my aging self. The physical likeness which is so undeniable reminds me that these particular intergenerational obligations cannot be denied. Through my aging parents I begin to empathize with other old people.

As for our children, the genetic tie also becomes more important as they age. (Infants exact worship always.) We value our growing children not as personal property or as personal achievements, but partly because they are biologically like us, like our mates, and like our other family members. My genes are shared with my parents and siblings after all, and my biological child shares in these family resemblances. Biological similarities can make it easier for me to understand and be attuned to a child of my flesh, akin to me and mine.

The biological link to children is a particularly useful support for parents in the crisis time of adolescence. In this trying period of separating and achieving independence, many members of a family might choose to divorce (if not murder) each other if they could. The irreversible biological bond helps hold parents to their task; one's parental authority is augmented when the parent-child tie is irreversibly "just the way it is," courtesy of nature's genetic throw, with no undoing possible. Like it or not, we're all in this family together.

When one's children become adults and move out into their grown-up lives, the family's daily encounters and mutual exchanges lessen. But kinship ties and mutual aid still operate over a distance, buffer setbacks, and enhance celebrations and triumphs.[8] When grown children marry and begin having their own families, the sense of ongoing biological kinship becomes renewed by the appearance of grandchildren.

Of course this appreciation of biological kinship and the renewal of new generations in a family could not happen without the human ability to make and honor permanent psychosocial procreative commitments, be they implicit or explicit. Marriage (like adoption) is an explicitly chosen commitment that binds legally; promises imbue relationships with the moral obligation to give nurture and support for life. The interaction of personal commitments and biological intergenerational ties has given support for the traditional definition of a family used by census takers as "two or more persons living together related by blood, marriage or adoption." This defintion has sometimes been amended to "an intimate community related by blood, marriage or adoption for the whole of life."[9]

Gay and Lesbian Families

I think most observers could accept this definition as a prototypical definition of a family. But does this mean that no other forms of family life, such as a gay or lesbian family, could be included? After all, every prototype or definitional category includes many instances which do not fit into the category exactly.[10] Human beings, unlike computers, are experts in understanding the need for what has been called that "fuzzy logic" in which the definitions and boundaries so necessary for ordered existence are flexible, in order to include certain cases that share overlapping characteristics with the prototype.

I would argue that gay or lesbian households that consist of intimate communities of mutual support and that display permanent shared commitments to intergenerational nurturing share the kinship bonding we observe and name as family. If marriage were legally available, many permanently committed gays and lesbians would gladly seek the symbolic communal affirmation that the prototypical definition of family provides. When adoption is available to gay and lesbian families, they adopt children. For that matter, blood ties are present in the many gay and lesbian families where biological children from a previous marriage exist.

Fortunately, more and more families of origin adapt to new conditions and now openly accept and include their gay and lesbian members along with their partners. Traditional families respond to family love and loyalty, and integrate their adult gay children into their kinship networks. In fact the support and advocacy of many heterosexual family members has been one factor in the progress toward social acceptance that the gay and lesbian movement has enjoyed in recent years.

To discriminate against gay and lesbian families in custody disputes or adoptive and foster children decisions, one would have to assert and argue a difficult position that is surely unacceptable to most feminists. A case would have to be made that sexual orientation makes a major difference in the whole personality, behavior, and moral functioning of an individual person. This contention is almost as impossible to prove as asserting that gender identity determines the whole of personality. While some feminist and gay and lesbian activists may attempt to exaggerate and valorize differences between men and women or between gay and straight people, I do not think they can prove their assertions by the psychosocial evidence.[11]

Human persons are complex systems made up of many multiple dimensions and subsystems that function together as emerging wholes with complex personal identities. Emerging gender and sexual orientation programs appear in the course of a child's development and produce virtually irreversible outcomes which then shape and are shaped by psychosocial environments. Developments in gender and sexual orientation take their place among many other programmed developments, such as linguistic, affective, cognitive, and moral developmental predispositions, which operate to produce the overall configuration of personal identity. Whole persons are more than either their gender identities or their sexual orientation, or, for that matter, their active sexual functioning and behavior. Gender identity and sexual orientation are partial strands of a multidimensional tapestry of development. A person may not choose gender identity or sexual orientation; but persons do choose how they live, act, and form their moral character.

When people know morally mature and admirable gay and lesbian persons living fruitful professional and personal lives, prejudices and stereotypes can be overcome. Today many loving and faithful gay and lesbian couples live exemplary family lives, nurturing their biological and adoptive children in caring ways. They are powerful counterexamples to the idea that gay and lesbian families must be pathological or produce homosexual children. The fact that most homosexuals grew up in straight families helps to make the case that some biological factor is more important in producing homosexuality than any configuration of family dynamics.

Unfortunately it is also true that many gay couples often face the problems of social discrimination, harrassment, and isolation. Some families of origin do not accept their homosexual members. Without access to civil marriage, gay and lesbian families can enjoy only tenuous legal standings. But even without civil marriage, new movements to grant domestic partnerships have helped these families. It is heartening to see that many more gay couples are able to keep custody of their biological children and become adoptive and foster parents. After all, the criteria in custody and adoptive decisions is the same for heterosexuals and homosexuals. The question to be asked is whether these specific persons and this family can offer children good nurturing support and proper socialization. Surely gay families, like other families, will come in different degrees of adequacy. The criteria of acceptance in both homosexual and heterosexual families is the ability to provide what has been called "an average expectable environment" and "good-enough parenting." These are the criteria by which custody decisions, child abuse decisions, adoptive and foster care decisions are decided for everyone in the society. No community committed to the common good and the well-being of children could abandon all criteria of acceptable parenting and family living in the name of privacy or liberty. We do not countenance incest, violent abuse, or medical, emotional, or educational neglect—even if we cannot always enforce our norms of protection. The question always is where to draw the line in giving individuals permissive liberty when the question of children's welfare is involved.

The availability of alternative reproductive technologies presents new moral dilemmas. Even if one affirms, as I do, that there should be no discrimination against gay and lesbian couples or homosexual families in custody or adoption decisions, the ethics of using new collaborative reproductive technologies to form any kind of family—whether gay or straight—remains. Feminists can recognize that inclusive definitions of the family and nondiscriminatory criteria for adoptive parents do not automatically solve the ethical question as to how individuals of either gender or any sexual orientation should use reproductive technologies.

Ethics of Reproduction

Reproductive decisions are always a complex ethical challenge because they involve potential third parties (the children-to-be) who are unable to participate in the decision, and yet whose well-being will be completely dependent upon the decisions made. Children in good-enough families require decades of arduous care and the expenditure of socioemotional and financial resources on the way to adulthood. Because of their unique needs, children are especially vulnerable to neglect, abuses of power, and emotional scarring. Bringing a child into the world is always a morally serious undertaking.

Today, with the availability of contraceptive technologies and with new knowledge of fertility, children are not inevitably conceived when heterosexual intercourse takes place. Similarly, human infertility is no longer inevitable, because a variety of medical interventions may remedy the condition. With more freedom and technological control over reproduction, voluntary conscious decisions to try to produce a child, or to avoid having a child, become moral actions. Clearly society has not settled the contentious question of using technologies to avoid birth, as seen by bitter conflicts over abortion and sex selection, and to a lesser extent, disagreements over contraception and sterilization. Nor have we settled what technological interventions in conceiving children would count as morally acceptable.

What goals and motivations should a person or a couple have in reproducing, and what means to what ends are acceptable? It is a daunting challenge to arrive at an adequate ethics of responsible reproduction.[12] To my mind, an appropriate feminist ethics of reproduction should apply to females, males, heterosexuals, or gay persons, without bias or discrimination. Such an ethic should take into account the concerns of individual adults, the well-being of children, and the general good of the whole society. Here Alison Jaggar's cautions appear pertinent: "Feminist approaches to ethics must understand individual actions in the context of broader social practices." Harmful side effects can appear from "the symbolic and cumulative implications of any action as well as its immediately observable consequences."[13]

In the issue of forming families, questions arise over goals and which technological measures are appropriate for use. Feminists and others who value the potential goods of the family and genetic ties of kinship can well understand the strength of any individual's desire to have children and to have one's own children. It appears unexceptional that gay and lesbian persons desire to form families and have children. Of course no feminists could maintain that procreation is *required* for either female or male fulfillment, but most feminists who are not radical separatists would concur that the choice to engage in childbearing, child-rearing, and family life can be a good and worthwhile life plan.

Yet individual desires can hardly be enough justification for undertaking parenthood. Even an individual's readiness to make a permanent commitment to the long-term nurture of a child is not enough. Morally responsible persons must not only be ready to commit themselves to the parental enterprise but must also think of the child and its long-term needs. They must judge whether they can provide an adequate child-rearing environment and enough good-enough parenting to fulfill their moral responsibilities. Along with such considerations there are the questions of what means and strategies will be morally appropriate to gain a child for themselves. As Gandhi wisely avowed: "means are ends in the making"; so the means used to obtain a goal must be chosen carefully. An adequate reproductive ethic should seek ends and use means that respect the good of all the participating individuals along with the moral good of the communities in which individuals will live.

Baby kidnapping and baby buying have been morally condemned and prohibited. Such practices have been judged to be immoral because it is universally recognized that persons should never be kidnapped, nor bought or sold like objects. Forced procreation through rape is an even more abhorrent crime that has been inflicted upon women. Other more subtle coercions to obtain other people's children have also occurred, as when Argentinian political prisoners' children were stolen for adoption, or Native American children were taken from their parents.

When employing a long-term perspective on the human condition, I believe it can be generally agreed that the well-being of most children most of the time is best served when genetic, gestational, and social parenting are not separated. In the evolution of mammalian, primate, and human parenthood, the contact and continuity with genetically related newborn offspring provides the best protection for the survival and welfare of the next generation—and the third generation to come. Reptilian eggs laid in the sand and abandoned, for instance, are open to a host of predators and disasters. (Modern instances of careless abuse in sperm banks, irresponsible embryo experimentations, or doctors using their own sperm to inseminate the eggs of their patients would be modern examples of the breakdown of protection when genetic, gestational, and social parenting are separated.)

Asymmetry in biological relationships within families can be shown to produce negative social effects in a population. Both evolutionary psychologists and sociologists can attest to the claim that human stepparents, especially males, are more likely to neglect or abuse children not their own. Much of the alarm over divorce and reconstituted families has been generated because of the unexpected difficulties children of divorce experience, effects lasting even into their own adult formation of families.[14] While theoretical arguments against Western culture's operating norms of family structure can be made, practical human experience attests to the positive outcomes for children when reared by two committed, nurturing, sexually bonded, biological parents supported by two intergenerational kinship networks. Ideological claims that new experimental forms of family living would be better at socializing children have to argue their case, contending with an enormous amount of existing evidence to the contrary.

Adoptive arrangements appear morally unproblematic because when children are born whose parents cannot take care of them, then a separation of genetic, gestational, and social parenting is already effected by some unforeseen emergency or crisis. The altruistic rescue of these children by heterosexual couples, gay and lesbian couples, or single persons is admirable. Being reared by a committed parent or, better yet, two parents, appears better than institutional rearing without a parent. At least a form of family with kinship bonds is created. There is also a great deal of historical and cross-cultural evidence that the custom of adoption is an old human institution, much used in many cultures to supplement family formation and to meet the unforeseen contingencies of reproductive life.

In modern American society we find many adoptive families, many blended and reconstituted families, and many single-parent families, with both heterosexual and homosexual members who are admirably meeting the needs of children. The crux of the moral question, however, is whether homosexual or heterosexual persons should use alternative collaborative reproductive technologies to initiate the creation of families in which genetic, gestational, and social parenting are separated intentionally.

Adoption does not serve as the correct model to use to justify collaborative reproduction. The analogy fails because it is a careless argument that confounds situations in which new lives have already been brought into existence with situations in which lives have not yet come into being, and will only come into being through acts of will employing medical reproductive technological interventions and third parties. Individual cases which after the fact may be seen as successful exceptions do not justify encouraging general practices which will still be experimental for the children involved. This is all the more true when the long-term cumulative effects of using such methods may involve negative social and symbolic side effects.

In my judgment, alternative collaborative reproductive technologies which employ third parties are harmful to the common good and to individuals who are involved—the gestational mothers, egg donors, sperm donors, recipient families, and the children so conceived. I do not think that the use of third-party collaborative reproduction can protect women's dignity, encourage mens' moral responsibility for their children, or serve the familial bonding necessary for multigenerational families to flourish. Intentionally using medical technology to break apart genetic, gestational, and social parenting by the use of third-party collaborative reproduction breaks down the moral responsibility and personal integrity embodied individuals should exercise in the use of their reproductive powers.

Women's well-being is endangered in third-party collaborative reproduction particularly in the case of contract pregnancy. The notorious Mary Beth Whitehead case brought a great deal of critical feminist analysis to the issues involved in such contracts. Contract birthgivers, of course, are actually the biological mothers of their children. (Similarly, sperm "donors" are biological fathers, whoever the recipient, whether a heterosexual married couple, a single mother, or a lesbian couple—whatever the legal forms that are employed.)

When a child is born through a pregnancy contract, the woman has become a womb for hire, a means to an end. Most feminists have pointed out that women, particularly enslaved women, have spent generations escaping from the status of a breeder or baby machine as defined by their wombs. Wet nurses and prostitutes have been other women whose sexual and reproductive functions have been isolated and coopted into service for pay. To morally countenance contract pregnancy with all the control over the woman during pregnancy that such a contract calls for, reduces women to a part object, even if this practice is not deemed to be overt baby selling.

Women may consent to these contracts, but the money and social rewards offered as an inducement insure that affluent, socially dominant persons will hire women who are economically deprived. Whether it is a male, male couple, female, or heterosexual couple who hire a gestator to bear a child, there is an unequal relationship set up, in which a woman's most intimate personal capacities for reproduction are rented and thereby alienated. The emotional bond between mother and child must be broken by agreement; detachment from the child and an abdication of responsible control for the child's future are required. If a contract birthgiver has a husband and children, the marital relationship also is controlled for the duration of the pregnancy, and the birthgiver's children will see their half-sibling given away at birth. The contracting party also can require abortion if there is some unfortunate development in the pregnancy.

Male donors or biological fathers are also selling, or giving away, their capacities and responsibilities for reproductive outcomes when they allow or sell their sperm to be used to father children. They too become breeders and a means to an end. Sperm donors, along with egg donors, are giving away the procreative functions and genetic identities which they received from their parents. The resulting child is cut off from a biological parent and part of its biological kinship network. Since secrecy is the usual order of the day in donations, a further problematic factor is added to the families formed in this way and to the families of donors.

Confusions over family lineages and medical genetic histories are a serious drawback to third-party collaborative reproduction. Other feminist critics have worried over the control given to medicine and physicians when these transactions are put into their hands. Still other critics have seen the medical resources expended on expensive and often unsuccessful reproductive technologies to be an unfair allocation of scarce medical resources in society. Yet sperm donation technology is not high level or expensive, as "turkey baster babies" prove. The major moral reservations surrounding third-party reproduction do not lie so much in perpetuating economic injustices as in the fact that such practices are breaking the kinship bonds and the moral accountability necessary for responsible exercises of reproductive power.

A child conceived by third-party collaborative reproduction explicitly becomes a made-to-order product of a parent's will and desire to reproduce. Control becomes a paramount value. Males (either gay or heterosexual) hire women to give them a child to rear. And women (either lesbian or heterosexual) who procure sperm are determined to experience pregnancy as well as rear their own child. Even when no money changes hands, there is an inevitable commodification of a child conceived by technology and a third-party collaborator.

These children enter into a family in a different and less than equal way than all the other entrants in the kinship network; they must live and exist under the pressure of being the optimal babies ordered up as a means to the end of satisfying parental desires.[15] As we become more sensitive to the morality of responsible parenthood we come to see how important it is that a child be accepted and responded to as a unique gift. Children conceived by heterosexual intercourse also should not have to bear the status of a trophy child, or the child who is only instrumentally valued because it fulfills a parent's plan or extrinsic goal. Adolescents may want to have a baby to love them, or misguided couples may want a baby to hold their marriage together, and so on. We do not think these motivations do justice to the dignity of a child, or bode well for the need to see one's child as an intrinsically valuable human life with his or her own separate needs and inalienable rights.

Babies grow up and become children, adolescents, and adults who cannot help but be affected by their origins. "Whose child am I?" is a natural question. Adoptive children ask, "Why did my parents give me up?" and children of sperm donors, contract birthgivers, and egg donors will not be spared questions of identity whether they grow up in heterosexual homes or gay or lesbian homes. Persons think more about their own beginnings and lineage when they begin to form their own families. Procuring the baby that one desires is never the end of a procreative drama.

As for cultural side effects, do we really want to encourage the idea that babies can be manufactured, procured, or given away, rather than received as gifts to parents who will feel morally obliged to rear their children responsibly? Children already worry about their security and the stability of their families. More to the point, it seems socially destructive to encourage and approve donors in an emotional detachment and abdication of responsibility for their biological offspring—already a problem with young males in our society. Then there are the broken kinship ties that ensue. This is particularly paradoxical since persons who use alternative third-party reproductive technologies recognize the strength of their own procreative desires for their own biological children. To form their own families they must discount and break apart, as the case may be, other biological ties between mothers, fathers, half-siblings, grandparents, and other relatives.

Sensitive to these concerns, a few adoptive parents and some gay and lesbian couples have pursued new "open family" options to let a child know and remain within all of his or her biological and social kinship networks. These parents give up the more usually desired exclusive control to be gained from anonymity and secrecy. While the biological mothers and fathers still must abdicate their roles as fully functioning residential parents, they retain an interest and a connection with the child they fathered or mothered. Some unusual gay and lesbian sperm donor arrangements claim that their children can now have four parents, two gay males (the biological father and his partner) and two lesbian females (the biological mother and her partner).[16] These arrangements are most difficult for the nonbiological gay parents, who have trouble grappling with this new form of family asymmetry. Whether such children in such newly constructed families will benefit remains to be seen. The adults are taking the risk that they can conduct an innovative social experiment without harming their children.

Naturally, any experiments with the lives of children in new family arrangements can never be proved harmful before the fact. If one must have evidence of concrete negative psychological or social consequences to individuals proved by the requisite social science studies *before* prohibiting innovative experiments, then nothing reproductive technology might be able to accomplish could ever be prohibited. Perhaps eighty-five-year-old heterosexual or gay couples could have their own biological children to lessen the painful prospect of dying. Or single males could bear children with eggs procured from female fetuses that have been aborted. With more biological discoveries, the species barrier may be broken and transspecies animal-human offspring could provide a more responsive pet (or animal companion), one which is more challenging than a kitten but less demanding than a child. All of these experimental procedures could be initiated by good people with the most sincere motivation.

My point, of course, is that while reproductive technologies are the result of humankind's wonderful and good capacities to invent and create, they must, like all technologies, be judged and shaped to serve morally worthy and appropriate human goals for individuals and for the human community. And when it comes to deciding new questions about the family and reproduction, there is no substitute for moral discernment and good judgment. Fortunately, feminists, with their unique moral sources, have a valuable contribution to make to these challenges of our time.

Notes

1. See David Popenoe, *Disturbing the Nest: Family Change and Decline in Modern Societies* (New York: Aldine de Gruyter, 1988); Arlene Skolnick, *Embattled Paradise: The American Family in an Age of Uncertainty* (New York: Basic Books, 1991).

2. A.F. Robertson, *Beyond the Family: The Social Organization of Human Reproduction* (Berkeley: University of California Press, 1991).

3. David Braybooke, *Philosophy of Social Science* (Englewood Cliffs, N.J.: Prentice-Hall, 1987), pp.31–33.

4. See *After Eden: Facing the Challenge of Gender Reconciliation*, ed. Mary Stewar Van Leeuwen, Annelies Knoppers, Margaret L. Koch, Douglas J. Schuurman, and Helen M. Sterk (Grand Rapids, Mich.: William B. Eerdmans, 1993).

5. Peter J. Wilson, *Man the Promising Primate: The Conditions of Human Evolution* (New Haven: Yale University Press, 1980).

6. Jerome Kagan. 1983, *The Nature of the Child* (New York: Basic Books, 1983); Robert Wright, *The Moral Animal* (New York: Basic Books, 1994); Steven Pinker, *The Language Instinct: How the Mind Creates Language* (New York: William Morrow and Company, 1994); Carrol E. Izard, *The Psychology of Emotions* (New York: Plenum Press, 1991).

7. For an extreme statement of the suspicious view see Jeffner Allen, "Motherhood: The Annihilation of Women," in *Mothering: Essays in Feminist Theory*, ed. Joyce Trebilcot (Totowa, N.J.: Rowman & Allanheld, 1983).

8. Alice S. Rossi and Peter H. Rossi, *Of Human Bonding: Parent-Child Relations Across the Life Course* (New York: Aldine De Gruyter, 1990); *Parenting Across the Life Span: Biosocial Dimensions*, ed. Jane B. Lancaster, Jeanne Altmann, Alice S. Rossi, and Lonnie R. Sherrod (New York: Aldine De Gruyter, 1987).

9. Statement of the U.S. Roman Catholic Bishops on the Family, "Follow the Way of Love," *Origins* 23 (December 2, 1993).

10. Gerald M. Edelman, *Bright Air, Brilliant Fire: On the Matter of the Mind* (New York: Basic Books, 1992), pp. 233–237.

11. See Rhoda Unger and Mary Crawford, *Women and Gender: A Feminist Psychology* (New York: McGraw-Hill, 1992).

12. For a sampling of the literature, see *Having Children: Philosophical and Legal Reflections on Parenthood*, ed. Onora O'Neill and William Ruddick (New York: Oxford University Press, 1979); Jeffrey Blustein, *Parents and Children: The Ethics of The Family* (New York: Oxford University Press, 1982); Paul Lauritzen, *Pursuing Parenthood: Ethical Issues in Assisted Reproduction* (Bloomington: Indiana University Press, 1993).

13. Alison M. Jaggar, "Feminist Ethics: Projects, Problems, Prospects," *In/Fire Ethics* 2, no. 3 (1993), p. 6. This essay orignally appeared in Claudia Card, ed., *Feminist Ethics* (Lawrence: University Press of Kansas, 1991).

14. E. Mavis Hetherington and Josephine D. Arasteh, eds., *Impact of Divorce, Single Parenting, and Stepparenting on Children* (Hillsdale, N.J.: Lawrence Erlbaum Associates, 1988); Lenore J. Weitzman, *The Divorce Revolution* (New York: Free Press, 1985).

15. For a statement of these problematic issues of commodification, see Mary Gibson, "Contract Motherhood: Social Practice in Social Context," in Alison M. Jaggar, ed., *Living with Contradictions: Controversies in Feminist Social Ethics* (Boulder: Westview Press, 1994), pp. 402–419.

16. Laura Benkov, *Reinventing the Family: The Emerging Story of Lesbian and Gay Parents* (New York: Crown Publishers, 1994).

Part VI

Images We Don't Need

14

The Idea of Fatherhood

Sara Ruddick

Should we recognize sexual difference between parents? More precisely, should we endorse an idea of distinctive Fatherhood? These are very odd questions. Throughout the world people distinguish between mothers and fathers; mothers and fathers, in turn, usually differ in their conceptions and styles of parenting. Yet I used to believe that we should strive to eliminate, in thought as well as practice, the idea of distinctive Fatherhood. I welcomed the "new father," a man who participated fully in the work and responsibilities of child care. But I saw no reason not to count an engaged male parent as a "mother" and many reasons not to grant him distinctive paternal characteristics. David Blankenhorn, a father-advocate to whom this paper is something of a response, presents my previous position accurately:

> Today's . . . story of fatherhood largely assumes that fatherhood is superfluous. . . . Fatherhood as a distinctive role for men is either unnecessary or undesirable. . . . There are not—and ought not to be—any key parental tasks that belong essentially and primarily to fathers. . . .[1]

Recently I have begun to wonder if it is not conceptually and politically risky to deny sexual difference and paternal distinctiveness. Does the idea of gender-inclusive parenthood or, my preference, male-inclusive motherhood, reflect a fear of sexuality as well as of sexual difference? Is it possible to explore the meaning of birth without acknowledging men's as well as women's distinct procreative activities? Does the erasure of difference in parenting make it difficult to speak or even to think about the deeply gendered character of parents' lives?

Despite these questions, I remain unconvinced by arguments that there not only are but should be distinct paternal and maternal "roles" and "tasks." More important, I believe that distinctive Fatherhood is a regulative ideal which has harmed women, has probably harmed children, and may harm men. My utopian hope is that acknowledging distinctive Fatherhood (and therefore motherhood) might become an occasion for developing an *ethics* of sexual difference. But I also fear that, in the absence of such an ethics, the affirmation of sexual difference between parents will yield the usual suspects: increased subordination of women, compulsory heterosexuality, and intolerance of multiply diverse modes of parental life.

Parenting is, in the first instance, a complex, ongoing *work* of responding to children's needs in particular economic and social circumstances.[2] As the term "parent" suggests, this work is not *prima facie* associated with either sex. To be sure, almost every culture distinguishes maternal from paternal work. Generally speaking, the younger the children, the more physical their demands, the more time-consuming their care, the more likely that the work of caring for them will be assigned to women. But this sexual division of parental labor could be entirely a consequence of patriarchal ideologies.

The question I want to address is whether there is anything in the "nature" of children, women, or men that requires a sexual division of parental labor even in postpatriarchal societies. One familiar reply to this question is that women are "by nature" capable of child care in ways that men are not. I believe that men can participate fully and ably in all parental activities. If men now appear to be less effective than women in some aspects of parenting, this is a consequence of different preparation for parenthood. The insufficiencies of male parents are also exaggerated by sentimental, mystifying views of the talents of female parents. But the affirmation of female mothering, or, correlatively, the denial of mothering abilities to men, is not the subject of this paper.

My concern is not with male parents' alleged deficiencies but rather with their allegedly distinctive *abilities* and "functions." These allegedly distinctive paternal virtues are currently the subject of intense conversation. Fathers are said to be missing from theories and practices of families, especially from feminist theories, especially from African-American families. Their absence is said to be a principal cause of serious social ills, especially the poverty of their children, their own and their sons' violence, and their sons' frantic yet failed "masculinity."[3] Father presence conjoined with an idea of distinctive Fatherhood is offered as the remedy. John Edgar Wideman, pained by white racism's denial of fatherhood to African-American men and their sons, translates theoretical and social absence of fathers into personal longing:

Who is listening and searching as I am for a father's voice, not to prove anything to anybody, but so it will be remembered. Live on.[4]

The longing for fathers and pain in their absence is real; the presence in children's lives of effectively caring men is a blessing. But I am troubled by the arguments of father-advocates. I am not persuaded by the statistical analyses of the dangers of father absence but I will address these only briefly. I want primarily to question the *idea(l)* of distinctive Fatherhood persuasive in the literature. This ideal, I believe, mystifies the character of parental work, harms men—would-be fathers—as well as women, and privatizes child care to the detriment of children and their communities. This ideal also lends itself to coercive and cruel regulation of family life.

The Idea(l) of the Father

Ideas of Fatherhood diverge radically within and among cultures. According to an idea of Fatherhood widely endorsed in the United States, a father is defined by the functions he fulfills. Two paternal functions, provision and protection, are fairly straightforward. The third involves a complex exercise of paternal authority, paternal legitimation, discipline, and the right to punish. A father is also defined by the family relationships in which he participates. Ideally he is the biological progenitor of his children and the husband of their mother.

Consider first the function of paternal provision. A parent is a provider to the extent that he or she gets and then delivers the goods a child needs. To take a simple example, a providing parent obtains, prepares, and presents food to a child. One parent alone could get and plant seed, harvest a crop, cook and serve the produce, inveigle children to eat or help them to share scanty provisions. In most cases, the ability to provide depends upon many peoples' labor. A parent enters into a chain of provision which runs from seed to child, sometimes through the parent's bodily labor, most dramatically in the nursing of an infant, most routinely in activities like planting and harvesting produce, chopping wood, designing and building a house.

How does it come to seem that a male parent is, distinctly, the parental provider? First, getting the means to acquire goods is separated from actually acquiring them. For example, getting money to buy food is separated from standing in line, selecting, perhaps bargaining, then purchasing. Acquisition is separated, though less so, from delivery, for example preparing and feeding with all of its social complexities. The first link in this chain is then assigned to fathers: fathers provide whatever is required—for example cash—in order for someone to acquire and deliver the goods. This distinct paternal provision is the most distant from children and also often from home; I therefore refer to it as "distant provision."

Distant provision is assigned to fathers for three kinds of reason. "Distance" is a general characteristic of Fatherhood; the closer, the more intimate the parental work, the more likely it is to be assigned to women. Secondly, fathers are said to provide more of the means to acquire than mothers, or husbands more than their wives. Most telling, distant provision is said to be more integral to *paternal identity* in the eyes of women and children as well as men. In Blankenhorn's words, for fathers "the provider role is an assumption, a given," "a part of parenthood."[5] Children too see "fatherhood" but not "motherhood" in their parents' wage labor. By contrast, women may be seen or see themselves as *less* effective parents when they spend a considerable part of their days getting the means to get the goods, that is, "working."

I do not dispute these connections between Fatherhood and distant provision. I agree that an employed father who works "outside" has an aura of distance, especially if he also engages in sports or other social life "outside" and cuts himself space at home, behind a newspaper, in front of television, "out" in the yard. I accept statistical evidence that fathers currently provide more of the means to get the goods than mothers or at least than wives. I would, however, underscore a second fact: many women distantly provide, frequently with little or no supplementary male provision. I agree that, at least in the social circles of my childhood—roughly white, upwardly striving, Protestant, middle-class suburbia—paternal identity was tied to, and maternal virtue nearly opposed to, distant provision. I would note, however, that this connection between gender identity and parental provision is far less strong in my current circle of acquaintances and unravels altogether, as debates about welfare and workfare make crystal clear, if mothers are poor, especially if they are not white.

Let us assume, however, that (most) fathers see themselves and are seen as distant providers. There are nonetheless several disadvantages to making distant provision nearly constitutive of Fatherhood. Emphasis on distant provision, getting the means to get the goods, obscures the complex daily activities of providing. It comes to seem "natural," for example, to count men as primary providers even if women—whether or not they also distantly provide—spend many hours lining up to buy food and preparing and serving it. Identifying distant provision with provision *tout court* also obscures activities undertaken by men that are indispensable to providing, ranging from the stereotypical, relatively distant dishwashing and garbage disposal to intimate caregiving acts such as enticing a child to take the medicine someone—perhaps the father himself—has procured or helping her dress herself in the clothes someone has made or acquired. Emphasis on distant provision also obscures the fact that many men engage intensively in fatherlike activities with children for whom they do not, and sometimes cannot, distantly provide. Some are "otherfathers" (to adapt a phrase of Patricia Hill Collins)—men from a neighborhood or community who act toward children in "fatherly" ways,[6] some participating actively in the details of their daily care. To make "distant provision" a necessary feature of Fatherhood renders their actual fathering invisible.

Where fathers do distantly provide, the belief that such provision is distinctly valuable may undermine paternal relationships. Too often the one who earns also controls, inspiring resentment and manipulative hypocrisy in the controlled. Good family men are said to celebrate provision as a "bedrock responsibility" only within a larger context of paternal service. But the idea of "service," while less reductive than the idea of paternal cash, is also problematic. Those who serve, for instance, are liable to resent their obligations, assert rights over the served earned by service, and demand service in return.

Finally, and most important in my view, ascribing distant provision to fathers makes a fundamental aspect of child care both intrinsically private and highly dependent on economic and social conditions in which the father lives. As many social critics insist, fathers can distantly provide only if they have the means—usually the jobs—to do so. More deeply, *parenting* is the responsibility of communities, states, a parental generation. To be sure, children benefit from provision in a household (a refugee camp or an orphanage are usually inferior substitutes). Also, bracketing complexities in family relationships, it is usually better for children if households have more than one distant provider, especially where social services are underfunded. But even households with two or more distant providers also require multiple kinds of sustenance from a variety of social institutions. Some parents may appear to need no "outside" help with provision, but they are almost always already benefiting from the distribution of economic goods and from a variety of more or less hidden social services.

Let me turn now to the second paternal function: protection. A commitment to protect is a primary, perhaps constitutive, characteristic of parental work: to be a "parent" means, *inter alia*, to be someone who sees children as vulnerable and who *attempts* to respond to vulnerability by protecting rather than assaulting or neglecting them.[7] While both mothers and fathers are protective, fathers are sometimes said to protect differently. They may, for example, worry less about a child's emotional suffering, more about physical illness,[8] be less preoccupied with daily dangers, more concerned with preparing their children for "an uncertain and dangerous future."[9] These are differences of degree and subject to cultural and individual variation; to be a parent is to attempt to protect.

Nonetheless, mothers, fathers, and children often see men as more effectively protective of their children, especially against physical intrusion or assault. A mother and wife, for example, is evidently proud that her husband avenged the theft of their daughter's and another child's bike:

> My daughter was about seven. We had just bought her a brand-new bike. The bike was outside on the front lawn. My daughter . . . went outside and the bike was gone. Meanwhile a little boy down the street . . . [also] said his bike was stolen. My husband gets in his van. . . . You know what he did? He took the van right to where the kids were and

knocked them off both the bikes and they ran. Now, not only had he saved my daughter's bike, but the little kids down the street's. I mean everybody, the whole neighborhood, knew what he had done. My daughter was so proud of her daddy saving their bikes.[10]

Manly protection is symbolically extensive. As a father protects his children and home, so a soldier protects his country, a president his people. The mother/wife/citizen honors the protector. During the bombing of London in World War II, the current queen mother, then wife to the king, offered her compatriots the comfort of symbolic patriarchal protection:

The children will not leave without me, I will not leave without the King, and the King will never leave.[11]

This myth of fatherly protection seems to me a strange dream. In many families, it is fathers whose bodies and egos elicit "protective" material service and emotional cosseting. When fathers are toughly protective they can be dangerous to children. The father knocking child-thiefs off bikes might well hurt these "bad" children; tough fathers, especially if enraged or armed, can imperil anyone who provokes them.[12] Even if he is restrained, the tough father suggests that, although he is surely stronger and more authoritative than, for example, thieving kids, physical force is his only recourse. This model of protection may put his children at risk in circumstances where to be tough is hazardous.

Oddly enough, father advocates often insist on fatherhood as a way of civilizing *males*. If men *were* inherently violent, a view I have strongly contested elsewhere,[13] the hope that fatherhood might calm them is unfounded. Children's demands and provocations try the nonviolence of even the most disciplined parents, female or male. Paternal—or parental—"rights" excuse or actually encourage violence among those already inclined to bully and hurt. As studies of family violence and numerous memoirs reveal, children often become targets of their own fathers' injurious force.

The fantasy of fatherly, or more generally, manly protection is also harmful to women insofar as it suggests that we need not learn to protect ourselves. Many times women defend themselves from assault with no protective man in sight. Often it is the very man who is meant to protect, and who does indeed on other occasions act as protector, who endangers "his" woman. The fantasy of male protection also falsifies the experience of women and men assaulted by racism and poverty, for whom safety is nearly impossible and fatherly or motherly protection is at best a partial and heartbreaking compensation for community failure.[14]

The obligation to protect, construed as an individual manly duty, also misleads fathers and mothers who are socially secure. The best that any parents can do is to create protective *communities*. This requires accepting the limits of parental power to control a world in which children are inevitably subject to danger. And it means extending a measure of protective concern to all the children within reach (and to their sometimes dangerous fathers or mothers). It is banal but perhaps still necessary to remind ourselves that children are safest when the circumstances of their lives are safe: when adults act, and are seen to act, fairly; when ideals of justice are enacted and also tempered with patience and compassion; when lethal weapons are unavailable to the enraged; when despair is met not only with comfort but with effective aid. This safety cannot be ensured by any combination of parents but only by collective and deliberate policies to which parents can contribute.

The third and most complex paternal function is concerned not so much with fatherly activities as with values a father "represents." Fathers are meant to be of the world and to present the world to their children, insisting especially on its harsher aspects.[15] Symbolically, fathers represent reality in opposition to the comforts and protectiveness of maternity. Morally, fathers are judges with the authority to discipline and punish. Fathers legitimate a child in the society and legitimate society's demands on the child. Put gently, as John Edgar Wideman puts it,

> Father stories are about establishing origins and through them legitimizing claims of ownership, of occupancy and identity. They connect what's momentary and passing to what surpasses, materiality to ideal.[16]

Put *in extremis*, a fatherless child is lost in chaos and confusion, comforted by illusions, enervated by soft love.

This depiction of paternal value and authority is consonant with a philosophical tradition that assigns reason to men, defines rationality partly by contrast with emotion, particular attachment, and practicality, then assigns these traits to women and to lower-class, less "developed" men. This account of authority is also elaborated in certain, especially Lacanian, versions of psychoanalytic theory and in theories of moral development.

To simplify greatly, psychoanalytic theorists often depict a child still attached to his (or presumably her) mother as presocial and a creature of illusion, especially illusions of mutually symbiotic unity with its mother and of its own omnipotence. A father disturbs this unity and disrupts these illusions. As a result of this paternal intervention, the child admits to several realities. To cite one pertinent example, he acknowledges the reality of sexual difference and the fact of male procreation; he sees that the world is "teeming with [other and independent] life" rather than being a child's creation, "just as, thanks to the father's act and his penis, the mother's body is teeming with children."[17]

Many psychoanalytic theorists are quick to reject correlations of symbolic paternity with characteristics of actual fathers. The "father represents reality by reason of his very existence,"[18] not because male parents are actually more moral, lawful, intellectual, or authoritative than mothers. But the fantasy that without actual male fathers children are seriously damaged is culturally expressed in numerous adult beliefs and practices: for example that a father—and only a father—provides distantly, bringing power from outside into the mother's house as into her body; that a "father and his penis represent a protection against chaos, confusion and the mists clouding the mind";[19] that a father is the "head" of a family which, lacking him, is decapitated—deviant and broken.

Belief in paternal rationality can also be supported by recent studies of moral development, associated most prominently with Carol Gilligan. These "different voice" developmental theories have been read as claiming that men are more likely than women to articulate rules, defend rights, and insist on fair play and just punishment. Women, by contrast, are said to be less concerned with rights and punishment than with resolutions of conflicts within the context in which they arise. Readers of these theories make far sharper, more "essentialist," gender distinctions, and far less nuanced moral distinctions, than their authors.[20] But ironically, the cruder interpretations of (mis)readers are often echoed by adult children, especially sons, who describe fathers as the more distant, judgmental, rule-governed, world-representing parent.

> The first rule of my father's world is that you stand alone. Alone, alone, alone.... My mother's first rule was love. She refused to believe she was alone.... My father, present or not, evoked boundaries. The rules of the house. My duties, chores, responsibilities.... I was certain my mother needed me. My father never expressed such a need.[21]

> Compared to a mother's love, a father's love is frequently more expectant, more instrumental, ... a bit farther away, more distant and contingent.[22]

> Paternal attachment to breadwinning [distant provision] is neither arbitrary nor anachronistic.... Breadwinning is objective, rule-oriented, and easily measurable. It is an instrumental, goal-driven activity in which success derives in part from aggression.[23]

Lacanian theories seem intended to buttress distinctive paternal authority while different-voice theories intend to legitimate a voice culturally defined as "feminine." Nonetheless both kinds of theories can be used to substantiate the *belief* in a father who is authoritative, rule-governed, distant, and just. Such beliefs, especially if they are resonant with cultural fantasies, tend to be self-confirming.

It is important, therefore, to recognize the modesty and limits of developmental theory and to name fantasy as fantasy even while recognizing its power. Children do not need fathers to separate from mothers. In the absence of violence, disease, and despair, children's delight in their emerging motility and mentality, the allure of neighborhood and friends, the fascinations of "nature" and the exhilaration of tasks mastered, propel them into a "love affair with the world."[24] Nor, in the absence of fantasy is there any reason to believe that female or male parents inherently represent justice, care, reality, or conscience. Nor does a child's close, "unseparated" intimacy with his or her mother prevent him from moving out into the world and feeling real there.

> She was always there with me. . . . A rare night I spent in somebody else's house, visualizing myself as my mother might see me, was the surest way to make myself feel *real*. . . . She was *there* like the internal words and rhythms of consciousness are there. A closeness and intimacy the opposite of oppressive, since her presence freed me, helped me grow and expand.[25]

Whatever its source in fantasy or basis in current social life, belief in distinctly male conscience, authority, and reason is dangerous. The ascription of authority to men brings in its train the worst of fatherhood: a right, often conjoined with real power, to intrude, humiliate, exploit, and assault. But the price of paternal authority is evident not only in its abuses. Parents who mean to be egalitarian and child-respecting often struggle against their own patriarchal habits of according the last word and final judgment to fathers. Children and wives write of coming to fear a father even when he didn't mean to cause and poignantly regrets the fear he created. Women have written tellingly of their loss of cognitive or moral authority in father- and husband-dominated families. Daughters especially, but also sons, testify to their confusion, resentment, and contempt when confronted with the submissiveness of a mother who in their eyes is powerful and, in the absence of the father, often trustworthy. Sons but also daughters lament the man they might have known if only he were not camouflaged by distant authoritative Fatherhood.[26]

Despite this testimony, father-advocates insist that children without fathers suffer in numberable ways; the dangers of fatherlessness outweigh the dangers of Fatherhood. Since fathers relish paternal authority and take pride in distant provision and protection we—social theorists, mothers, and children—should believe in Fatherhood, or at least pretend to believe in order to keep fathers home. I myself am unconvinced by reports of the dangers of fatherlessness.[27] But even if the harm of father absence were more convincing, it is not clear what lessons to draw. In what ways might communities compensate, or help families to compensate, for the absence of fathers? This question, if it were asked, for example, about war widows, rather than never-married, nonwhite mothers, would probably provoke reflective discussion and the subsequent invention of services that benefited most children without stigmatizing any.

Even if I were convinced that father absence harmed children I would reject a quasi-contractual view that promises men that they can be (seen as) providers, protectors, and unchallenged judges if only they will stay home or at least act fatherly from a distance. I don't believe that this strategy will work for negligent men, I don't believe that it's necessary for caring men. But this is only one possible response to father absence. The presence of caring men in children's lives is a blessing for them and for the men who care. Were we, collectively, to take up the task of enabling men to be parents, to share fully in this gender-inclusive work, the ideal of distinctive Fatherhood would, I have tried to suggest, be more of an obstacle than an aid.

Toward an Ethics of Sexual Difference[28]

Everything I have said so far recommends adopting a gender-inclusive ideal of parenthood in which women and men care for children according to their talents and temperaments. If men and women can participate in every aspect of mothering from changing infant's diapers to showing up at the jail when a teenager is arrested, why would anyone affirm, rather than strive to eliminate, sexual difference? Indeed in most contexts, for political and personal reasons, I advocate an ideal of gender-inclusive parenting or, even more, of male-inclusive mothering.

Yet I also begin to wonder about costs paid and possibilities lost in this determined erasure of sexual difference. I want now to suggest some bases of my doubts, not to persuade but to open a conversation. In this spirit I identify three motives not so much for affirming as for refusing to deny sexual difference and distinctive Fatherhood.

The first motive concerns sex and has only indirectly to do with parenting. Ways and acts of naming sexual specificity offer one poignant early schooling in the meaning of difference itself. To speak very generally, adopting aspects of psychoanalytic theory, the first ego is a bodily ego. Children's sense of their body, and therefore their sense of themselves as subjects, is both sexed and sexual. This does not mean that a child recognizes sexuality as such. Rather, children are spurred to learn difference through the exploration of their own bodies, especially their genitals, and through the mysterious, often misinterpreted sexualities they witness.

But children also predictably mislearn difference. Notoriously, for example, they may believe that girls have had penises taken from them. More suggestively and generally, when they are very young, children may wish "to polymorphously incorporate the organs and abilities of both sexes," to wish and therefore believe that their bodies include *all* sexual possibilities. Somewhat later—in the so-called oedipal phase—"the child repudiates all that is other and insists that what he (or she) has is the only thing. . . . Everything [s/he] can't have is (worth) nothing."[29] Both of these fantasies resonate in adult speech: I am everything, but if I have to recognize you, then let me be the only real and good thing there is.

In a poignantly intense sexual and familial context, children might learn, and parents might relearn, to name their sexual specificities. Where parents are differently sexed, or where children are differently sexed from each other or a parent, this requires acknowledging sexual difference. By contrast, in such a family a determined denial of difference could leave in place fantasies of being the only good thing there is. More subtly, where parents are differently sexed, refusing to name difference obscures the power and fact of family sexuality.

But naming and accepting sexual difference has no simple implications for parenting. Acknowledging sexual difference does not involve identifying distinct parental functions since, as I have argued, there are none. Nor does acknowledging sexual specificity or sexual difference require living with differently sexed parents. Children learn that bodies are *sexual* through exciting self-exploration and through sensuous, erotic relationships which they experience or witness. This would be true if there were only one sex or several sexes. Naming sexual specificity requires only that *where sexual difference exists* it too be named rather than denied or mystified.

My second motive for distinguishing fathers from mothers is to acknowledge the importance of birthgiving. Notwithstanding scientific and philosophic fantasies to the contrary, to be "pregnant" with new life is still and only to be a *woman* whose body and embodied willfulness is the ground and condition of each new original being who lives. Elsewhere[30] I have explored the idea, which I first heard from birthgivers themselves, that the experience of birthgiving is sometimes intellectually transformative and gives rise to what I call "natal reflection." Natal reflection, and more generally maternal thinking, is distorted by a sentimental or hysterical identification of birth with mother/female or by an inflation of the importance of birthgiving to parenting. But natal reflection is also distorted by the personal or political need continuously to deflect the sexual exclusiveness of the birth experience—"we are pregnant," "we're due the sixteenth." At best, sexual difference in birthgiving and the relation of birth to the mothering that follows provoke natal reflection and become its topic.

Only women give birth. Yet both male and female bodies are inherently procreative. I would welcome a richer, more imaginatively elaborated understanding of male bodies as procreative. Men—and also many women—appear to apprehend male sexual bodies reductively, focusing on the (erect) penis. Were men to understand early and richly the procreativity of their bodies they might more easily recognize their relation to children as given. This might meliorate the contractual view that offers men authority and distinctive identity in return for being distant providers and staying around.[31] It might then also be easier to recognize the challenge of imagining responsible but not possessive procreation, a conceptual and moral task they could share with girls and women.

More generally, I believe that a richer apprehension of the symbolic and moral meaning of birth is necessary and central to respecting bodily life, including bodily death. Respect for human natality has to include male as well as female procreative experiences and desires. Only men can create and relate the richer story of male sexual procreativity which I would like to hear. But any such story will require a sober respect, neither grandiose nor sentimental, for biological fathering and its limited but clear relation to female birthgiving.

My final reason for not wanting to deny distinctive Fatherhood has to do with demands of contemporary conversations about parenting. Parents almost everywhere lead highly gendered lives.[32] Whatever their intentions, they are seen as mothers *or* fathers in a society in which sexual difference is enforced. Unless we recognize Fatherhood, we, feminists or mothers or social theorists, cannot converse with other mothers, feminists, or theorists, cannot compare experiences, share hopes, or even resist the distinction between mothers and fathers.

In my own work I have increasing felt the need to talk about *mothering*, not as male-inclusive but as a work in which women engage. Many issues which I want to understand—child abuse, for example, or adolescent birthgiving—involve both women and men and involve them quite differently. More generally, I fear that what Martha Fineman calls the "neutering" of mother denies the history, and usually the current practice of female mothering, including women's unjustly disproportionate responsibilities for child care. It also mystifies women's psychological experience of mothering and ultimately disrespects virtues and ways of thinking labeled "maternal."[33]

Finally, as father searchers and father advocates testify, fathers do not disappear into parenthood, still less, as I once hoped, into mothering. They are present, perhaps most poignantly in their absence that attracts, like a magnet, fantasies of a paternal protection, provision, and authority that are slipping away or just out of reach. Even the physically and historically present "new father" remains on the scene as a man, sexually distinct, redefining masculinity and masculine parenting, for his daughters as well as his sons. Consider, to cite one example, Robin Kelley's admonition:

> Dads should spend a lot more time with their daughters playing *their* games on *their* terms. Don't think for a minute that playing with dolls or make up, hopscotch or jacks, ought to be mom's domain, or that every Barbie needs a GI Joe. Those dads who feel uncomfortable playing girls games ought to get over it or get some counseling.[34]

Replacing "dads" with "parents" or with "moms" (and necessarily leaving out the "mom" already there) not only undercuts Kelley's advice but changes the meaning entirely.[35]

If we ignore fathers, fantasies and ideologies of Fatherhood remain unchecked; the task, as I see it, is to talk about fathers differently. I imagine men thinking intently about their children-in-the-world and about the world that fathering reveals to them. But these men, unlike many fathers and mothers before them, will not need to distinguish polemically the father from the mother, to profess a paternal identity, to claim for fathers distinctive value. From these men, I imagine, we could hear transformed and transformative expressions of *paternal* thinking which neither feared nor exploited sexual difference.

Yet even as I begin to think in terms of mothers and fathers I remain troubled by the associations of "Fatherhood." Given the persistence of patriarchal ideologies, sexual difference is more likely than not to be used in the service of domination; procreativity of women or men is more likely than not to lead to possessiveness and, again, to domination. It seems almost impossible to respect bodily and historical difference without trying to spell it out in psychological theory or divisions of labor. But any attempt to spell out difference, to say fathers are like this, mothers like that, only mothers can do this, only fathers do that, resurrects mystifying dangerous fictions of provision, protection, and authority, of domination and subordination.

Moreover, as I mentioned only in passing, the very idea of Fatherhood brings in its train a specific family paradigm which is exclusionary and coercive. This is, in part, a liability of any assertion of dyadic difference. Difference tends to complete itself in a couple: master-slave, woman-man, perhaps black and white. Whatever the terms, and however horrendous the relationship, subject and other are mutually constitutive. One alone, then, is lacking her other. In the Fatherhood conversation a single parent, a single mother especially, is seen not only as incomplete but as whole only when completed by a male parent. The dyadic couple then excludes anything outside itself; occupies the entire conversational space.

Whether or not these liabilities of effacement and exclusion are inherent in claims of difference, many father advocates seem prepared to exclude. For example, male procreativity and heterosexual birthgiving are in no way harmed by the mere existence of other ways of conceiving. Yet some propose to outlaw sperm donation,[35] thus limiting possibilities of mothering for lesbian women, heterosexual women without partners, or heterosexual couples for whom sperm donation is the only or preferred form of conception. Another example: neither sexual difference nor parenting require heterosexuality. Yet despite the multiple injuries to children and adults of heterosexual bigotry, father advocates usually take for granted and often wish to legislate the heterosexuality of parents.

Just because Fatherhood, like motherhood, has been used to judge and exclude, it is not enough merely to tolerate "diversity" in sexual life and family arrangements. Advocates of distinctive Fatherhood have to find ways to *actively* recognize, symbolically and socially, gay fathers, single fathers, "otherfathers"—the multifarious caring, responsible men in children's lives. Certainly I would not advocate distinguishing fathers from mothers in the absence of an *ethics* of sexual difference, an ethics which contests longstanding misogyny and heterosexual bigotry, which resists the cruelty and coercion that have attended the idea of Fatherhood.

It seems to me, at least in 1996, in the United States, extraordinarily difficult to acknowledge sexual difference without either falling into old habits of domination or embarking on imperialist intrusions into others' lives. It remains very tempting to adopt the safe-speak of "parenting." Perhaps my final, odd, reason for wanting to acknowledge sexual difference is that it is so difficult to do so. It is a challenge to relish female and male procreativity, mothers and fathers, without suffering under the illusion that one's own sex, one's own sexuality, one's own procreative act, one's own way of living is the only thing there is or should be. It is an effort to create a nonimperialist ethics of sexual difference, in the midst and in respect of the poignant complexities of sexual lives. This effort is not only necessary but exciting. By contrast, gender inclusion seems morally fearful if also morally safe.

Acknowledgments

I thank Hilde Nelson, William Ruddick, and Marilyn Young for useful comments on an earlier draft.

Notes

1. David Blankenhorn, *Fatherless America* (New York: Basic Books, 1995), p. 67.
2. On the controversial subject of "children's" needs and "maternal" or "parental" work, see my *Maternal Thinking*, 2d ed. (Boston: Beacon Press, 1995), and the new preface to this edition.
3. The fatherhood literature is especially concerned with sons. See for example, John Edgar Wideman, *Fatheralong* (New York: Pantheon Books, 1994), p. 64. "Ideas of manhood, true and transforming, grow out of private, personal exchanges between fathers and sons." Robin D.G. Kelley in "Countering the Conspiracy to Ignore Black Girls" takes direct issue with fathers' exclusive focus on males. Manuscript, courtesy of the author.
4. Wideman, *Fatheralong*, p. 64. John Wideman's *Fatheralong* is a book as much about race as about fathers, a book in which anyone speaking of fathers must necessarily speak of race. So for example, immediately after speaking of masculine identity as forged in conversations between fathers and sons, he writes:

    Yet for generations of black men in America this privacy, this privilege has been systematically breached in a most shameful and public way. Not only breached but brutally usurped, mediated by mayhem, murder, misinformation. (p. 64)

    More generally:

    If you're a black man gazing through the nursery window at your newborn son, whatever else you're feeling, love, joy, wonder, gratitude, the tipsiness of the universe whirling around you as you step aside, make room for a new star at the dead center, you cannot entirely escape the chill of the cloud passing momentarily between you and your boy. The cloud of *race*. (p. 69 and *passim*).

5. Blankenhorn, *Fatherless America*, pp. 212, 109.
6. Patricia Hill Collins, *Black Feminist Thought* (New York: Routledge, 1991).
7. This definition of "parent" depends upon construing parenting work. If parents are identified in biological or legal terms, as they often are, then many "bad" parents don't protect. See *Maternal Thinking* and the preface to the second edition.
8. Diane Ehrensaft, *Parenting Together: Women and Men Sharing the Care of Their Children* (Urbana: University of Illinois, 1990), p. 112.
9. Blankenhorn, *Fatherless America*, p. 214.
10. Blankenhorn, *Fatherless America*, p. 214.
11. From the television special, *The Windsors*, on the present British royal family.
12. The *New York Times*, Dec. 13, 1995, tells of three young girls shot by their fathers, who took them for intruders.
13. See, for example, *Maternal Thinking*, chap. 7.
14. For the particular concern of African-American parents with their children's survival, see Patricia Hill Collins, "Shifting the Center: Race, Class and Feminist Theorizing about Motherhood" in *Representations of Motherhood*, ed. Donna Bassin, Margaret Honey, and Meryle Mahrer Kaplan (New Haven: Yale University Press, 1994), pp. 56–74.
15. See Wideman, *Fatheralong*, p. 50.
16. Wideman, *Fatheralong*, p. 63.
17. Janine Chasseguet-Smirgel, "Being a Mother and Being a Psychoanalyst: Two Impossible Professions," in *Representations of Motherhood*, p. 117. I chose Chasseguet-Smirgel because she is self-critical about Fatherhood fantasies and nonetheless idealizes fathers.
18. Chassguet-Smirgel, p. 117.
19. Chassguet-Smirgel, *passim*, and p. 123.
20. For a sense of the complexity of the "justice/care" framework see Virginia Held, ed., *Justice and Care* (Boulder: Westview Press, 1995).
21. Wideman, *Fatheralong*, pp. 50–51, 85.
22. Blankenhorn, *Fatherless America*, p. 219.
23. Blankenhorn, *Fatherless America*, p. 116.
24. The phrase is Louise Kaplan's, from *Oneness and Separateness* (New York: Touchstone Books, 1978), esp. chap. 5.
25. Wideman, *Fatheralong*, p. 84, first italics mine.
26. On women's loss of cognitive authority see Hilde Nelson, "Sophie Doesn't: Families and Counterstories of Self-Trust," *Hypatia* 11, No. 1 (1996), 90–103. Wideman laments: "One mistake had been treating my father as if a father always required a capital F. As long as I carried a deity, a natural force in my mind, I couldn't see the man on the seat beside me." *Fatheralong*, p. 14.
27. The samples on which statistics are based are often small and the questions simple. Researchers seem to relish the harms of the fatherlessness they report. Absence is itself a crude notion admitting of degrees. Even where harm is "proven," it is often not clear that the absence of a *father* is to blame. Are two distant providers or disciplinarians better than one whatever the sex? Do

researchers insist on the benefits of heterosexual couples when intergenerational, collective child rearing might be equally beneficial? I can at most agree with Frank Furstenberg, who suggests, roughly, that a good father is better than none but a bad father is worse than no father at all and that "the seemingly obvious benefits for children of paternal participation in disrupted (or even intact) families cannot be assumed without stronger evidence to this date." Frank Furstenberg and Kathleen Mullin Harris, "When Fathers Matter/Why Fathers Matter: The Impact of Paternal Involvement on the Offspring of Adolescent Mothers," in *The Politics of Pregnancy*, ed. Annette Lawson and Deborah Rhodes (New Haven: Yale University Press, 1993), p. 191.

28. The phrase "sexual difference" echoes Luce Irigaray. When I first began thinking about fatherhood I was influenced by Irigaray. But ultimately my concerns are so dissimilar that I would, if I could, find a distinctive, equally useful term.

29. Jessica Benjamin, "The Omnipotent Mother," in *Representations of Motherhood*, p. 140.

30. In "Thinking Mothers/Conceiving Birth," in *Representations of Motherhood*, chap. 1.

31. This point was made in discussion by Mitt Regan of Georgetown Law School.

32. The very useful term "gendered lives" comes from Martha Fineman, *The Neutered Mother, the Sexual Family, and Other Twentieth-Century Tragedies* (New York: Routledge, 1995), pp. 12–13 and *passim*.

33. Martha Fineman, *The Neutered Mother*, *passim*.

34. Robin Kelley, "The Conspiracy to Ignore Black Girls."

35. Blankenhorn is upset by the very idea of sperm donation and proposes outlawing it.

15

Sexuality, the Family, and Nationalism

Bat-Ami Bar On

During the past few years it has become easier to be a lesbian, a gay man, or a bisexual in Israel.[1] The Israeli sodomy law, a remnant from the British Mandate beginning with the British conquest of the area after World War I and ending in May of 1948, has not been enforced since 1963, but in 1988 same-sex sexual conduct was actually decriminalized. Since 1988 several legal cases, some reaching BAGATZ (the Israeli Supreme Court) for adjudication, have all been resolved in a manner favorable to lesbians, gay men, and bisexuals. The egalitarian tendency that the Court has been exhibiting can also be observed in the acts of the Israeli Knesset (Israel's one-house parliament) which has passed legislation that can be used to prosecute cases of discrimination based on sexual orientation. Moreover, some members of the Knesset, like Yael Dayan and Amnon Rubinstine, have been very committed to extending equal rights to lesbians, gay men, and bisexuals. In addition, one can see a trend toward egalitarianism in the acts of municipalities like that of Tel-Aviv, which has a special committee on the legal rights of lesbians, gay men, and bisexuals and has moved to protect these rights. Finally and unlike the U.S. military, TZAHAL (the IDF or Israeli Defense Forces), which has permitted lesbians, gay men, and bisexuals to serve in the military, has also reversed policies that assumed that they pose a greater security risk than heterosexuals and has began granting full top security clearance to them.

The equality that lesbians, gay men, and bisexuals are beginning to experience in Israel is not merely legally formal but has a culturally public aspect too. Thus, for example, several international conferences of Jewish lesbians, gay men, and bisexuals have been held in Israel. Both Hollywood films, like *Philadelphia*, and slightly more marginal films, like *The Crying Game*, were quite successful in Israel, as were the plays *Angels in America* and *M. Butterfly*. And the Tel-Aviv museum exhibited Robert Mapplethorpe's pictures. The culturally public aspect of the growing equality of lesbians, gay men, and bisexuals in Israel has a local flavor too. So, for example, a national Pride Day began to be celebrated in June of 1993, and like other lesbian, gay, and bisexual public events and issues, it is generally covered sympathetically by the Israeli media. Pictures by an openly Jewish-Israeli lesbian and an openly Jewish-Israeli gay man about overtly lesbian and gay topics were exhibited in Tel-Aviv and Jerusalem. Films by Amos Gutman, who was a gay filmmaker, have been acclaimed in the Jewish-Israeli press. And Israel now also has a small but active lesbian, gay, and bisexual café and disco culture which helps forge more of a sense of a community among those who seek entertainment at places like the Café at Nordau or go dancing at Zman Amiti.

According to Jewish-Israeli lesbian, gay, and bisexual activists, the movement toward legally formal equality and the growth of a culturally public space for lesbians, gay men, and bisexuals is their achievement and would have not happened without their work.[2] I am not about to dispute this claim since I am convinced that social activism is always involved in the making of profound changes.[3] Yet I think that this claim needs to be contextualized, and what strikes me about the Israeli situation is that the extension of legally formal equality and a culturally public space to lesbians, gay men, and bisexuals has been taking place at the same time that the Jewish-Israeli family is changing.[4] Furthermore, the equality and recognition have followed hard on the heels of major, even if incomplete and still uncertain, transformations in Israel's economic and political situation: Israel is moving into a possibly still underminable[5] yet nevertheless more peaceful coexistence with neighboring Arab states and the Palestinians, and is also becoming a capitalist center for a region that encompasses Southwest Asia and North Africa and a few Mediterranean countries marginal to Europe, like Turkey, Cyprus, and Greece.[6]

A trend toward a legally formal and culturally public egalitarianism for lesbians, gay men, and bisexuals seems to quite often follow and coincide with liberalizing changes of the family, at least in the West.[7] At the same time, however, because in Israel the Jewish-Israeli family has been among the material and ideological cornerstones of the Zionist nation-building project,[8] changes in the family seem to require changes in this project. It is contested but real changes in the Zionist nation-building project, I believe, that are suggested by the regional changes in Israel's political and economic situation,[9] and they are as linked to the trend toward the legally formal and culturally public egalitarianism for lesbians, gay men, and bisexuals in Israel just as they are linked to the liberalizing changes of the Jewish-Israeli family, the two acting together to reconstitute gender, sexuality, and their intersections, at least for Jewish-Israelis.[10]

I

Among the local reflections regarding the constitution of Jewish-Israeli gender, sexuality, and their intersections in the context of the Zionist nation-building project is the film *Machboim*.[11] *Machboim* means literally "hiding places" and is a children's game with versions that are similar to and versions that are a bit different from "Hide and Seek."

In the film, the playing of the game "Machboim" loses its innocence because the players, a group of adolescent Jewish boys in Jerusalem just before the 1948 Jewish-Israeli War of Independence, turn the game into a hunt for Jews who spy for either the British Mandate or the Palestinians. The boys learn about the possibility that such Jewish spies are operating in their neighborhood as they listen from a hiding place to a secret neighborhood meeting organized by the Haganah (the moderate left-based Jewish underground predecessor of the IDF). The boys' primary suspect is David Balaban, the tutor of one of their number, Uri. The audience knows Balaban is not the real spy but the boys do not till much later, after the real spy is executed by members of the Haganah. The boys suspect Balaban because he seems different from other young men of his age, symbolized for them by apparently tough older brothers who are members of Zionist underground units. Balaban, who served with the Notrim (an openly armed unit of Jewish guards), is a biology student at the Hebrew University interested in teaching in elementary school and does not belong to any of the Zionist undergrounds. Moreover, he questions the current Zionist ideological projections in one of his sessions with Uri, problematizing for him the meaning of the idea of an enemy which till then Uri took to refer to the English, Palestinians, or other Arabs. The boys' imagination is being molded not only by the Haganah but also by the right-wing ETZEL (Iyrgun Tzvai Leumi) radio, and by late '30s and '40s U.S. and European spy movies mostly produced in the context of World War II. Under these influences, while they are in a hiding place in a Jerusalem park during an actual game of "Machboim," the boys see Balaban talking with a Palestinian man with whom they will see him speak and exchange notes a few more times, and doing so in Arabic, a language that they recognize but do not understand. For Uri, though, this is mostly confusing and troubling since he is fond of his tutor and reluctant to believe immediately that Balaban is a traitor.

The penultimate sequence of the film begins with information about an action against Balaban planned by a Zionist underground unit. One learns about the plan with Uri, who is told about it by another boy from his group. This boy learned of the plan from his brother, who is a member of the Zionist underground unit that is planning the action against Balaban. The boys had earlier told the brother about Balaban, because they took his suspected spying very seriously. They were surprised to find the brother condescending to them, plainly considering them not manly enough yet, lacking as they were in facial hair, and, therefore too impatiently jumping to participate in the Zionist struggle. The boys do indeed take that struggle very seriously, swearing alliance to it in initiation rituals imitating the secret swearing-in of the Zionist undergrounds. The brother's unit is undertaking the action to punish Balaban, but Uri is not told what the punishment is for, only that it is not for spying.

Uri, at first, defended Balaban to the group, thereby losing status and trust. Still, not being convinced of Balaban's innocence he secretly follows him and searches his apartment. There he finds pictures of a Palestinian man, the very same man with whom Balaban was seen several times by the group. When Balaban finds him in the apartment, Uri refuses to listen as Balaban tries to assure him that he is not a spy and tells him that there are aspects of his life about which Uri does not know anything and about which he cannot talk. Unconvinced, and feeling betrayed and hurt, Uri leaves to join his group.

Demoted from leadership due to what his group perceives as his split loyalties, Uri is not told that the meeting place has been changed, and he initially cannot find the group. Hearing from the boy who has assumed the group's leadership that Balaban is not a spy after all, Uri rushes back to Balaban's place. Looking through the window, he sees him and the Palestinian man sitting half-naked on Balaban's bed. The two are not exchanging secrets as spies might. Instead they are exchanging lovers' tenderness. Uri is confused. Yet before he can decide what to do, he becomes a witness to the Zionist underground unit attack on Balaban and his Palestinian lover. In the attack the apartment is vandalized and the lover is beaten to death while Balaban is made to watch. As Balaban is held down forcefully, shouting "no," his shout is echoed by Uri.

II

What this sequence of the film makes quite clear is that what pre-Israeli-Independence adolescent Jewish boys in the '40s had to learn as they played "Machboim" were not only certain skills that may be useful to them once they are allowed by older men to join the Zionist struggle; they also had to learn to be worthy of inclusion in the groups that undertook the Zionist nation-building project, hence of the special bonds of the brotherhood of comrades-in-arms in a struggle for national liberation assumed by its participants to be transformatively redemptive.[12] To rehearse for this they needed to do more than test each other's courage, loyalty, and stamina. They also had to rehearse in ways that at one and the same time constituted their (soon to be) Jewish-Israeli nationality,[13] their gender as toughly masculine,[14] and their sexuality as strictly heterosexual.

The group's complicity in the brutal killing of Balaban's Palestinian male lover and through it in the terrorization of Balaban made of the boys a different kind of group. The moment of the attack was for the boys what, following Freud, has been termed a primordial founding moment.[15] During this moment the boys submitted to the "Law of the Father." They did so not by partaking in the murder of "the Father" but by complicity partaking in the murder of the one who ought to be their "Other,"[16] the Palestinian homosexual lover of a Jewish homosexual man who refused the rigid national, gender, and sexuality boundaries that the boys were supposed to internalize as they created their interiority.

Only in this way could boys grow to be like today's Yehoyada Mandeel. Yehoyada, or Yo Yo, is a sixteen-year-old Jewish-Israeli boy who for the past three years has been participating in the "Seeds for Peace" summer camp in Maine. There he has established a growing friendship with Laith Arafeh, a sixteen-year-old Palestinian boy who lives on the West Bank. Yo Yo's interiority is revealed in the last paragraph of Sara Rimer's *New York Times* article about the two boys. She writes:

> Yo Yo grew serious. "In two years I am going to go into the Israeli Army. In two years I am going to have a gun in my hand. Naturally, it will be my nation first. Laith feels the same way."
>
> Laith looked his friend in the eye. "If you were in a jeep, and I threw stones at the jeep, would you shoot me?"
>
> Yo Yo did not hesitate. "I can't tell you I would not," he said.[17]

III

There is no Jewish-Israeli film like *Machboim* about adolescent Jewish girls in the pre-Israeli-independence period and little that clarifies what they had to do to constitute their nationality, gender, and sexuality. The one woman that *Machboim* focuses on, Uri's mother, is present primarily through her absence from her home and family. Home is where she is expected to be, yet is permitted not to be, because she extends her maternal skills and nurturing warmth to Jewish refugee children orphaned, or presumed to have been orphaned, during the Nazi Judeocide. Because she is mobilized to mother many children rather than just her own child, and so does her duty in the service of the Zionist nation-building project, her absence from her home is tolerated.

The mobilization of Uri's mother into service for the Zionist nation-building project as the mother of many children is in line with a traditional gendered division of labor.[18] Yet *Machboim* points out that despite this, women and men in the pre-Israeli-Independence period were projected ideologically as quite equal. The film does so by positioning both of Uri's parents as similarly absent, his father also working actively in the service of the Zionist nation-building project outside his home and away from his family. In addition, it is Uri's grandfather who takes on Uri's care and nurturance and the household chores that would have been Uri's mother's. The film shows a woman leading the neighborhood Haganah meeting and in doing so hints at women's participation in the Zionist undergrounds. And, though teaching is considered a woman's occupation, when Balaban tells Uri's grandfather about his intent to teach in the elementary school, the grandfather repeats a Zionist slogan that approves of teaching as among the best forms of participation in the Zionist nation-building project.

Machboim's presentation of a different but equal gender-egalitarianism is subtly undermined by showing Uri's grandfather as quietly upset with and critical of Uri's mother's plan to return to her work after a short visit home. The film also shows Uri as quietly longing to have his mother home and for himself, and also fighting with her. Both imply his criticism of her neglect of him, particularly when he responds to her worries that he is playing games that endanger his life by saying that he does not care if he dies. And, much less subtly, *Machboim* undermines the Zionist ideological projection of gender-egalitarianism by showing that the boys are socialized in a single-sex group and without any contact with girls. Moreover, aside from Uri, who has an ambiguous relationship with Balaban, the boys are shown as totally idealizing for themselves the Zionist warrior males in their environment, which is, according to *Machboim*, of course, what they are really expected to do.

By undermining the Zionist ideological projection of gender-egalitarianism in the ways it does, *Machboim* calls attention to the normative force behind women's assignment to traditional familial roles in the pre-Israeli-Independence period, as well as to the fact that it was an assignment to socially inferior roles. At the same time, though, *Machboim* suggests that the Zionist nation-building project did not leave these roles unaffected. Rather, it transformed them by turning the nation into the primary extended family that women had to care for. For Uri's mother this transformation is so complete that she invites Uri to join her refugee children at the institution in which she was working, a move that for her eliminated the tension between her duties to her personal family and her duties to her national one.

It is not only fictional characters like Uri's mother who gesture at the transformation of women's roles under the Zionist nation-building project. A few days after the assassination of Israel's Prime Minister Yitzhak Rabin in November 1995 by Yigal Amir, the assassin's mother asked the forgiveness of Leah Rabin, thereby holding herself accountable for her son's deeds. Her failure, as she seems to have understood it, was to raise a child who murdered the head of Israel's government, an act that she characterized as "betraying us," where the "us" could be read as signifying Amir's family or all Jewish-Israelis and perhaps all Jews. To the extent that Amir's mother felt any conflict between her familial and national allegiances, she resolved them by disassociating herself from her son and declaring their connection so attenuated by Amir's deeds that it became "merely biological."[19]

The elimination of the tension between a personal family and the larger society is among the most important conditions for group conformity.[20] Since the Zionist nation-building project was quite successful, one can suppose that group conformity was as common among girls in the pre-Israeli-

Independence period as it was among boys, and that they came to create their interiority in ways that made it possible for them to accept their social assignment to their traditional familial roles within the nation. Still, one needs to leap imaginatively from the well-documented and carefully analyzed experience of boys in the pre-Israeli-Independence period to the experience of girls. If one does so by following the critical format offered by *Machboim*, the obvious question one must ask is: If the Jewish homosexual man represents a culpable psychopedagogical refusal of the rigid national, gender, and sexuality boundaries that Jewish-Israeli heterosexual men have to abide by, does the Jewish lesbian woman represent the same kind of refusal of national, gender, and sexuality boundaries that Jewish-Israeli women have to abide by and, therefore, must she too be punished for psychopedagogical purposes?

IV

About midway in her oral history,[21] Ora Yarden, whose parents came to Palestine from Europe in the '30s yet lost families to the Nazi Judeocide, and who was born in 1946, states;

> Israel is very conservative when it comes to marriage and family. It's a Jewish state and in Jewish culture, family is very important. If you are not married by twenty-four, then something must be wrong with you. When I was twenty-eight, my father said, "It's better to be a divorcée than an old maid of forty no one wants."[22]

Yael Omer's oral history[23] confirms Yarden's perception of Israeli society as conservative when it comes to marriage and family. Omer, whose parents came from Greece and Morocco and who was born in 1961, married when she was twenty-one, and at twenty-seven, when interviewed, was struggling with the fact that she was also a lesbian, something she discovered just two years after marrying. She said, as she was thinking through a solution to her situation:

> Maybe I could be like a friend of mine in town: married for sixteen years, raised her kids, then went with a woman after that.... Yes, I think, sixteen years and then the children will be more or less adults, and then I can be lesbian again! Because when you are older, the criticism from society is not so great. You've made your duty already, you've had your kids, it's fine if you want to have some fun! I could split my life in two: one half regular, the other half me, myself. It's not good that this is the way, but it's going to help me to cope with everything.[24]

Omer, like Yarden, feels the social pressures to which Yarden returns toward the end of her interview when she also theorizes about being a Jewish-Israeli lesbian in Israel. Yarden claims:

The political situation here has great hostility toward lesbians. In Israel, we live in a military, very conservative society. Women have a certain role—period. Of course, women are supposed to do what they are supposed to do all over the world—but more so here: raise kids, raise the men for the army, take care of soldiers. A lesbian is a real threat to this structure. She says: "I'm not taking care of your soldiers or raising new soldiers. I'm not taking part in these war games you play all the time." In addition, since Israel is a religious country, there are all kinds of religious laws against us.[25]

Yarden describes the Jewish-Israeli lesbian as refusing the national identity a Jewish-Israeli woman is expected to have by refusing her social assignment to a traditional familial role in the personal and national families, a role that requires that a woman see herself as feminine (insofar as this connotes nurturance) and as heterosexual (insofar as this connotes reproduction). This assignment, as Shira Markowitz's oral history[26] clarifies, still has an aspect of service to the nation that has to be fulfilled outside the personal family that Omer considers a duty and feels compelled to obey. Markowitz, who was born in 1963 in the U.S. to parents originating in Russia and Germany, immigrated to Israel with her parents when she was seven. She describes one of her military assignments, saying:

Next I was sent to the Hermon, a mountainous, snow-covered region on the Syrian border. A unit of soldiers was stationed there and I was to be their "platoon clerk," a job coveted by army women. There is one woman in a fighting unit of sixty or seventy men, and while she has a technical side to her work—she takes care of the mail, things like that—mostly the role means being a *woman*. She's expected to be motherly—to be affectionate, to bake cookies for the boys, to listen to their problems with their girlfriends. A few of them fall in love with her, she usually falls in love with one of the officers—it is a role a lot of women want.[27]

Markowitz, who joined the antiwar movement while still in the military and came out as a lesbian after her military service, confirms Yarden's sense of the Jewish-Israeli lesbian as refusing a strict national identity as a Jewish-Israeli heterosexual woman by refusing her social assignment to a traditional familial role. She adds:

I had a hard time with this role—I felt that it was not all right that I couldn't be these things. I was trying but it did not work. Now I don't feel bad about it. In fact, I feel rather proud.[28]

Yarden, who is also a peace activist, is no less proud than Markowitz. Nonetheless, she has a sense of a deferred danger. At the moment, she thinks that the danger that Jewish-Israeli lesbians may face is deferred because masculine Jewish-Israeli hostility is focused on the Palestinians. She states:

> Still, we're a small enough group so we are not harassed. In Israel, it's the Palestinian who gets all the shit. As a Jew, even if I'm a lesbian—I am still privileged. So, if I don't make too much noise, they leave me in peace and continue harassing the Palestinians.[29]

V

Given Euro-American models of analysis, it is interesting and important to note that it is not a transgressive sexuality but the refusal of a social role assignment that is the focus of Jewish-Israeli lesbians' explanations of the threat that they pose to Jewish-Israeli society and could be punished for. Their situation has been framed by Zionism, which, like the European revolutionary movements that influenced it,[30] tended toward puritanical sublimation and the redirection of eroticism. In Zionism's case, eroticism has been directed primarily toward the land of Israel. Having redirected eroticism toward the land, Zionism could center-stage the social roles that people were expected to assume as they shouldered their share of the revolutionary burden. This is what the Jewish-Israeli lesbians see themselves as refusing to do and as a result, understandably, they see themselves as rupturing the Jewish-Israeli social order.

Elena is a twenty-seven-year-old immigrant from Uruguay who has been in Israel for just seven years. She says:

> In the last year I have sometimes felt I don't want to get older here in Israel. I am getting tired of the Israeli mentality, I am tired of the Intifada, worrying, having to be afraid of stones or petrol bombs. But I don't see myself back in Uruguay, and I don't see myself anywhere else. I know Israel is making terrible mistakes. But I *like* Israel inside me. If I leave Israel, I will worry about it. I get angry because I expect my people, victims of the Holocaust, to be better. It's disgusting to see that we are not better. We are the same as the Germans, the Americans—countries that do horrible things. Either I can live in Israel or I can't, but I will always be concerned about Israel; I will always consider myself a Jew and an Israeli. It does not matter what Israel does; I will be concerned about it.[31]

Nurit D., Israeli born in 1949 to Nazi Judeocide survivors, uses a somewhat different idiom to express feelings similar to those of Elena. She says:

> I cannot forgive Jews who treat others like anti-Semites treat us. I expect more from Jews; it's like feminists and lesbians. I'm appalled by what we're doing to the Arabs. . . . But, of course, it is a vibrant beauti-

ful country. For a long time it was the realization of the ultimate Zionist dream. Now I've outgrown Zionism, but it still has weight for me. It
was an enormous feat of redemption for a whole people. It's just a pity
it was at the expense of somebody else. But, in and of itself it was a
magnificent feat. I don't think any Jew who lives here for enough time
to become really acclimated can leave it and be whole, ever again.[32]

Not having released themselves from the familiar discourse, Elena and
Nurit D. can still prioritize Jewish-Israelis and their concerns and marginalize the Palestinians. This, if Yarden is right, is in their self-interest as Jewish-Israeli lesbians, though, given the rise in violence against women in
Israel,[33] not in the long run. Yet how can they release themselves from the
familiar discourse when the alternative to their analysis of their situation
is the Euro-American model, focusing as it does on transgressive sexuality?
At this point, an analysis of the Jewish-Israeli situation that focuses on
Jewish-Israeli lesbians' transgressive sexuality seems incapable of making
that situation intelligible. Still, things are changing for Jewish-Israeli lesbians, as they are for all Jewish-Israelis, due to the regional changes in Israel's political and economic situation. Among the consequences of this for
Elena is a more fragmented sense of herself that separates her lesbian perspective from other perspectives she has. And she claims:

Israel is getting more occidental. For gay life, it's good. But, I look at Israel not only from a lesbian point of view. . . .[34]

With a fragmentation of this kind, it is possible that Jewish-Israeli lesbians will begin to analyze their situation in new terms, perhaps even trying to theorize it with a focus on their transgressive sexuality. Whichever
turn Jewish-Israeli lesbian analysis takes, however, it must continue to pay
attention to the unique local situation and cannot be blind to the current
transformations of the Zionist nation-building project. While despite Benjamin Netanyahu's success in the 1996 elections this project may appear
less nationalist, due to the current peace process and the territorial con-
cessions it involves,[35] there are ways in which it is attempting to revive itself, and more subtly than through the forms of mobilization and acts of
the Jewish-Israeli right wing. Right now the Jewish-Israeli state is responding in a straightforwardly classical modernist way[36] to the effects of
the regional changes in its political and economic situation on people's
sense of identity. It is attempting to reintegrate them, obviously so in the
case of Jewish-Israeli lesbians, gay men, and bisexuals to whom a legally
formal and culturally public egalitarianism has been extended, into a new
organic whole.

The offer of integration is extremely seductive, especially in the case of
a group as marginal to their society as Jewish-Israeli lesbians can be. Their
marginality may free them somewhat but also creates a yearning to belong

that is palpable in the Jewish-Israeli lesbian oral histories. They are products of Jewish-Israeli state and society, constituted to feel this yearning and respond to it by rebonding as much as they can to the imagined Jewish-Israeli collectivity. Membership in this collectivity is, after all, an important source of meaningfulness at the level of everyday life.[37] To accept the offer, though, is to accept an offer that is not made to redress the alienation of Jewish-Israeli lesbians. Even if it were, it would still be complicit in perpetuating the alienation of the Palestinians, the "Others" for the Zionist nation-building project.

That in Israel an offer of integration to a Jewish-Israeli collectivity reinscribes the alienation of the Palestinians has become poignantly clear in the wake of Rabin's assassination. The assassination was followed by calls for national unity because it was taken to signal a rift in the body-politic that was deeper than had been thought, and interpreted as shattering an innocent belief in the existence of shared national taboos. The fragmented body-politic addressed by the calls did not include all Israeli citizens, a substantial number of whom are Palestinian, but only Jewish citizens of Israel, and perhaps all Jews. In addition, while the calls were made and responded to emotionally and politically with a certain "coming together"[38] of Jewish-Israelis, the investigation into the assassination showed that Rabin's assassin, Yigal Amir, belonged to a Jewish-Israeli, religious, right-wing group that had plans to attack members of the Israeli government and to violently terrorize Palestinians in their autonomous enclaves in the West Bank and Gaza. The investigation also revealed that the security arrangements made for Rabin were lax because the Shin Bet (Israel's secret security forces) and Israeli police were prepared only for an attack by Palestinians.

It is painful not to answer a yearning to belong. Still, as painful as it may be to keep oneself from uniting fully with the Jewish-Israeli collectivity, in the present Israeli conditions, one must prioritize the cacophony and chaos of democracy over the satisfaction of a unifying and oppressing inclusion.

Acknowledgments

I would like to thank my Middle-East Gender Formation Research Group, part of the Regional Economies and Cultures Project, Lisa Tessman, and Mary Jane Treacy for discussions that helped me think about issues pertinent to this essay, Hilde Nelson for her editorial help, and my union—UUP—for grants that helped with my research.

Notes

1. One of the best sources for information about the situation of lesbians, gay men, and bisexuals in Israel is the archived collections, especially of newspaper articles, at the Haagudah Le-Shmirat Zchuiot Haprat Le-Maan Homosexualim, Lesbiot, Ve-Bisexualim Be-Israel (the Society for the Protection of Personal Rights for Gay Men, Lesbians, and Bisexuals in Israel, or SPPR)

Center at 28 Nachmani Street in Tel-Aviv (P.O. Box 37604, Tel-Aviv 61375, Israel). The SPPR also has useful publications and references.

2. This is a point that was emphasized to me in an interview with Amit Kama, the Executive Director of SPPR.

3. For a general discussion of movements for social change see Samir Amin, Giovanni Arrighi, Andre Gunder-Frank, and Immanuel Wallerstein, *Transforming the Revolution: Social Movements and the World-System* (New York: Monthly Review, 1990). For a discussion of lesbian, gay men, and bisexual progressive movements see Margaret Cruikshank, *The Gay and Lesbian Liberation Movement* (New York: Routledge, 1992).

4. See information and discussion in Leslie Hazelton, *Israeli Women: The Reality Behind the Myths* (New York: Simon and Schuster, 1977), Dafna Israeli, Ariela Friedman, and Ruth Shrift, eds., *The Double Bind: Women in Israel* (Tel-Aviv: Hakkibutz Hameuchad, 1982 (Hebrew)), and Barbara Swirski and Miriam Safir, eds., *Calling the Equality Bluff: Women in Israel* (New York: Pergamon, 1991).

5. This is the hope of Jewish-Israelis on the further right and especially religious right, as well as of movements on the Arab and Palestinian side, like Hizballa, Hamas, and the Muslim Brotherhood, and is why they have resorted more and more to violent terrorism.

6. See Yoav Peled, "From Zionism to Capitalism," *Middle East Research and Information Project* 25/3–4 (May-June/July-August 1995), pp. 13–17.

7. This is fairly obvious in the history of the U.S. See a discussion of the relationship between the two for England in David T. Evans, *Sexual Citizenship: The Material Construction of Sexualities* (London: Routledge, 1993), pp. 69–70.

8. In Israel almost everything has been linked to the Zionist nation-building project. (See Anita Shapira's work on the Jewish-Israeli revolutionary ethos in *Visions in Conflict* [Tel-Aviv: Am Oved, 1989 (Hebrew)].

9. In *The Long Twentieth Century* (London: Verso, 1994), Giovanni Arrighi discusses the relationship between state and capitalist formations. See also Joel Bauman, "Designer Heritage: Israeli National Parks and the Politics of Historical Representation," *Middle East Research and Information Project* 25/5 (September–October 1995), pp. 20–24.

10. Though probably not only. See Naomi Chazan and Mariam Mar'i, "What Has the Occupation Done to Palestinian and Israeli Women? A Dialogue," in Tamar Mayer, ed., *Women and the Israeli Occupation: The Politics of Change* (New York: Routledge, 1994), pp. 16–32.

11. *Machboim* (1980) was written and directed by Dan Wolman.

12. For a sympathetic discussion of the Zionist nation-building project, see Shlomo Avineri, *The Making of Modern Zionism: The Intellectual Origins of the Jewish State* (New York: Basic Books, 1981). For a more critical discussion see Bernard Avishai, *The Tragedy of Zionism: Revolution and Democracy in the Land of Israel* (New York: Farrar Straus Giroux, 1985).

13. See Amos Elon, *The Israelis: Founders and Sons* (New York: Holt, Rinehart, and Wilson, 1971).

14. See David Biale, *Power and Powerlessness in Jewish History* (New York: Schocken, 1986) and especially Chapter 6, "Israel and the Meaning of Modern Sovereignty," pp. 145–176, as well as Paul Breins, *Tough Jews: Political*

Fantasies and the Moral Dilemma of American Jewry (New York: Basic Books, 1990) and especially Part 2, "From Masada to Mossad: A Historical Sketch of Tough Jewish Imagery," pp. 75–168.

15. Freud discusses the primordial founding moments for groups in several texts beginning with *Totem and Taboo* (1912–1913). He eleborates systematically on the subject of groups that are not kin-based in *Group Psychology and the Analysis of the Ego* (1921).

16. See Ilan Peleg's discussion of the othering of Arabs in Israel in his "Otherness and Israel's Arab Dilemma," in Laurence J. Silberstein and Robert L. Cohn eds., *The Other in Jewish Thought and History* (New York: New York University, 1994), pp. 258–280.

17. Sara Rimer, "A Camp Sows the Seeds of Peace: Arab and Israeli Teen-Agers Talk, Listen and Make Friends," *New York Times* (September 3, 1995), p. 16.

18. Generally, for a Jewish-Israeli film, this functions to position women as inferior. See Orly Lubin, "The Woman as Other in Israeli Cinema," in Silberstein, and Cohn eds., *The Other in Jewish Thought and History*, pp. 305–325.

19. Amir's mother's interview with Israeli TV was reported in Israeli newspapers, a summary of which is on the Internet, courtesy of the Israeli consulate in New York (http://www.israel-mfa.gov.il). The *Boston Globe*, November 10, 1995, reported the interview on p. 11.

20. This is implied by Freud's work on group psychology and developed by Herbert Marcuse in "The Obsolescence of the Freudian Concept of Man," in *Five Lectures: Psychoanalysis, Politics, and Utopia* (Boston: Beacon, 1970), pp. 44–61, an essay that seems even more suggestive when read in juxtaposition with Eli Zaretsky's *Capitalism, the Family, and Personal Life* (New York: Harper and Row, 1976).

21. Ora Yarden (edited by Irene Klepfisz) in Tracy Moore, ed., *Lesbiot: Israeli Lesbians Talk About Sexuality, Feminism, Judaism, and Their Lives* (London: Cassell, 1995), pp. 53–76.

22. Yarden, p. 64.

23. Yael Omer (edited by Melanie Braverman) in Moore, ed., *Lesbiot*, pp. 77–87.

24. Omer, p. 86.

25. Yarden, pp. 72–73.

26. Shira Markowitz (edited by Alexis Danzig) in Moore, ed., *Lesbiot*, pp. 105–115.

27. Markowitz, p. 110.

28. Markowitz, p. 110.

29. Yarden, p. 73.

30. See Greta N. Slobin's discussion of Russia, the primary model for socialist Zionists, the rulling elite in pre-Israeli-Independence and into Israel's first three decades, in "Revolution Must Come First: Reading V. Aksenov's *Island of Crimea*," in Andrew Parker, Mary Russo, Doris Sommer, and Patricia Yaeger, eds., *Nationalisms and Sexualities* (New York: Routledge, 1992), pp. 246–259.

31. Elena (edited by Kate Chandler) in Moore, ed., *Lesbiot*, pp. 32–33.

32. Nurit D. (edited by Spike Pitsberg) in Moore, ed., *Lesbiot*, pp. 131–132.

33. See Simona Sharoni, "Homefront as Battlefield: Gender, Military Occupation, and Violence Against Women," in Tamar Mayer, ed., *Women and the Israeli Occupation: The Politics of Change* (New York: Routledge, 1994), pp.

121–137.

34. Elena, p. 31.

35. The appearances can be quite misleading. See Edward W. Said, "Oslo I to Oslo II: The Mirage of Peace," *The Nation* 261, No. 12 (October 16, 1995), pp. 413–420.

36. See Cindy Patton's discussion in "Tremble, Hetero Swine," in Michael Warner, ed. *Fear of a Queer Planet: Queer Politics and Social Theory* (University of Minnesota, 1993), pp. 143–174.

37. For discussion, see my "Meditations on National Identity," *Hypatia* 9, No. 2 (Spring 1994), pp. 40–62.

38. The popular "coming together" political response consisted of a sway of public opinion toward Labor Party peace policies, which repudiated the Jewish-Israeli religious right-wing claim to represent the majority. The less extreme secular Jewish-Israeli right wing presented itself as belonging with everyone else by distancing itself from the extreme right wing. So did some of the less extreme religious Jewish-Israeli right wing.

16

The Family Romance:
A *Fin-de-Siècle* Tragedy

Diana Tietjens Meyers

A century ago in the midst of the political, artistic, and intellectual foment of *fin-de-siècle* Vienna, Freud published "The Aetiology of Hysteria" (1896). This paper contains the shocking revelation that patients suffering from hysteria were sexually abused during childhood and the provocative explanatory hypothesis that the symptoms of hysteria are consequences of this abuse. Some scholars maintain that Freud never denied the high incidence of sexual abuse of children and was troubled by it throughout his life; others maintain that Freud's handling of this matter calls into question his personal and scientific integrity.[1] What is incontrovertible is that Freud soon repudiated the explanatory hypothesis put forward in "The Aetiology of Hysteria." In subsequent accounts of the genesis of neurosis, veridical recollections of early sexual abuse are replaced by recollections of incestuous childhood desires and fantasies of their consummation. Embellishing his initial account by interiorizing the substance of his patients' poignant testimony, Freud invented the elegant baroque conceit that became known as psychoanalysis.

On centennial, not to say millennial, cue, the issue of father-daughter incest has recently resurfaced with all the ferocity and vitriol that psychoanalysts associate with the return of the repressed. The revival of this dormant controversy has unsettled contemporary family life and injected a note of urgency into the by-and-large sluggish political, artistic, and intellectual climate of *fin-de-siècle* postindustrial society. Especially in the United States, large numbers of women are accusing their fathers[2] of having sexually abused them when they were young, and their supporters are engaged in pitched scholarly, media, and courtroom battles defending recovered memory against skeptics.

My aim in this paper is to propose a way of interpreting the phenomenon of recovered memory that moves beyond the prevailing "Did it happen, or didn't it?" construal of the debate. In Section 1, I critically examine four prominent views of recovered memory, and I argue that none strikes the right balance between the epistemic opacity of the past and the obligation to respect women who claim to remember childhood sexual abuse after a long period of amnesia. In Section 2, I turn to the role of culturally furnished figurations in autobiographical memory, and I consider how different versions of Freud's family romance are used to figure disparate adult outcomes for women—marriage and motherhood, on the one hand, and hysteria or multiple personality disorder, on the other. Focusing on the rhetoric of autobiographical memory in conjunction with the contribution of autobiographical memory to self-definition reorients the discussion of recovered memory. Instead of stubbornly trying to answer the often unanswerable question "Which of these two people is telling the truth?" we can ask which psychological conditions the trope of sadistic incest aptly figures and whether this figuration is necessary or fruitful. Section 3 argues that feminist therapists and scholars have reason to develop alternatives to the family romance. In Section 4, I explore some implications of my analysis with respect to a basic issue in feminist theory, namely, how to conceive the self. Some feminists have sought to reclaim women's experience of multiplicity and to defend the multiplicitous self. I urge, however, that using the trope of sadistic incest to figure multiplicity impedes this reclamation project. Both for purposes of psychotherapy and for purposes of feminist theory, it is time to displace the family romance and to replace it with tropes that support feminist emancipatory aims.

1. The Controversy over Recovered Memory

That autobiographical reality is as much a matter of literary form as documentable content seems to be a truism among psychologists who study memory. Still, it does not follow that autobiographical reality is merely subjective. On the contrary, it is intersubjective in many and sundry ways. What does follow is that the personal past is not straightforwardly retrievable and also that the personal past is highly malleable. Of course, neither of these facts stops anyone from confidently representing her past—the minor details as well as the momentous crises and formative watersheds—to herself and others. This is by no means surprising, for however contestable, manipulable, and revisable memory may be, it anchors personal identity. The continuity of one's memory sequence sustains one's sense of ongoing individual existence, and one interprets one's experience and choices and ascribes meaning to one's life in part by invoking memories.

In this context, it is obvious why recovered memories of childhood sexual abuse are both explosive and problematic. Likewise, it is predictable that accounts of the standing of these reports would proliferate. There are three principal accounts currently in contention. Jeffrey Masson, Judith Herman, and Lenore Terr are prominent among those who credit the memories.[3] They believe that child victims commonly repress experience of trauma, especially repeated trauma, and although Herman cautions against injudiciously using hypnosis or drugs to extract memories of abuse, she joins Masson and Terr in holding that there should be a presumption that patients' memories are veridical reports of actual incidents. Taking sharp issue with this view, Frederick Crews debunks recovered memories as suggestions implanted in vulnerable and pliant women by irresponsible, perhaps nefarious, psychotherapists and authors of self-help books.[4]

Ian Hacking proposes a more complex view of recovered memory. He does not deny that some patients are accurately reporting specific abuses, nor that therapists and self-help books can induce susceptible individuals to believe they were abused. However, he observes that these alternatives do not account for all of the cases. According to Hacking, intentional action is indeterminate, for there are many correct ways to describe a single act. Moreover, as new descriptions become available, people can redescribe and reexperience past events. Consider, for example, a "less flagrant" form of abuse that gave a child a "shady feeling of sexual discomfort" at the time. She may not forget her feelings of peril and intimidation even though she is not familiar with the concept of child abuse. If at a later time, she becomes acquainted with the concept of child abuse and the narrative possibilities this concept authorizes, she may fill in scenes that blame her distress on the other person's conduct. Now she remembers being sexually abused as a child. Even conduct that was considered innocuous at the time can be interpreted in light of new concepts. Retroactively revising the past, such recasting accounts for additional cases of recovered memory.[5]

Plainly, it is a virtue of Hacking's view that it respects the testimony of women who are remembering childhood trauma. Yet some will surely find his view promiscuously inclusive. His account of "semantic contagion" entails that there is almost no woman alive today who could not reasonably profess to have been sexually abused in childhood. That girls are victims of incest becomes a historically conditioned tautology. Yet Hacking draws back from this conclusion. Insisting on preserving the distinction between true and false beliefs about one's past, he defends the value of lucid self-knowledge.[6]

The territory of memory is notoriously treacherous. Once we relinquish the untenable idea that remembering is like playing a tape one has recorded on an interior video camera (this is Hacking's simile), we are obliged to acknowledge that memory is full of holes. Moreover, it is often impossible to determine which features of an incident one registered at the time and which features one picked up in later conversations with other participants or from other reports. The miscellaneous materials of memory are cobbled into narratives that include selected materials while omitting others and that could be framed and organized in indefinitely many ways.[7] Rehearsal helps to preserve memories. Yet, people relate their experiences in stories fashioned for particular audiences, and these retellings may erode memory.[8] It is amazingly easy to induce people to believe that they are remembering major events that never happened to them.[9] It is extremely difficult to persuade people that they are misremembering events if their recollections are vivid and detailed, form a coherent sequence, and maintain characterological consistency.[10] Dissolving the distinction between recalling an experience, on the one hand, and believing an experience took place or imagining that it did, on the other hand, is an ever-present danger. Although Hacking resists subjectivizing memory by appealing to shared, though contestable and modifiable, conventions of language use, it is not clear that he altogether avoids conflating these phenomena.

The obligation to show respect for rememberers and their recollections, coupled with the overwhelming evidence of the incompleteness, the variability, indeed, the downright unreliability of memory is confounding. This baffling conjunction of a compelling moral imperative with insuperable epistemic opacity may make Freud's psychoanalytic solution seem attractive. On his view, recovered memories are reports of repressed childhood fantasies of seduction, and these fantasies are constituents of psychic reality. Psychic reality is the unconscious inner world where wishing is indistinguishable from doing a certain act or being subjected to a certain treatment and where the effects of wishing on personal well-being may be as profound as the effects of acting or undergoing. A girl's repressed fantasies of incest may lead to neurosis later in her life. Women who report childhood sexual abuse but whose parents and siblings adamantly and convincingly deny it are neither lying, nor are they altogether deluding themselves. They are reporting actual past experience of a riveting fantasy.

By positing psychic reality, Freud supplies real events for psychoanalytic interpretations to correspond to and a way out of the either-it-happened-or-it-didn't dilemma. Although psychoanalytic theory holds that the deliverances of memory require a bit of professional decoding since they may conflate fantasies with interpersonal incidents, it upholds the veracity of psychoanalytic patients and the basic reliability of memory. Thus Freud's fantasy-packed psychic reality secures the truthfulness of women suffering from hysteria or multiple personality disorder and vindicates a qualified affirmation of the veridicality of their memories. Concomitantly, it avoids besmirching the reputations of their fathers.

Recovered memory generates a triadic antinomy of memory and morals. By consigning recovered memories to psychic reality, Freud obtains a neat correspondence between his patients' recollections of sexual molestation and their childhood experience at the price of suppressing or, at least, sidelining the possibility that their fathers really raped or otherwise molested them. Moreover, he opens his clinical practices to the charge of suggestion, for psychic reality may be nothing more than a fabrication that the therapist persuades the impressionable patient to embrace. Masson, Herman, and Crews revert to a more commonsensical distinction between true and false memories, but at the cost of indiscriminately countenancing or dismissing recovered memories. Masson and Herman merely pay lip service to what they seem to regard as the remote possibility that a father accused of incest is innocent. However, unqualified support for recovered memory claims neglects a substantial body of empirical data demonstrating the mercurial workings of memory, and it scorns out of hand the testimony of anyone who denies the truth of these accusations. In contrast, Crews's impatience with women who report recovered memories of childhood sexual abuse and his contempt for therapists who ally themselves with these women are undisguised. Crews's apostate antipathy for psychoanalysis blinds him to the real possibility that the long-run psychological impact of incest may assume a number of different forms. Hacking proffers a subtle account of memory that is faithful to related social practices. Although Hacking distances himself from many women who allege that they were sexually abused, his account does not preclude solidarity with them. However, his account blurs the line between beliefs representing facts about the past and beliefs projecting present anxieties onto the past. Evidently, no account of memory and recovered memory is free of serious liabilities.

2. Figurations of Sexuality and the Family—The Cultural Cache

A second truism among psychologists who study autobiographical memory is that people generally rely on a cultural stock of figurations to recount their past. Literary and artistic originality are rare, and most people appropriate culturally furnished figurations. It would be a mistake, though, to think of recollection as a two-stage process in which one starts with a bit of raw memory material and then articulates it via selected figurations. Rather, the figurations guide and shape recollection from the start.[11] To some extent, people are captives of their culture's repertory of figurations. It takes a conscious effort to become aware of and to criticize ubiquitous figurations, especially those that are integral to a cultural worldview, and it takes a great deal of assiduous self-monitoring to begin to extricate one's thinking from these figurations. To understand recovered memory, then, we must consider what culturally entrenched figurations are fueling this phenomenon.

Figurations of gender, sexuality, and family relations are multifarious, pervasive, and captivating.[12] Among the most potent of these figurations is Freud's family romance. According to Freud, the Oedipus complex and its resolution explain the emergence of normal gender, that is, heterosexuality with the aim of procreation. For a girl, the Oedipus complex commences when she discovers that she lacks a penis, a deprivation which she takes for castration.[13] Angry with her mother for not endowing her with this supremely valuable organ, and repelled by her mother who is castrated too, the girl falls in love with her father. Not only does her father have a penis, but also he can give her a penis substitute in the form of a baby. Eventually, the girl will detach her affection from her father and transfer it to a male peer whom she will marry and have children with. Having made this transition, she achieves "femininity," and the curtain rings down.

But, of course, the family romance is a drama that is never out of production. The culmination of psychic development, the Oedipus complex is reenacted in every generation of every family with mother, father, and daughter or son as conscripted dramatis personae. Its plot embodies the meaning of the family as a site of procreative heterosexuality and as a transmitter of procreative heterosexuality. Its continuous run ceaselessly reaffirms that meaning.[14] Incest is, then, the reigning metaphor of the heterosexual mother (or father).

Although Freud regards the family romance as a childhood fantasy that becomes a prime component of psychic reality, I have classified it as a figuration. Here, I follow Elizabeth Abel, who likens psychoanalysis to fairy tales.[15] Both genres situate prototypical characters in memorable stories that interpret experience and guide conduct, and both are widely disseminated. On this view, we can understand the power of the family romance without becoming embroiled in sterile controversy over infantile sexuality and the fantasies it may or may not kindle. As long as this image of family relations is a cultural staple that is imparted to each new generation, it will be constitutive of the cognitive and emotional substrate of perception and memory, including self-perception and autobiographical memory.

In a discussion of Freud's theory of original fantasies, Jean Laplanche and J.-B. Pontalis characterize these fantasies in a way that also illuminates the view I am proposing. Laplanche and Pontalis claim that original fantasies take the form of skeletal, impersonal, present-tense scenarios, and they urge that this form facilitates psychological assimilation of these fantasies.[16] The daughter's version of the family romance might be schematized as follows: a daughter falls in love with a father, and she becomes a wife and a mother. This deceptively simple scenario resonates with the solemn grandeur of ancient Greek mythic tragedy, with the fatuous yet needling taunt of Freud's more recent portrayal of women's anatomical deficit and characterological shortcomings, and with the unnerving cacophony of current news exposés of epidemic child abuse. Consolidating all of these cultural currents in a single emblematic narrative, the family romance is so culturally and psychically entrenched that it seems impervious to critique and virtually impossible to dislodge. The trope of father-daughter incest structures our conception of womanhood and hence our beliefs, expectations, and feelings about women.

Still, the family romance is not our sole source of imagery for gender and sexuality. Indeed, the family romance derives some of its power from its parasitic tie-in to other figurations in a vast cultural cache. Here I shall only adumbrate the dimensions of this cache by mentioning a few well-known images that are plainly relevant to recovered memory. Male heterosexuality is commonly personified as a predatory and voracious hunter or beast.[17] Correlatively, women are commonly figured as sexual targets or prey, although they may also be figured as lascivious whores bent on leading upright men astray.[18] Eroticized images of prepubescent girls often depict these minors as seductive gamines or waifs.[19] The oscillation between figurations representing women and girls as innocent and ones representing them as depraved, and between figurations representing men as violent and ones representing them as honorable sets the stage for what we might think of as unauthorized productions of the family romance.

I have considered the scenario for happy wives and fulfilled mothers. But what about other women? Freud supplied a number of plots with different denouements—including the lesbian, the female professional, and the hysteric. How is the hysteric, the precursor of the multiple, portrayed? Here is a synopsis of Freud's nineteenth-century staging of the family romance with that plot twist interpolated: a father seduces a daughter, and she represses this shameful experience and develops hysteria. And the twentieth-century update of this tragic scenario: a father forces sex upon a daughter, and she dissociates and develops multiple personality disorder. A rather whimsical tenor offsets the sordidness of the *fin-de-siècle* Viennese figuration of hysteria—a father romancing a daughter.[20] In the United States today, however, the figuration of multiple personality disorder, which presages recovered memory, is obscene and stark—a father savagely violating and wantonly exploiting a daughter. Unambiguous sadism supplants ambiguous romance.

3. Figuring One's Life

In many cases, memories of childhood sexual abuse raise no more doubt than any other memory. Either the individual has always remembered these assaults (I mean, the memories have never been less retrievable than other memories), or credible corroboration of a recovered memory is forthcoming.[21] However, there are also many bewildering cases in which a recovered memory is met with resolute denial. The woman making the allegations is sincere and deeply wounded, while the man denying the charges is honest and loving. If there is no reason to believe that the woman has fallen into the clutches of an overzealous therapist, and if there is no feasible way to obtain relevant evidence about the past, it is impossible to decide between the irreconcilably opposed positions. These impasses that pit the obligation to respect persons in the present against the epistemic opacity of the past are best approached by placing autobiographical rhetoric in the context of the functions of autobiographical memory.

Memory can resemble a radio announcer's blow-by-blow description of a sporting event: I said, "...."; you said, "...."; I said, "...."; and so on.

Sometimes this sort of bare word-for-word recall is precisely what is needed—say, to settle a dispute about the terms of an agreement. But obviously this kind of account leaves out important facts about how one perceived the interaction at the time. Thus, memory often introduces elements of manner and subjectivity: I said, "...", you acidly joked, "...", I blanched and retorted, "..."; and so on. This sort of recollection might be germane, for example, to a determination of provocation. Such memory is informationally packed and motivationally intelligible. But except in the immediate aftermath of an incident (and not always then), people are seldom able to recall such minute detail. They are left with summaries: we fought bitterly over such-and-such, or, maybe just, we quarreled. Thin though these memories may seem by comparison, they suffice for many purposes, such as explaining the awkwardness of an encounter or seeing the need to initiate a rapprochement. Not only is the content of memories of particular actions, responses, or exchanges restricted by the limits of human retentive and retrieval capacities, but it is also edited and reedited, depending on how the memory is being used to conduct social relationships or to make sense of one's life.

The case of life stories is parallel. People remember their lives by telling stories that excerpt key episodes, and string these episodes together according to themes, such as traits of character, values, aims, norms, exigencies, and so forth. These stories are varied to suit different audiences and different purposes. A politician would hardly tell the same life story to her lesbian partner, to the voters, and to her five-year-old grandchild. Moreover, these narratives can be distilled and condensed. One's story of one's scientific quest might be captured in an image of oneself as an astronaut, or one's story of one's erotic escapades might be captured in an image of oneself as a Don Juan. When autobiographical narratives are encoded in self-figurations, memory's contribution to self-definition becomes salient.

Self-definition pursues the intrinsic value of self-knowledge along with the instrumental value of figuring out how to lead as rewarding a life as one can. Sometimes, one takes a retrospective view and searches one's past in order to better understand oneself and anticipate one's future prospects.[22] In the process of self-definition, the distinction between memory and self-description can dissolve, for self-figuration easily elides the present and the past. In summing up one's life in a trope, one simultaneously represents one's past experience and one's present condition. This may seem unexceptionable since most people believe that they are largely, if not wholly, products of their past experience. However, the trope of summing up misleadingly suggests that memory works by digesting a superfluity of detail and extracting a figuration. Remembered experience constrains autobiographical figuration, to be sure, but the relation between remembered experience and figuration is not unidirectional. As we have seen, people seldom derive narrative forms and figurations from their experience. They typically adopt ready-made plot templates and tropes of life trajectories or personality types, and they remember their experience as these culturally furnished literary devices ordain. Thus, a self-definitional trope one embraces in the present is constitutive of one's recollected past—it provides thematic threads for life stories; it highlights certain incidents and obscures others; it prompts one to impute certain attitudes and intentions to oneself and others, and to dismiss other interpretations as implausible.[23] The past inherits the present.

Still, figurative self-definition can seem paradoxical, for a figuration can aptly symbolize one's present and can provide an advantageous springboard into the future without accurately representing one's past. A timid scientist whose research has been rather pedestrian might accent an emerging self-confidence and perhaps improve her chances of doing more innovative work in the future by figuring herself as an adventurous explorer. But because people generally believe that the past determines the present, and because they see memory as a guarantor of personal identity, they are disposed to see continuity between their past and their present. This disposition poses a danger that self-figuration will lead people to falsify the past. The danger becomes acute when an apt figuration of oneself in the present has not been derived from one's past and has instead been appropriated from a cultural cache. The trope of the adventurous explorer may color the scientist's memory in rosy hues. Downplaying the disappointing results of her research program while underscoring the boldness of the (indefensible) hypothesis she proposed, she may remember her professional persona as less mousy and more forceful. Slightly exaggerating the extent to which her present self-confidence is latent in her past may be harmless. But if her self-figuration persuades her to remember the lackluster work she has done as a trove of momentous discoveries and to convert decisive refutations of her work into plaudits, her memories of her professional accomplishments run squarely afoul of the facts. She is falsifying the past and deceiving herself.

Trouble arises when people misapprehend and misuse the rhetoric of self-definition. They may mistake figurations for literal truths, and they may proceed to literalize these images by filling in mundane details that personalize them and expand them into autobiographical narratives.[24] Whereas self-figuration is a way of answering the question, "What does it mean to be this way—to have these needs, to lack these skills, to experience these feelings, etc.?" literalization transmutes a self-figuration into an answer to the question, "What caused me to be this way?" Since memory plays a pivotal role in self-definition, and since self-figuration structures memory, keeping these questions disentangled is no mean task.

The temptation to literalize self-figurative discourse is almost irresistible when the figurations are images of childhood scenes. Indeed, it seems that Freud surrendered to this siren call. His theory of psychic reality is a sophisticated compromise between the therapeutic value of figurative discourse and the allure of literal discourse. According to Freud, a girl's infantile desire latches onto an iconic tableau—a father seducing a daughter. By individualizing the features of the daughter and the father to match her own and those of her father, and by locating the action in a familiar setting, the girl spins a personalized fantasy of incest that will prove devilishly difficult to distinguish from a childhood incestuous assault. In contrast, Julia Kristeva trenchantly characterizes psychoanalysis as "a scene of metaphor production."[25] Psychoanalytic interpretations are animated mainly by imagination, and their primary medium is figurative language.[26] For Kristeva, memory is incidental to the talking cure, and nothing is gained by recasting self-figurations as life stories.

Plainly, feminists cannot endorse a conception of self-definition or a psychotherapeutic method that altogether excludes memory. Such an approach would distract women from identifying the social causes of their suffering and induce them to personalize the political. Whether a woman's problems stem from discrimination at work or from childhood sexual abuse, curtailing unfair or persecutorial practices presupposes recognizing them, and recognizing them presupposes remembering being harmed by them. If victims of wrongful practices turn inward and figure their selves in an upbeat way that enables them to feel better instead of tracing their suffering to its source, they will never challenge oppressive institutions or call malign individuals to account. Feminist analysis and activism cannot dispense with memory.

Still, it is not always possible to trace one's problems to their cause(s). The aetiologies of many of one's traits, desires, feelings, and the like are sketchy and speculative at best. In many cases of recovered memory, there is no way to reach a well-supported judgment about the accuracy of one's memories. In such cases, I believe, the best course is to regard the sadistic incest scenario as a figurative window onto one's present and to remain agnostic about its relation to one's past. Where the past is epistemically opaque, self-definition must be insulated from memory.

Psychic states that a sadistic incest scenario could aptly figure readily come to mind. They include feeling damaged where one is most vulnerable and least mendable, suffering from persistent, unsoothable anxiety, living in fear of spontaneity that might reveal one's terrible deficiencies, and feeling aggrieved by a vague, unrectifiable wrong. All of these complaints are amenable to this figuration, and, to judge by my experience, all of them are appallingly widespread among contemporary women. If it is true that people tend to adopt culturally furnished figurations and elaborate these figurations into autobiographical narratives, it is understandable that some fathers are perplexed and injured by their daughters' allegations of sexual abuse. Likewise, it is understandable that many of the women making these charges are unshakable in their conviction that they were sexually assaulted. After all, the sadistic incest scenario does aptly figure their present psychic condition, and the narrative analogue of figurative aptness is factual accuracy. Moreover, since shifting from the self-definitional figurative mode to the autobiographical narrative mode produces closure and relieves the terrible anguish attendant upon agnosticism about childhood trauma, the benefits of believing in a literalized sadistic incest scenario may overpower an individual's qualms about its credibility. Nevertheless, I would submit that gaining a subtle and complex understanding of the meaning of one's psychic makeup is both emotionally satisfying and helpful in bringing about felicific change.[27] When identifying the causal antecedents of one's suffering is not possible, figuring one's life is the key to figuring out one's life.

4. The Family Romance and Feminist Politics—
Cultural Critique and Social Change

Apart from the light the sadistic incest scenario may or may not shed on a particular individual's past, there are several perspectives from which feminists must evaluate this trope. One is the prospective aim of self-definition. It is necessary to ask not only whether a self-figuration aptly symbolizes one's present condition, but also whether it is conducive to a more rewarding life. Does the sadistic incest scenario now in currency help women to overcome constraints and to lead satisfying lives, or, like its predecessor, the trope of castration and penis envy, does it stifle women's potential and divert them into a cramped, subordinate social niche? Since the clinical evidence that is now available is spotty and contradictory, it would be premature to hazard an answer to these questions.

From another angle, however, assessing the merits of the sadistic incest scenario need not await well-wrought, longitudinal studies. I have furnished no protocol for distinguishing literalized self-figurations from ordinary autobiographical narratives in controversial cases, nor, as my recommendation for agnosticism implies, do I expect one to materialize. Certainly, an apparently honest and loving father's vigorous protestations of innocence do not suffice to identify literalized self-figurations. Those who are principally concerned with issues of legal and moral responsibility for child abuse might consider this lacuna fatal to my account. However, I would argue that, on the contrary, my account has the virtue of pinpointing the menace of the family romance while at the same time showing why this menace need not be tolerated. What is most deplorable about the sadistic incest scenario is the grave disservice it does to women who are not entirely certain about their memories of abuse and to incest victims, both those who are certain about their abuse and those who are not.

For women who have recovered memories of incest but who also have reason to question whether these memories are accurate, the cultural circulation of this trope together with its widespread use to figure various sorts of dissatisfaction, frustration, and dislocation virtually guarantees that their doubts will never be satisfactorily resolved. Since nothing internal to these memories distinguishes them from literalizations of self-figurations, many of these individuals are doomed to a tormenting state of autobiographical limbo. However, if this trope were taken out of circulation, there would be no more reason to doubt memories of childhood sexual abuse than there is to doubt memories of affectionate paternal nurturance. Thus, the pruning of the figurative repertory that I am proposing would redound to the benefit of women in psychotherapy and their therapists. They would have less difficulty determining whether the problem needing treatment was childhood incest, and better diagnosis would presumably speed recovery. For the sake of women who are confused and distraught by recovered memories, then, I would urge feminists to repudiate the family romance.

In addition and even more sobering, the ubiquity of the sadistic incest scenario impeaches the testimony of individuals whose fathers have sexually assaulted them. The fact that it is always possible that a woman has seized upon this figuration and literalized it provides a ready and credible defense for the most scurrilous fathers. To countenance the cultural prevalence of this figuration is to perpetuate a major obstacle to prosecuting real villains. Since other figurations could be devised to represent the miseries and sorrows that the sadistic incest scenario is presently being used to represent, feminists have every reason to oppose it and to champion alternative figurations. For the sake of the untold numbers of real incest victims, then, I would urge feminist therapists and theorists to marshall their critical powers to dispose of the family romance once and for all and to dedicate their imaginative powers to crafting counterfigurations that better serve the interests of women.[28]

Nothing I have said blunts feminist critiques of gender and the family that take aim at child abuse in the home, nor does my view of recovered memory stymie feminist initiatives that seek to reform the criminal law in ways that make it more likely that child abusers will be convicted and punished. It is indisputable that incestuous child abuse is sufficiently prevalent to justify concerted feminist opposition. Moreover, since displacing the family romance would create a cultural climate in which victims' claims would be less suspect, my view complements these other feminist approaches. Once the family romance and its pathological variants have been retired from the repertory, there will cease to be any respectable excuse for distrusting women who accuse their fathers of sexually abusing them.

5. The Family Romance and Feminist Reclamation—
   Obstacles and Prospects

I would like to conclude by reflecting on the implications of the foregoing view of recovered memory for the larger project of feminist theory. Reclaiming women's experience has been an important dimension of this project. So far, it seems to me that feminists have had their greatest success in reclaiming women's experience of motherhood. Lately, however, feminist reclamation efforts have moved in an intriguing new direction, namely, women's experience of multiplicity. I would like to offer some observations regarding the impact that the figurations I have been discussing have on this undertaking. Before I do, however, let me stress that my conjectures should not be blown out of proportion. I am not claiming that culturally entrenched figurations of multiplicity exhaust the obstacles impeding feminist reclamation, but I do think these figurations are obstacles that should not be underestimated.

To put the view I want to advance in context, it is worth briefly reviewing the history of the feminist bid to reclaim motherhood. Central to the overall critique developed at the beginning of second-wave feminism was a critique of motherhood. The economic disadvantages were documented; the missed opportunities for personal fulfillment were chronicled; the undercurrent of social contempt for motherhood was exposed. This critique alienated many women who were already mothers or who wanted to become mothers. Yet it is indisputable that it fastened on real and serious problems. Subsequently, feminists sought to address the needs of mothers and to increase their options by demanding concrete changes like family leave, affordable, high-quality day care, flex-time work schedules, and so forth. A change in feminist rhetoric accompanied these policy demands—a change that was not limited to toning down the critique. More significantly, motherhood was reconceived and revalued partly through feminist counterfigurations.

Freud's family romance looks like it has a happy ending—girls grow up to be mothers. But if maternity means pursuing a penis equivalent to compensate for an irremediable anatomical lack, maternity can hardly be cause for feminist rejoicing. For motherhood to be reclaimed, it must be refigured in ways that express auspicious meanings, like gladly bestowing life on and/or caring for a precious child. To the extent that Freud's family romance clings to the activity of mothering, motherhood eludes feminist reclamation. That, I would venture, explains why so many psychoanalytic feminists have devoted so much attention to creating counterfigurations of motherhood.[29] They are seeking to displace established figurations of maternity that distort its meaning and belittle the contributions of mothers. They are seeking to figure maternity in a way that is conducive to women's emancipatory aims.

Turning now to the project of reclaiming multiplicity, I think it is possible to discern a similar pattern. No feminist account of the self would be complete without an account of oppositional agency and, specifically, an account of how feminist critique can emerge and how feminist initiatives can be mounted. Many feminist theorists have pointed out that a complex, nontransparent self is needed to undergird an account of feminist agency. A number of feminists who are sympathetic to postmodernism have proposed to understand the complex, nontransparent self as a multiplicitous or plural self.

María Lugones's influential work illustrates the turn to multiplicity. Lugones maintains that she is constructed differently in different social worlds—in the Anglo world, she is serious; in the Latino world, she is playful.[30] For Lugones, this is not a case of being a playful person who is inhibited in some social milieux but not in others.[31] Rather, she insists that she is a different person in each social context (albeit a person who remembers what it is like to be the other person), and she concludes that she is a multiplicitous self.[32]

What is at stake in this line of thought becomes clear in an important paper by Naomi Scheman. After explicating the evils consequent upon fetishizing a unified self, Scheman embraces the multiplicitous self.[33] But plainly a multiplicitous self is in danger of succumbing to terrifying and paralyzing fragmentation. Scheman concedes this liability: "The most striking and clear-cut cases of internal multiplicity are cases of multiple personality, a pathological condition typically caused by severe childhood abuse."[34] Multiple personality is a defense against devastating child abuse, often including incestuous sexual assault. By creating a "bad" alter who deserves the brutality heaped upon her, a child can rationalize her suffering and avoid condemning an adult whom she needs to trust and whose love she needs.[35] Her need to protect herself from knowledge of the vicious harm she has endured may eventually bring about a proliferation of alters, that is, multiple personality disorder.

For women, the multiplicitous self is associatively linked to multiple personality disorder and incestuous childhood sexual assault. In other words, a dysfunctional condition brought on by unforgivable parental behavior figures multiplicity. It is no wonder, then, that the road to reclaiming multiplicity has proven nearly impassable—it is booby-trapped. No one wants to embrace pathology and victimization, and there is an alternative course that is by no means unattractive. Arguably, working to eradicate child abuse—to reform family relations and create a family environment in which dissociation would not be psychologically necessary—makes more sense than identifying with multiplicity. More tellingly, feminists cannot maintain that culturally entrenched figurations of gender generally have a profound effect on thought and yet theorize as if they were exempt from this pernicious influence. Accordingly, there is reason for feminists to proceed cautiously in conceptualizing multiplicity, since the trope of incest-driven alter formation is presumably shaping this theorizing.

Incest is a shattering experience that often leads to a shattered condition. As Scheman points out, therapists seek to repair this damage by persuading different alters to communicate with one another and to agree to some cooperative arrangements.[36] Unfortunately, the alters of multiple personality disorder are a fractious throng, and they mightily resist collaboration.

Now, this description of multiple personality disorder is strikingly reminiscent of some well-known philosophical accounts of the state of nature, and it brings to mind feminist critiques of social contract theory. Feminists have argued that the contractarian conception of the individual as an independent, self-interested atom denies interdependency and the need for care, and also that modeling justice on a bargain reached by wary rivals yields an impoverished vision of social relations.[37] Feminists must reject conceptions of the self that repeat the mistakes they have diagnosed in social contract theory. Conceiving the self as an internal population of self-interested, mutually competitive, unitary individuals would be counter-productive as a foundation for an account of feminist agency. Feminist values and demands cannot be construed as those that no internal self would veto. Since living in a society structured by male dominance ensures that most women have internalized traditional feminine norms, most women have an internal self that will refuse to endorse emancipatory values and demands. Women may have other internal selves that support feminist aims, but these selves need not prevail in the negotiation process.

I am not arguing for jettisoning the multiplicitous self.[38] Nor am I accusing Scheman of lapsing into theorizing the self as an internal population of possessive individualists. Indeed, her text guards against this very trap by tendering a diverse array of figurations of multiplicity.[39] This leads me to believe that Scheman would agree that feminists need vigilantly to resist some of the implications of figuratively linking multiplicity to multiple personality disorder.[40]

My point is that reclamation requires reconception, as well as revaluation. Reconceiving the multiplicitous self requires figuring it in a more felicitous way, for multiplicity will remain in the grip of the picture of an internal mob of warring alters and the connotations of pathology and victimization that this picture conjures up unless it is refigured. It would be naive to suppose that a figuration so durable and deeply embedded in Western culture as the one connecting multiplicity and incest can be severed by counterfigurative fiat,[41] and it would also be a betrayal of women who have been subjected to unspeakable abuse to try to suppress this figurative history. Nevertheless, it would be self-defeating to let multiplicity be absorbed by the trope of incest.

Happily, the counterfiguration project I am advocating is already under way. As I mentioned a moment ago, Scheman cites African, African-American, Latino, and lesbian figurations of multiplicity. I would also like to commend Ruth Leys's psychoanalytic counterfiguration to readers' attention. Ironically dubbing multiplicity "the scandal of dedifferentiation," Leys refigures multiplicity as primordial mimetic identification with the mother.[42] Since I do not have space to explore these counterfigurations here, I must confine myself to urging feminists to build on this groundbreaking counterfigurative work. Thus, I close by opening another inquiry—an inquiry that I believe holds promise for preventing this *fin de siècle* from turning into a dead end for feminism.

Acknowledgments

I am grateful to Susan Brison, Hilde Nelson, and Jennifer Radden for helpful comments on an earlier draft of this paper.

Notes

1. For defense of Freud, see Jean Laplanche and J.-B. Pontalis, "Fantasy and the Origins of Sexuality," *The International Journal of Psychoanalysis* 49 (1968), pp. 1–18 at 6; Teresa Brennan, *The Interpretation of the Flesh* (New York: Routledge, 1992), p. 29. For criticism of Freud, see Jeffrey Moussaieff Masson, *The Assault on Truth: Freud's Suppression of the Seduction Theory* (New York: Harper Collins, 1992), p. xxxiii and throughout; Judith Lewis Herman, *Trauma and Recovery* (New York: Basic Books, 1992), pp. 13–14.

2. These allegations are not exclusively against biological fathers. Stepfathers, cohabiting male partners, visiting boyfriends, and male relatives are often charged with sexual abuse of girls, as well. However, for the sake of parsimony, I shall use "father" to refer to all of these possible culprits.

3. Masson, *Assault on Truth*; Herman, *Trauma and Recovery*; Lenore Terr, *Unchained Memories: True Stories of Traumatic Memories, Lost and Found* (New York: Basic Books, 1994).

4. Frederick Crews, "The Revenge of the Repressed," *The New York Review of Books* 41, No. 19 (1994), pp. 54–60 and 41, No. 20 (1994), pp. 49–58.

5. Ian Hacking, *Rewriting the Soul: Multiple Personality and the Sciences of Memory* (Princeton: Princeton University Press, 1995), pp. 235–249.

6. Hacking, *Rewriting the Soul*, pp. 258–267.

7. Jerome Bruner, "The 'Remembered' Self," in *The Remembering Self: Construction and Accuracy in the Self-Narrative*, ed. Ulric Neisser and Robyn Fivush (New York: Cambridge University Press, 1994), p. 53.

8. Elizabeth F. Loftus and Leah Kaufman, "Why Do Traumatic Experiences Sometimes Produce Good Memory (Flashbulbs) and Sometimes No Memory (Repression)?" in *Affect and Accuracy in Recall*, ed. Eugene E. Winograd and Ulric Neisser (New York: Cambridge University Press, 1992), pp. 215–216, 219.

9. Elizabeth F. Loftus, "The Reality of Repressed Memories," *American Psychologist* 48, No. 5 (1993), pp. 518–537 at 532–533.

10. Ross and Buehler, "Creative Remembering," in *The Remembering Self*, pp. 227–229.

11. For discussion of the role of figurations in structuring thought and feeling, see Helen Haste, *The Sexual Metaphor* (Cambridge: Harvard University Press, 1994), pp. 36–47.

12. See Haste, *The Sexual Metaphor*; Sander L. Gilman, *Difference and Pathology: Stereotypes of Sexuality, Race, and Madness* (Ithaca: Cornell University Press, 1985); Eva Feder Kittay, "Woman as Metaphor," *Hypatia* 3 (1988): 63–86; Phyllis Rooney, "Gendered Reason: Sex, Metaphor, and Conceptions of Reason," *Hypatia* 6, No. 2 (1991), pp. 77–103; Genevieve Lloyd, "Maleness, Metaphor, and the 'Crisis' of Reason," in *A Mind of One's Own*, eds. Louise Antony and Charlotte Witt (Boulder, Colo.: Westview Press, 1992); Diana Tietjens Meyers, *Subjection and Subjectivity: Psychoanalytic Feminism and Moral Philosophy* (New York: Routledge, 1994).

13. Since it is not relevant to recovered memory, I shall leave aside the boy's Oedipus complex.

14. For discussion of the inextricability of the Oedipus complex from the meaning of the institution of the family, see Kaja Silverman, *Male Subjectivity at the Margins* (New York: Routledge, 1992), pp. 35–51.

15. Elizabeth Abel, "Race, Class, and Psychoanalysis? Opening Questions," in *Conflicts in Feminism*, eds. Marianne Hirsch and Evelyn Fox Keller (New York: Routledge, 1990), p. 191.

16. Laplanche and Pontalis, "Fantasy and the Origins of Sexuality," pp. 13–14.

17. Wendy W. Williams, "The Equality Crisis: Some Reflections on Culture, Courts, and Feminism," in *Feminist Legal Theory*, ed. Katharine T. Bartlett and Rosanne Kennedy (Boulder, Colo.: Westview Press, 1991), p. 20; Patricia S. Mann, *Micro-Politics: Agency in a Postfeminist Era* (Minneapolis: University of Minnesota Press, 1994), pp. 29–30.

18. Haste, *The Sexual Metaphor*, pp. 172–173; Catharine MacKinnon, "Feminism, Marxism, Method and the State: An Agenda for Theory," *Signs* 7 (1982), pp. 515–544, at 530; Sandra Lee Bartky, *Femininity and Domination* (New York: Routledge, 1990), pp. 73–74.

19. In addition to child pornography, see the photographs of Charles Dodgson and the paintings of Balthus. For discussion of nineteenth-century literary treatments of this theme, see Gilman, *Difference and Pathology*, pp. 39–58.

20. I find it an interesting sidelight that Freud also figures the mother as a child molester—in the course of routine bathing and dressing, the mother stimulates her baby's genitals and sexually arouses it. However, the image of the mother/seductress has never caught on. If women's credentials as benign caregivers were figuratively compromised, who could be trusted to do this work? This suggests a second source of resistance to this image, namely, that it is highly threatening to the sexual division of labor. If women were figured as untrustworthy with small children, how could their continued subordination as designated unpaid caregivers be rationalized? There is too much at stake socially and politically for womanhood to be figured as a sexually aggressive mother.

21. The hyperprivacy in which sexuality is shrouded in many cultures complicates matters. Not only are there usually no nonparticipating witnesses to sex acts, but also we usually don't talk about our sexual experience. To the extent that memory depends on rehearsal, then, sex memory is weak. In this connection, it is interesting that the typical abuser's efforts to create a conspiracy of silence around the incestuous acts may counteract the frailty of sex memory. In order to secure the child's silence, the abuser reminds the child not to tell. Thus, abusers may speak of incest more than people usually speak of sex, and if so, memories of incest may be strengthened.

22. Near the end of her recounting of a Parisian concierge's autobiographical history of modern France, Bonnie G. Smith comments, "It now became clear that during the past few weeks Mme Lucie had reached the end of memory. In the depths of old age, present and future prospects had disappeared from her perspective on life, so she lost sight of the past." *Confessions of a Concierge* (New Haven: Yale University Press, 1985), p. 150.

23. Notice, by the way, that if cultures are thought to be implanting suggestions by purveying figurations, hardly any perception or memory will be unconta-

minated by suggestion. On this sweeping view of the scope of suggestion, the charge of suggestion that is pivotal to Crews's critique of recovered memory would lose all force.

24. I want to distinguish this claim from Hacking's account of memories constituted through semantic contagion (*Rewriting the Soul*, pp. 238, 257). As Hacking points out, once people have categorized their experience (say, as child abuse), they may proceed to fill in their memory of this experience with category-appropriate events (say, incidents of sexual molestation). If I understand Hacking correctly, his view is that semantic contagion is part of the phenomenon of veridical memory formation. Whether a memory derived from semantic contagion is veridical or not depends on the memory practices that are in force in a particular culture at a particular time, and these practices are shaped by memoro-politics.

I agree that literalizing a self-figuration could yield a veridical memory. Memory is cued in many different, sometimes mysterious ways, and there is no reason to deny that self-figuration can prompt veridical memories. But contrary to Hacking's view, I am suggesting that literalizing figurations often confuses backward-looking memory with forward-looking self-direction and also that, although memoro-politics may determine what people count as a veridical memory, it does not determine what is a veridical memory. Suppose that a scenario of being subjected to clitoridectomy in childhood gained currency as a trope expressing certain psychic scars. It seems unlikely that there would be any temptation to literalize this figuration, but if there were, it is obvious that no memory practice could by itself transform a literalization of this trope into a veridical memory. Only a woman's discovery that her clitoris had been surgically removed (without her knowing it at the time or despite her having forgotten it in the meantime) could certify the accuracy of the memory. Why, then, suppose that whether a memory that literalizes a figuration of an event for which there is no lasting physical evidence is veridical or not depends entirely on memory practices shaped by memoro-politics? When Hacking affirms that he regards truth and factuality as basic and unproblematic (*Rewriting the Soul*, p. 250), he seems sympathetic to this line of thought, for in these passages he seems to be denying that memory reduces to a circumlocutious discourse of prospective self-definition. Yet, his predominant concern with the malleability of memory practices and the power of these practices to authenticate people's recollections seems to belie this sympathy.

It is clear, in contrast, that Elizabeth Loftus and Katherine Ketcham share my concern with distinguishing between discourses of autobiographical memory and discourses of self-definition (*The Myth of Repressed Memory* (New York: St. Martin's Press, 1994, pp. 265–267)). I strongly object to the tone of relentless skepticism about recovered memory that pervades their book, and I do not endorse their suggestion that psychotherapy abandon its concern with autobiographical memory—if a patient has suffered childhood trauma, remembering it may be crucial to her recovery. Nevertheless, I think it is important to recognize that the incest scenario can be appropriated as a self-figuration and that the aptness of this figuration does not depend on the individual's having been sexually assaulted in childhood.

25. Julia Kristeva, *Tales of Love*, trans. Leon S. Roudiez (New York: Columbia University Press, 1987), p. 276.

26. Jerome Bruner remarks, "[I]f the Self is a remembered self, the remembering reaches far back beyond our own birth, back to the cultural and language forms that specify the defining properties of a Self" ("The 'Remembered' Self," p. 53). This observation is instructive with respect to the drift I have noted from self-figuration to autobiographical narrative. If a key feature of the self is its temporal continuity, self-definition cannot rest with self-figuration, for self-figuration is atemporal and leaves out the sequences of episodes that endow the self with continuity through time. Thus, the self-definitional discourse of "metaphorization" that Kristeva advocates will be liable to deteriorate into the discourse of autobiographical narrative unless adjustments are made in our conception of the self. Kristeva is right, then, to couple her enthusiasm for self-definition through self-figuration with a call for a nonunitary, destabilized conception of the self.

27. For discussion of psychoanalysis' harnessing of the transformative power of metaphor, see Kristeva, *Tales of Love*, pp. 13–16; also see Marcia Cavell, *The Psychoanalytic Mind: From Freud to Philosophy* (Cambridge: Harvard University Press, 1993), pp. 96–97.

28. My critique of the family romance raises interesting questions about the history of this trope in Western culture. It is possible that Freud and his followers did women an unintended service by bringing this trope into cultural currency, for its presence in the figurative repertory may have been instrumental in enabling many women to remember and testify to childhood incest. Thus, this trope may have helped to gain attention for this heretofore well-concealed harm. Whether or not this is so, I am convinced that this stock figuration has now become counterproductive from the standpoint of women's interests.

29. See, for example, Nancy Chodorow, *The Reproduction of Mothering* (Berkeley: University of California Press, 1978) and Julia Kristeva, "Stabat Mater," in *Tales of Love*. For discussion of feminist psychoanalysis as counterfiguration, see my *Subjection and Subjectivity*, pp. 62–91.

30. María C. Lugones, "Playfulness, 'World'-Travelling, and Loving Perception," *Hypatia* 2, No. 2 (1987), pp. 3–19, at 9.

31. Lugones, "Playfulness," p. 14.

32. Lugones, "Playfulness," p. 14.

33. Naomi Scheman, *Engenderings: Constructions of Knowledge, Authority, and Privilege* (New York: Routledge, 1993), pp. 96–105.

34. Scheman, *Engenderings*, p. 102.

35. Herman, *Trauma and Recovery*, pp. 103–107.

36. Scheman, *Engenderings*, p. 103.

37. Annette C. Baier, "The Need for More than Justice," in *Science, Morality, and Feminist Theory*, ed. Marsha Hanen and Kai Nielsen (Calgary: The University of Calgary Press, 1987); Virginia Held, "Feminism and Moral Theory," in *Women and Moral Theory*, ed. Eva Feder Kittay and Diana T. Meyers (Totowa, N.J.: Rowman and Littlefield, 1987).

38. Elsewhere I have defended a version of the multiplicitous self; see Meyers, *Subjection and Subjectivity*, pp. 146–147. For a promising proposal to model the dynamics of the multiplicitous self on strategies for forging "responsible agency" among the members of an oppressed community, see Claudia Card, *The Unnatural Lottery: Character and Moral Luck* (Philadephia: Temple University Press, 1996), chap. 2.

39. Scheman, *Engenderings*, pp. 100–103. It is worth noting that none of Scheman's alternatives to figuring multiplicity as multiple personality disorder stem from the dominant Anglo-European culture that gave us the family romance. Scheman's alternative figurations originate in African, African-American, Latino, and lesbian cultures.

40. In conversation, she has assured me that she does.

41. This point should be underscored. As I remarked earlier, although Freud articulated the family romance in a particularly compelling way and popularizations of psychoanalysis subsequently broadcast this figuration far and wide, in various versions this figuration has been in circulation virtually throughout recorded Western history. The family romance is, then, deeply embedded in Western culture, and it is durable. While I fully recognize how difficult it will be to supplant it (for related discussion, see Meyers, *Subjection and Subjectivity*, pp. 52–56, 113–115), I would nevertheless maintain that it is a task that feminists must undertake.

42. Ruth Leys, "The Real Miss Beauchamp: Gender and the Subject of Imitation," in *Feminists Theorize the Political*, ed. Judith Butler and Joan W. Scott (New York: Routledge, 1992), pp. 189, 201–203. I hope that Leys will not object to my characterizing her view as a counterfiguration of multiplicity. She positions her view as an explanation of why memories of childhood sexual abuse are not recoverable, but I think my reading is faithful to the spirit of her work. For my reasons for reading psychoanalytic developmental theory as an extended trope, see Meyers, *Subjection and Subjectivity*, pp. 12–14.

Contributors

Bat-Ami Bar On is Associate Professor of Philosophy and Women's Studies at the State University of New York at Binghamton. She has edited two collections of feminist readings in the history of philosophy, *Engendering Origins* and *Modern Engendering* (both SUNY Press, 1994). The primary focus of her work is violence in its multiple forms and guises; she has recently edited a special issue of *Hypatia* (Fall 1996), "Women and Violence."

Françoise Baylis is Associate Professor of Bioethics Education and Research on the Faculty of Medicine at Dalhousie University, Halifax, Nova Scotia. The author of a number of essays on topics in clinical ethics, she has also edited *The Health Care Ethics Consultant* and, with Jocelyn Downie, *Health Care Ethics in Canada*.

Judith Bradford is a doctoral student at Fordham University, Bronx, New York. She has an essay forthcoming in *Feminist Interpretations of Wittgenstein*, edited by Naomi Scheman, which is in the ReReading the Canon series from Penn State Press; another essay (with Crispin Sartwell) will appear in Naomi Zack's *Race/Sex* (Routledge). Her dissertation, in feminist epistemology, examines justification as a set of social practices and explores the connections between knowledge and the accreditation of speakers.

Cheshire Calhoun is Associate Professor of Philosophy and Director of Women's Studies at Colby College, Waterville, Maine. She works on the intersections between moral theory, feminist philosophy, and gay and lesbian studies. She has published (in *Ethics*, the *Journal of Philosophy*, and *Signs*, among others) on such topics as forgiveness, reproach, resistance to unjust practices, gender bias in ethics, lesbian/gay identity, and injustice regarding sexuality.

Sidney Callahan is Professor of Psychology at Mercy College, Dobbs Ferry, New York. She has written many books and essays, among them *Abortion: Understanding Differences* (Plenum, 1984) and *In Good Conscience: Reason and Emotion in Moral Decision Making* (HarperSanFrancisco, 1991), and is a regular contributor to *Commonweal*.

Jocelyn Downie is a philosopher and lawyer who has clerked for Chief Justice Lamer at the Supreme Court of Canada and is currently the director of the Health Law Institute of Dalhousie University. She has published articles in a variety of areas of health law and, with Françoise Baylis, recently edited *Health Care Ethics in Canada*.

John Hardwig is Professor of Philosophy at East Tennessee State University, Johnson City, where he also teaches in the medical school. He has published a number of essays in anthologies and such journals as *Ethics*, the *Journal of Philosophy*, and the *Hastings Center Report* on the ethics of personal relationships, social epistemology, and the role of families in medical treatment decisions.

Judith Hughes is Director of The Derwent Initiative in Newcastle upon Tyne, England. She is the author of several essays on children, including one that appeared in *Feminist Perspectives in Philosophy*, edited by Morwenna Griffeths and Margaret Whitford, and another in *Children, Parents and Politics*, edited by Geoffrey Scarre. She has written various books and articles with Mary Midgley.

Diana Tietjens Meyers is Professor of Philosophy at the University of Connecticut, Storrs. Her most recent book is *Subjection and Subjectivity: Psychoanalytic Feminism and Moral Philosophy* (Routledge, 1994). She is also the author of *Self, Society, and Personal Choice* (Columbia University Press, 1989) and *Inalienable Rights: A Defense* (Columbia University Press, 1985). She has edited two recent collections: *Feminists Rethink the Self* (Westview, 1996) and *Feminist Ethics and Social Theory: A Sourcebook* (Routledge, 1996).

Mary Midgley was formerly Senior Lecturer in Philosophy, University of Newcastle upon Tyne, England. She has had a special interest in problems of human nature and has written many books and articles on this subject. Among them are *Beast and Man* (Cornell University Press, 1978), *Wickedness* (Routledge, 1984), *Animals and Why They Matter* (University of Georgia Press, 1984), *The Ethical Primate* (Routledge, 1994) and, with Judith Hughes, *Women's Choices* (St. Martin's Press, 1983).

Michele M. Moody-Adams is Assistant Professor of Philosophy at Indiana University. She has published essays on the foundations of ethical theory, moral psychology and the theory of responsibility, political philosophy, applied ethics, and the theory and practice of feminism. She is the author of *Morality, Culture and Philosophy: Fieldwork in Familiar Places*, forthcoming from Harvard University Press.

James Lindemann Nelson is Professor of Philosophy at the University of Tennessee, Knoxville. He has written extensively in bioethics, particularly on the ethics of organ transplantation, allocation of scarce medical resources, care of the elderly, and surrogate decision-making, and he also writes about animal and environmental ethics. He has coauthored two books, *The Patient in the Family* (Routledge, 1995) and *Alzheimer's: Answers to Hard Questions for Families* (Doubleday, 1996), and coedits the Reflective Bioethics series for Routledge.

Hilde Lindemann Nelson is Director of the Center for Applied and Professional Ethics at the University of Tennessee, Knoxville. A former editor of the *Hastings Center Report*, she writes on issues in bioethics and feminist theory, and is the author (with James Lindemann Nelson) of *The Patient in the Family* and *Alzheimer's: Answers to Hard Questions for Families*. She coedits the Reflective Bioethics series for Routledge.

Linda Nicholson is Professor in the departments of Educational Administration and Policy Studies and Women's Studies at the State University of New York at Albany. She is the author of *Gender and History: The Limits of Social Theory in the Age of the Family* (Columbia University Press, 1986), the editor of *Feminism/Postmodernism* (Routledge, 1990), and the editor, with Steven Seidman, of *Social Postmodernism* (Cambridge University Press, 1995). She edits the Thinking Gender series for Routledge.

Susan Moller Okin is Professor of Political Science and Director of the Program in Ethics in Society at Stanford University. Raised in New Zealand, she is the author of *Women in Western Political Thought* (Princeton University Press, 1979) and *Justice, Gender, and the Family* (Basic, 1989). She is currently working on feminism and cultural differences.

Laura M. Purdy is Professor of Philosophy at Wells College, Aurora, New York. She has worked primarily in applied ethics, with a special focus on bioethics, reproduction, and the family. She has written two books—*In Their Best Interest? The Case against Equal Rights for Children* (Cornell University Press, 1992) and *Reproducing Persons* (Cornell University Press, 1996)—and has edited, with Helen B. Holmes, the collection *Feminist Perspectives in Medical Ethics* (Indiana University Press, 1992).

Elise L.E. Robinson is working toward her doctorate in dramatic arts at the University of California, Santa Barbara. Her focus is in feminist theater and narrative theory, and her dissertation develops the idea of theatrical counterstories as a means of political resistance and change.

Mary Romero is Professor in Chicana and Chicano Studies at Arizona State University. She has devoted much of her career to studying the working conditions of private household workers in the United States, examining the effect of such work on employees' families and on the future of race relations in particular. She has written one book, *Maid in the U.S.A.* (Routledge, 1992), and is completing another, based on the life narrative of the daughter of a live-in maid. She is coeditor of several anthologies in Chicana/o and Latina/o studies.

Sara Ruddick teaches philosophy and women's studies at Eugene Lang College, New School for Social Research, New York. She has contributed to many anthologies and coedited two, *Working It Out* (Pantheon, 1977) and *Between Women* (Beacon, 1984). She is the author of *Maternal Thinking: Toward a Politics of Peace* (Beacon, 1989).

Crispin Sartwell is Assistant Professor of Philosophy at the University of Alabama. He has published (in *American Philosophical Quarterly*, the *Journal of Philosophy*, and *Philosophical Studies*, among others) on aesthetics, epistemology, philosophy of mind, and Eastern philosophy, and has written two books: *The Art of Living* (SUNY, 1995) and *Obscenity, Anarchy, Reality* (SUNY, 1996). A third book, on African-American autobiography, is forthcoming.

Naomi Zack is Assistant Professor of Philosophy at the State University of New York at Albany. Her work in racial theory includes a monograph, *Race and Mixed Race* (Temple University Press, 1993) and an anthology, *American Mixed Race: The Culture of Microdiversity* (Rowman and Littlefield, 1995). *Bachelors of Science: Seventeenth Century Identity, Then and Now* (Temple University Press, 1996) reflects her interest in cultural studies and the history of philosophy.

Index

CPSIA information can be obtained
at www.ICGtesting.com
Printed in the USA
FFOW02n1503190116
20545FF